An Historical Account of the Rise and Progress of the Colonies of South Carolina and Georgia
Vol. II

by

Alexander Hewatt

Double 9
BOOKS

An Historical Account of the Rise and Progress of the Colonies of South Carolina and Georgia
Vol. II
by Alexander Hewatt

ISBN: 978-93-62200-97-6

Published by

DOUBLE 9 BOOKS

2/13-B, Ansari Road
Daryaganj, New Delhi – 110002
info@double9books.com
www.double9books.com
Tel. 011-40042856

ABOUT THE AUTHOR

Dr. Alexander Hewatt was South Carolina and Georgia's first historian, best remembered for his two-volume work "An Historical Account of the Rise and Progress of the Colonies of South Carolina and Georgia". He stayed loyal to the King during the American Revolution, which resulted in the seizure of his property and his expulsion in 1777. Hewat(t) was a Presbyterian minister who served in Charleston, South Carolina from 1763 until 1777. Following the publication of his History in 1779, Edinburgh University bestowed upon him an honorary DD doctoral degree. One of his sermons, as cited by Smollett, may provide insight into his nature. Every traitor worships gold, and he who shows faithful to his king and nation for a large reward will betray them both for a larger one. What method did Constantius Chlorus use to test the souls of his civil and military servants? We are told that, being friendly to the Christian religion and aware of how difficult it was to know the human heart, he assembled his officers and judges and proposed to them the following condition: either sacrifice to demons or leave the court and their positions to others, giving each the freedom of choice. By this strategy, he divided his servants into two groups: men of principle and men of the world.

CONTENTS

CHAPTER VII

[Sidenote] The form of legal governments.

From that period in which the right and title to the lands of Carolina were sold, and surrendered to the King, and he assumed the immediate care and government of the province, a new aera commences in the annals of that country, which may be called the aera of its freedom, security, and happiness. The Carolineans who had long laboured under innumerable hardships and troubles, from a weak proprietary establishment, at last obtained the great object of their desires, a royal government, the constitution of which depended on commissions issued by the crown to the Governor, and the instructions which attended those commissions. The form of all provincial governments was borrowed from that of their mother country, which was not a plan of systematic rules drawn before-hand by speculative men, but a constitution which was the result of many ages of wisdom and experience. Its great object is the public good, in promoting of which all are equally concerned. It is a constitution which has a remedy within itself for every political disorder, which, when properly applied, must ever contribute to its stability and duration. After the model of this British constitution the government of Carolina now assumed a form like the other regal ones on the continent, which were composed of three branches, of a Governor, a Council, and an Assembly. The crown having the appointment of the Governor, delegates to him; its constitutional powers, civil and military, the power of legislation as far as the King possesses it; its judicial and executive powers, together with those of chancery and admiralty jurisdiction, and also those of supreme ordinary: all these powers, as they exist in the crown, are known by the laws of the realm; as they are entrusted to Governors, they are declared and defined by their commissions patent. The council, though differing in many respects from the house of peers, are intended to represent that house, and are appointed by the King during pleasure, for supporting the prerogatives of the crown in the province. The Assembly consists of the representatives of the people, and are elected by them as the House of Commons in Great Britain, to be the guardians of their lives, liberties, and properties. Here also the constitution confides in the good behaviour of the representatives; for should they presume in any respect to betray their trust, it gives the people more frequent opportunities than even in Britain, of chusing others in their stead. The Governor convenes, prorogues, and dissolves these Assemblies, and has a negative on the bills of both houses. After bills have received his assent, they are sent to Great Britain for the royal approbation, in consequence of which they have the force of laws in the province. This is a general sketch of the royal governments, which are intended to resemble the constitution of Great Britain, as nearly as the local circumstances of the provinces will admit, and which, notwithstanding its imperfections, is certainly the best form of government upon earth. By the instructions which the Governor receives from time to time from England, his power no doubt is greatly circumscribed; but it is his duty to transmit authentic accounts of the state of his province, in order that the instructions given him may be proper, and calculated for promoting not only the good of the province, but also that of the British empire.

[Sidenote] Sir Alexander Cumming sent out to treat of peace with the Indians.

After the purchase of the province, the first object of the royal concern was, to establish the peace of the colony on the most firm and permanent foundation; and for this purpose treaties of union and alliance with Indian nations were judged to be essentially necessary. Domestic security being first established, the colonists might then apply themselves to industry with vigour and success, and while they enriched themselves, they would at the same time enlarge the commerce and trade of the mother-country. For this purpose Sir Alexander Cumming was appointed, and sent out to conclude a treaty of alliance with the Cherokees, at this time a warlike and formidable nation of savages. These Indians occupied the lands about the head of Savanna river, and backwards among the Apalachian mountains. The country they claimed as their hunting grounds was of immense extent; and its boundaries had never been clearly ascertained. The inhabitants of their different towns were computed to amount to more than twenty thousand, six thousand of whom were warriors, fit on any emergency to take the field. An alliance with such a nation was an object of the highest consequence to Carolina, and likewise to the mother-country, now engaged for its defence and protection.

[Sidenote] Brings with him to England seven Cherokees.

About the beginning of the year 1730, Sir Alexander arrived in Carolina, and made preparations for his journey to the distant hills. For his guides he procured some Indian traders, well acquainted with the woods, and an interpreter who understood the Cherokee language, to assist him in his negociations. When he reached Keowee, abort three hundred miles from

Charlestown, the chiefs of the lower towns there met him, and received him with marks of great friendship and esteem. He immediately dispatched messengers to the middle, the valley, and over-hill settlements, and summoned a general meeting of all their chiefs, to hold a congress with him at Nequassee. Accordingly in the month of April the chief warriors of all the Cherokee towns assembled at the place appointed. After the various Indian ceremonies were over, Sir Alexander made a speech to them, acquainting them by whose authority he was sent, and representing the great power and goodness of his sovereign King George; how he, and all his other subjects, paid a cheerful obedience to his laws, and of course were protected by him from all harm: That he had come a great way to demand of Moytoy, and all the chieftains of the nation, to acknowledge themselves the subjects of his King, and to promise obedience to his authority: and as he loved them, and was answerable to his Sovereign for their good and peaceable behaviour, he hoped they would agree to what he should now require of them. Upon which the chiefs, falling on their knees, solemnly promised fidelity and obedience, calling upon all that was terrible to fall upon them if they violated their promise. Sir Alexander then, by their unanimous consent, nominated Moytoy commander and chief of the Cherokee nation, and enjoined all the warriors of the different tribes to acknowledge him for their King, to whom they were to be accountable for their conduct. To this they also agreed, provided Moytoy should be made answerable to Sir Alexander for his behaviour to them. After which many useful presents were made them, and the congress ended to the great satisfaction of both parties. The crown was brought from Tenassee, their chief town, which with five eagle tails, and four scalps of their enemies, Moytoy presented to Sir Alexander, requesting him, on his arrival at Britain, to lay them at his Majesty's feet. But Sir Alexander proposed to Moytoy, that he should depute some of their chiefs to accompany him to England, there to do homage in person to the great King. Accordingly six of them agreed, and accompanied Sir Alexander to Charlestown, where being joined by another, they embarked for England in the Fox man of war, and arrived at Dover in June 1730.

[Sidenote] Who enter into a treaty of peace and alliance.

We shall not pretend to describe their behaviour at the sight of London, or their wonder and astonishment at the greatness of the city, the number of the people, and the splendour of the army and court. Being admitted into the presence of the King, they, in the name of their nation, promised to continue for ever his Majesty's faithful and obedient subjects. A treaty was accordingly drawn up, and signed by Alured Popple, secretary to the Lords Commissioners of trade and plantations, on one side; and by the marks of the six chiefs, on the other. The preamble to this treaty recites, "That whereas the six Chiefs, with the consent of the whole nation of Cherokees, at a general meeting of their nation at Nequassee, were deputed by Moytoy, their chief warrior, to attend Sir Alexander Cumming to Great Britain, where they had seen the great King George: and Sir Alexander, by authority from Moytoy and all the Cherokees, had laid the crown of their nation, with the scalps of their enemies and feathers of glory, at his Majesty's feet, as a pledge of their loyalty: And whereas the great King had commanded the Lords Commissioners of trade and plantations to inform the Indians, that the English on all sides of the mountains and lakes were his people, their friends his friends, and their enemies his enemies; that he took it kindly the great nation of Cherokees had sent them so far, to brighten the chain of friendship between him and them, and between his people and their people; that the chain of friendship between him and the Cherokees is now like the sun, which shines both in Britain and also upon the great mountains where they live, and equally warms the hearts of Indians and Englishmen; that as there is no spots or blackness in the sun, so neither is there any rust or foulness on this chain. And as the King had fastened one end to his breast, he defied them to carry the other end of the chain and fasten it to the breast of Moytoy of Telliquo, and to the breasts of all their old wise men, their captains, and people, never more to be made loose or broken.

"The great King and the Cherokees being thus fastened together by a chain of friendship, he has ordered, and it is agreed, that his children in Carolina do trade with the Indians, and furnish them with all manner of goods they want, and to make haste to build houses and plant corn from Charlestown, towards the towns of Cherokees behind the great mountains: That he desires the English and Indians may live together as children of one family; that the Cherokees be always ready to fight against any nation, whether white men or Indians, who shall dare to molest or hurt the English; that the nation of Cherokees shall, on their part, take care to keep the trading path clean, that there be no blood on the path where the English tread, even though they should be accompanied with other people with whom the Cherokees may be at war: That the Cherokees shall not suffer their people to trade with white men of any other nation but the English, nor permit white men of any other nation to build any forts or cabins, or plant any corn among them, upon lands which belong to the great King: and if any such attempt shall be made, the Cherokees must acquaint the English Governor therewith, and do whatever he directs, in order to maintain and defend the great King's right to the country of Carolina: That if any negroes shall run away into the woods from their English masters, the Cherokees shall endeavour to apprehend them, and bring them to the plantation from whence they run away, or to the Governor, and for every slave so apprehended and brought back, the Indian that brings him shall receive a gun and a watch-coat: and if by any accident it shall happen, that an Englishman shall kill a Cherokee, the King or chief of the nation shall first complain to the English Governor, and the man who did the harm shall be punished by the English laws as if he had killed an Englishman; and in like manner, if any Indian happens to kill an Englishman, the Indian shall be delivered up to the Governor, to be punished by the same English laws as if he were an Englishman."

This was the substance of the first treaty between the King and the Cherokees, every article of which was accompanied with presents of different kinds, such as cloth, guns, shot, vermilion, flints, hatchets, knives. The Indians were given to understand, "That these were the words of the great King, whom they had seen, and as a token that his heart was open and true to his children the Cherokees, and to all their people, a belt was given the warriors, which they were told the King desired them to keep, and shew to all their people, to their children, and children's children, to confirm what was now spoken, and to bind this agreement of peace and friendship between the English and Cherokees, as long as the rivers shall run, the mountains shall last, or the sun shall shine."

[Sidenote] Speech of a Cherokee warrior.

This treaty, that it might be the easier understood, was drawn up in language as similar as possible to that of the Indians, which at this time was very little known in England, and given to them, certified and approved by Sir Alexander Cumming. In answer to which, Skijagustah, in name of the rest, made a speech to the following effect:—"We are come hither from a mountainous place, where nothing but darkness is to be found—but we are now in a place where there is light.—There was a person in our country— he gave us a yellow token of warlike honour, which is left with Moytoy of Telliquo,—and as warriors we received it.—He came to us like a warrior from you.—A man he is;—his talk is upright—and the token he left preserves his memory among us.—We look upon you as if the great King were present;— we love you as representing the great King;—we shall die in the same way of thinking.—The crown of our nation is different from that which the great King George wears, and from that we saw in the tower.—But to us it is all one.—The chain of friendship shall be carried to our people.—We look upon the great King George as the Sun, and as our father, and upon ourselves as his children.—For though we are red, and you are white, yet our hands and hearts are joined together.—When we shall have acquainted our people with what we have seen, our children from generation to generation will always remember it.—In war we shall always be one with you. The enemies of the great King shall be our enemies;—his people and ours shall be one, and shall die together.—We came hither naked and poor as the worms of the earth, but you have every thing,—and we that have nothing must love you, and will never break the chain of friendship which is between us.—Here stands the Governor of Carolina, whom we know.—This small rope we show you is all that we have to bind our slaves with, and it may be broken.—But you have iron chains for yours.—However, if we catch your slaves, we will bind them as well as we can, and deliver them to our friends, and take no pay for it.—We have looked round for the person that was in our country—he is not here;—however, we must say he talked uprightly to us, and we shall never forget him.—Your white people may very safely build houses near us;—we shall hurt nothing that belongs to them, for we are children of one father, the great King, and shall live and die together." Then laying down his feathers upon the table he added: "This is our way of talking, which is the same thing to us as your letters in the book are to you, and to you beloved men we deliver these feathers in confirmation of all we have said."

The Cherokees, however barbarous, were a free and independent people; and this method of obtaining a share of their lands by the general consent, was fair and honourable in itself, and most agreeable to the general principles of equity, and the English constitution. An agreement is made with them, in consequence of which the King could not only give a just title to Indian lands; but, by Indians becoming his voluntary subjects, the colonists obtained peaceable possession. The Cherokees held abundance of territory from nature, and with little injury to themselves could spare a share of it; but reason and justice required that it be obtained by paction or agreement. By such treaties mutual presents were made, mutual obligations were established, and, for the performance of the conditions required, the honour and faith of both parties were pledged. Even to men in a barbarous state such policy was the most agreeable, as will afterwards clearly appear; for the Cherokees, in consequence of this treaty, for many years, remained in a state of perfect friendship and peace with the colonists, who followed their various employments in the neighbourhood of those Indians, without the least terror or molestation.

[Sidenote] Robert Johnson Governor.

About the beginning of the year 1731, Robert Johnson, who had been Governor of Carolina while in the possession of the Lords Proprietors, having received a commission from the King, investing him with the same office and authority, arrived in the province. He brought back these Indian chiefs, possessed with the highest ideas of the power and greatness of the English nation, and not a little pleased with the kind and generous treatment they had received. The Carolineans, who had always entertained the highest esteem for this gentleman, even in the time of their greatest confusion, having now obtained him in the character of King's Governor, a thing they formerly had so earnestly desired, received him with the greatest demonstrations of joy. Sensible of his wisdom and virtue, and his strong attachment to the colony, they promised themselves much prosperity and happiness under his gentle administration.

This new Governor, from his knowledge of the province, and the dispositions of the people, was not only well qualified for his high office, but he had a council to assist him, composed of the most respectable inhabitants. Thomas Broughton was appointed Lieutenant-governor, and Robert Wright Chief Justice. The other members of the council were, William Bull, James Kinloch, Alexander Skene, John Fenwick, Arthur Middleton, Joseph Wragg, Francis Yonge, John Hamerton, and Thomas Waring. At the first meeting of Assembly, the Governor recommended to both houses, to embrace the earliest opportunity of testifying their gratitude to his Majesty for purchasing seven-eight parts of the province, and taking it under his particular care; he enjoined them to put the laws in execution against impiety and immorality, and as the most effectual means of discouraging vice, to attend carefully to the education of youth. He acquainted them of the treaty which had been concluded in England with the Cherokees, which he hoped would be attended with beneficial and happy consequences; he recommended the payment of public debts, the establishment of public credit, and peace and unanimity among themselves as the chief objects of their attention; for if they should prove faithful subjects to his Majesty, and attend to the welfare and prosperity of their country, he hoped soon to see it, now under the protection of a great and powerful nation, in as flourishing and prosperous a situation as any of the other settlements on the continent. They in return presented to him the most loyal and affectionate addresses, and entered on their public deliberations with uncommon harmony and great satisfaction.

[Sidenote] Several indulgences granted the people.

For the encouragement of the people, now connected with the mother country both by mutual affection and the mutual benefits of commerce, several favours and indulgences were granted them. The restraint upon rice, an innumerated commodity, was partly taken off; and, that it might arrive more seasonably and in better condition at the market, the colonists were permitted to send it to any port southward of Cape Finisterre. A discount upon hemp was also allowed by parliament. The arrears of quit-rents bought from the Proprietors were remitted by a bounty from the Crown. For the benefit and enlargement of trade their bills of credit were continued, and seventy-seven thousand pounds were stamped and issued by virtue of an act of the legislature, called the Appropriation Law. Seventy pieces of cannon were sent out by the King, and the Governor had instructions to build one fort at Port-Royal, and another on the river Alatamaha. An independent company of foot was allowed for their defence by land, and ships of war were stationed there for the protection of trade. These and many more favours flowed to the colony, now emerging from the depths of poverty and oppression, and arising to a state of freedom, ease and affluence.

[Sidenote] Happy effects of peace and security.

As a natural consequence of its domestic security, the credit of the province in England increased. The merchants of London, Bristol, and Liverpool turned their eyes to Carolina, as a new and promising channel of trade, and established houses in Charlestown for conducting their business with the greater ease and success. They poured in slaves from Africa for cultivating their lands, and manufactures of Britain for supplying the plantations; by which means the planters obtained great credit, and goods at a much cheaper rate than they could be obtained from any other nation. In consequence of which the planters having greater strength, turned their whole attention to cultivation, and cleared the lands with greater facility and success. The lands arose in value, and men of foresight and judgment began to look out and secure the richest spots for themselves, with that ardour and keenness which the prospects of riches naturally inspire. The produce of the province in a few years was doubled. During this year above thirty-nine thousand barrels of rice were exported, besides deer-skins, furs, naval stores, and provisions; and above one thousand five hundred negroes were imported into it. From this period its exports kept pace with its imports, and secured its credit in England. The rate of exchange had now arisen to seven hundred *per cent. i. e.* seven hundred Carolina money was given for a bill of an hundred pounds sterling on England; at which rate it afterwards continued, with little variation, for upwards of forty years.

Hitherto small and inconsiderable was the progress in cultivation Carolina had made, and the face of the country appeared like a desert, with little spots here and there cleared, scarcely discernible amidst the immense forest. The colonists were slovenly farmers, owing to the vast quantities of lands, and the easy and cheap terms of obtaining them; for a good crop they were more indebted to the great power of vegetation and natural richness of the soil, than to their own good culture and judicious management. They had abundance of the necessaries, and several of the conveniencies of life. But their habitations were clumsy and miserable huts, and having no chaises, all travellers were exposed in open boats or on horseback to the violent heat of the climate. Their houses were constructed of wood, by erecting first a wooden frame, and then covering it with clap-boards without, and plastering it with lime within, of which they had plenty made from oyster-shells. Charlestown, at this time, consisted of between five and six hundred houses, mostly built of timber, and neither well constructed nor comfortable, plain indications of the wretchedness and poverty of the people. However, from this period the province improved in building as well as in many other respects; many ingenious artificers and tradesmen of different kinds found encouragement in it, and introduced a taste for brick buildings, and more neat and pleasant habitations. In process of time, as the colony increased in numbers, the face of the country changed, and exhibited an appearance of industry and plenty. The planters made a rapid progress towards wealth and independence, and the trade being well protected, yearly increased and flourished.

[Sidenote] A project formed for planting a new colony

At the same time, for the relief of poor and indigent people of Great Britain and Ireland, and for the farther security of Carolina, the settlement of a new colony between the rivers Alatamaha and Savanna was projected in England. This large territory, situated on the south-west of Carolina, yet lay waste, without an inhabitant except its original savages. Private compassion and public spirit conspired towards promoting the excellent design. Several persons of humanity and opulence having observed many families and valuable subjects oppressed with the miseries of poverty at home, united, and formed a plan for raising money and transporting them to this part of America. For this purpose they applied to the King, obtained from him letters-patent, bearing date June 9th, 1732, for legally carrying into execution what they had generously projected. They called the new province Georgia, in honour of the King, who likewise greatly encouraged the undertaking. A Corporation consisting of twenty-one persons was constituted, by the name of Trustees, for settling and establishing the Colony of Georgia; which was separated from Carolina by the river Savanna. The Trustees having first set an example themselves, by largely contributing towards the scheme, undertook also to solicit benefactions from others, and to apply the money towards clothing, arming, purchasing utensils for cultivation, and transporting such poor people as should consent to go over and begin a settlement. They however confined not their views to the subjects of Britain alone, but wisely opened a door also for oppressed and indigent Protestants from other nations. To prevent any misapplication or abuse of charitable donations, they agreed to deposit the money in the bank of England, and to enter in a book the names of all the charitable benefactors, together with the sums contributed by each of them; and to bind and oblige themselves, and their successors in office, to lay a state of the money received and expended before the Lord Chancellor of England, the Lord Chief Justice of the King's

Bench and Common Pleas, the Master of the Rolls, and the Lord Chief Baron of the Exchequer.

When this scheme of the Trustees with respect to the settlement of Georgia was made public, the well-wishers of mankind in every part of Britain highly approved of an undertaking so humane and disinterested. To consult the public happiness, regardless of private interest, and to stretch forth a bountiful hand for relief of distressed fellow-creatures, were considered as examples of uncommon benevolence and virtue, and therefore worthy of general imitation. The ancient Romans, famous for their courage and magnanimity, ranked the planting of colonies among their noblest works, and such as added greater lustre to their empire than their most glorious wars and victories. By the latter old cities were plundered and destroyed; by the former new ones were founded and established. The latter ravaged the dominions of enemies, and depopulated the world; the former improved new territories, provided for unfortunate friends, and added strength to the state. The benevolent founders of the colony of Georgia perhaps may challenge the annals of any nation to produce a design more generous and praise-worthy than that they had undertaken. They voluntarily offered their money, their labour, and time, for promoting what appeared to them the good of others, leaving themselves nothing for reward but the inexpressible satisfaction arising from virtuous actions. Among other great ends they had also in view the conversion and civilization of Indian savages. If their public regulations were afterwards found improper and impracticable; if their plan of settlement proved too narrow and circumscribed; praise, nevertheless, is due to them. Human policy at best is imperfect; but, when the design appears so evidently good and disinterested, the candid and impartial part of the world will make many allowances for them, considering their ignorance of the country, and the many defects that cleave to all codes of laws, even when framed by the wisest legislators.

About the middle of July, 1732, the trustees for Georgia held their first general meeting, when Lord Percival was chosen President of the Corporation. After all the members had qualified themselves, agreeable to the charter, for the faithful discharge of the trust, a common seal was ordered to be made. The device was, on one side, two figures resting upon urns, representing the rivers Alatamaha and Savanna, the boundaries of the province; between them the genius of the colony seated, with a cap of liberty on his head, a spear in one hand and a cornucopia in the other, with the inscription, COLONIA GEORGIA AUG.: on the other side was a represention of silk worms, some beginning and others having finished their web, with the motto, NON SIBI SED ALIIS; a very proper emblem, signifying, that the nature of the establishment was such, that neither the first trustees nor their successors could have any views of interest, it being entirely designed for the benefit and happiness of others.

[Sidenote] James Oglethorpe carries a colony to Georgia.

In November following, one hundred and sixteen settlers embarked at Gravesend for Georgia, having their passage paid, and every thing requisite for building and cultivation furnished them by the Corporation. They could not properly be called adventurers, as they run no risque but what arose from the change of climate, and as they were to be maintained until by their industry they were able to support themselves. James Oglethorpe, one of the Trustees, embarked along with them, and proved a zealous and active promoter of the settlement. In the beginning of the year following Oglethorpe arrived in Charlestown, where he was received by the Governor and Council in the kindest manner, and treated with every mark of civility and respect. Governor Johnson, sensible of the great advantage that must accrue to Carolina from this new colony; gave all the encouragement and assistance in his power to forward the settlement. Many of the Carolineans sent them provisions, and hogs, and cows to begin their stock. William Bull, a man of knowledge and experience, agreed to accompany Mr. Oglethorpe, and the rangers and scout-boats were ordered to attend him to Georgia. After their arrival at Yamacraw, Oglethorpe and Bull explored the country, and having found an high and pleasant spot of ground, situated on a navigable river, they fixed on this place as the most convenient and healthy situation for the settlers. On this hill they marked out a town, and, from the Indian name of the river which ran past it, called it Savanna. A small fort was erected on the banks of it as a place of refuge, and some guns were mounted on it for the defence of the colony. The people were set to work in felling trees and building huts for themselves, and Oglethorpe animated and encouraged them, by exposing himself to all the hardships which the poor objects of his compassion endured. He formed them into a company of militia, appointed officers from among themselves, and furnished them with arms and ammunition. To shew the Indians how expert they were at the use of arms, he frequently exercised them; and as they had been trained beforehand by the serjeants of the guards in London, they performed their various parts in a manner little inferior to regular troops.

[Sidenote] He treats with Indians for a share of their lands.

Having thus put his colony in as good a situation as possible, the next object of his attention was to treat with the Indians for a share of their possessions. The principal tribes that at this time occupied the territory were the Upper and Lower Creeks; the former were numerous and strong, the latter, by diseases and war, had been reduced to a smaller number: both tribes together were computed to amount to about twenty-five thousand, men, women and children. Those Indians, according to a treaty formerly made with Governor Nicolson, laid claim to the lands lying south-west of Savanna river, and, to procure their friendship for this infant colony, was an object of the highest consequence. But as the tribe of Indians settled at Yamacraw was inconsiderable, Oglethorpe judged it necessary to have the other tribes also to join with them in the treaty. To accomplish this union he found an Indian woman named Mary, who had married a trader from Carolina, and who could speak both the English and Creek languages; and perceiving that she had great influence among Indians, and might be made useful as an interpreter in forming treaties of alliance with them; he therefore first purchased her friendship with presents, and afterwards settled an hundred pounds yearly on her, as a reward for her services. By her assistance he summoned a general meeting of the chiefs, to hold a congress with him at Savanna, in order to procure their consent to the peaceable settlement of his colony. At this congress fifty chieftains were present, when Oglethorpe represented to them the great power, wisdom and wealth of the English nation, and the many advantages that would accrue to Indians in general from a connection and friendship with them; and as they had plenty of lands, he hoped they would freely resign a share of them to his people, who were come for their benefit and instruction to settle among them. After having distributed some presents, which must always attend every proposal of friendship and peace, an agreement was made, and then Tomochichi, in name of the Creek warriors, addressed him in the following manner: "Here is a little present, and, giving him a buffaloe's skin, adorned on the inside with the head and feathers of an eagle, desired him to accept it, because the eagle was an emblem of speed, and the buffalo of strength. He told him, that the English were as swift as the bird and as strong as the beast, since, like the former, they flew over vast seas to the uttermost parts of the earth; and, like the latter, they were so strong that nothing could withstand them. He said, the feathers of the eagle were soft, and signified love; the buffalo's skin was warm, and signified protection; and therefore he hoped the English would love and protect their little families." Oglethorpe accordingly accepted the present, and after having concluded this treaty limited by the nature of their government, was nevertheless great, as they always directed the public councils in all affairs relative to peace and war. It is true their young men, fond of fame and glory from warlike exploits, and rejoicing in opportunities of distinguishing themselves, will now and then, in contempt to the power of their old leaders, break out in scalping parties. To moderate and restrain the fiery passions of the young men, the sages find generally the greatest difficulties, especially as these passions are often roused by gross frauds and impositions. Unprincipled and avaricious traders sometimes resided among them, who, that they might the more easily cheat them, first filled the savages drunk, and then took all manner of advantages of them in the course of traffic. When the Indian recovered from his fit of drunkenness, and finding himself robbed of his treasures, for procuring which he had perhaps hunted a whole year, he is filled with fury, and breathes vengeance and resentment. No authority can then restrain him within the bounds of moderation. At such a juncture in vain does the leader of the greatest influence interpose. He spurns at every person that presumes to check that arm by which alone he defends his property against the hands of fraud and injustice. Among themselves indeed theft is scarcely known, and injuries of this kind are seldom committed; and had the traders observed in general the same justice and equity in their dealings with them, as they commonly practice among themselves, it would have been an easy matter with their wise and grave leaders to maintain peace in all the different intercourses between Europeans and Indians. Tomochichi acknowledged, that the Governor of the world had given the English great wisdom, power and riches, insomuch that they wanted nothing; he had given Indians great territories, yet they wanted every thing; and he prevailed on the Creeks freely to resign such lands to the English as were of no use to themselves, and to allow them to settle among them, on purpose that they might get instruction, and be supplied with the various necessaries of life. He persuaded them, that the English were a generous nation, and would trade with them on the most just and honourable terms; that they were brethren and friends, and would protect them from danger, and go with them to war against all their enemies.

Some say that James Oglethorpe, when he came out to settle this colony in Georgia, brought along with him Sir Walter Raleigh's journals, written by his own hand; and by the latitude of the place, and the traditions of the Indians, it appeared to him that Sir Walter had landed at the mouth of Savanna river. Indeed during his wild and chimerical attempts for finding out a golden country, it is not improbable that this brave adventurer visited many different places. The Indians acknowledged that their fathers once held a conference with a warrior who came over the great waters. At a little distance from Savanna, there is an high mount of earth, under which they say the Indian King lies interred, who talked with the English warrior, and that he desired to be buried in the same place where this conference was held. But having little authority with respect to this matter, we leave the particular relation of it to men in circumstances more favourable for intelligence.

[Sidenote] The colony of Switzers brought to Carolina.

While the security of Carolina, against external enemies, by this settlement of Georgia, engaged the attention of British government, the means of its internal improvement and population at the same time were not neglected. John Peter Pury, a native of Neufchatel in Switzerland, having formed a design of leaving his native country, paid a visit to Carolina, in order to inform himself of the circumstances, and situation of the province. After viewing the lands there, and procuring all the information he could, with respect to the terms of obtaining them, he returned to Britain. The government entered into a contract with him, and, for the encouragement of the people, agreed to give lands and four hundred pounds sterling for every hundred effective men he should transport from Switzerland to Carolina. Pury, while in Carolina, having furnished himself with a flattering account of the soil and climate, and of the excellence and freedom of the provincial government, returned to Switzerland, and, published it among the people. Immediately one hundred and seventy poor Switzers agreed to follow him, and were transported to the fertile and delightful province as he described it; and not long afterwards two hundred more came over, and joined them. The Governor, agreeable to instructions, allotted forty thousand acres of lands for the use of the Swiss settlement on the north-east side of Savanna river; and a town was marked out for their accommodation, which he called Purisburgh, from the name of the principal promoter of the settlement. Mr. Bignion, a Swiss minister, whom they had engaged to go with them, having received episcopal ordination from the bishop of London, settled among them for their religious instruction. On the one hand the Governor and council, happy in the acquisition of such a force, allotted each of them his separate tract of land, and gave every encouragement in their power to the people: On the other, the poor Swiss emigrants began their labours with uncommon zeal and courage, highly elevated with the idea of possessing landed estates, and big with the hopes of future success. However, in a short time they felt the many inconveniencies attending a change of climate. Several of them sickened and died, and others found all the hardships of the first state of colonization falling heavily upon them. They became discontented with the provisions allowed them, and complained to government of the persons employed to distribute them; and, to double their distress, the period for receiving the bounty expired before they had made such progress in cultivation as to raise sufficient provisions for themselves and families. The spirit of murmur crept into the poor Swiss settlement, and the people finding themselves oppressed with indigence and distress, could consider their situation in no other light than a state of banishment, and not only blamed Pury for deceiving them, but also heartily repented their leaving their native country.

[Sidenote] Eleven townships marked out.

According to the new plan adopted in England for the more speedy population and settlement of the province; the Governor had instructions to mark out eleven townships, in square plats, on the sides of rivers, consisting each of twenty thousand acres, and to divide the lands within them into shares of fifty acres for each man, woman, and child, that should come over to occupy and improve them. Each township was to form a parish, and all the inhabitants were to have an equal right to the river. So soon as the parish should increase to the number of an hundred families, they were to have right to send two members of their own election to the Assembly, and to enjoy the same privileges as the other parishes already established. Each settler was to pay four shillings a year for every hundred acres of land, excepting the first ten years, during which term they were to be rent free. Governor Johnson issued a warrant to St. John, Surveyor-general of the province, empowering him to go and mark out those townships. But he having demanded an exorbitant sum of money for his trouble, the members of the council agreed among themselves to do this piece of service for their country. Accordingly eleven townships were marked out by them in the following situations; two on river Alatamacha, two on Savanna, two on Santee, one on Pedee, one on Wacamaw, one on Watcree, and one on Black rivers.

[Sidenote] A struggle about lands.

The old planters now acquiring every year greater strength of hands, by the large importation of negroes, and extensive credit from England, began to turn their attention more closely than ever to the lands of the province. A spirit of emulation broke out among them for securing tracts of the richest ground, but especially such as were most conveniently situated for navigation. Complaints were made to the Assembly, that all the valuable lands on navigable rivers and Creeks adjacent to Port-Royal had been run out in exorbitant tracts, under colour of patents granted by the Proprietors to Cassiques and Landgraves, by which the complainants, who had, at the hazard of their lives, defended the country, were hindered from obtaining such lands as could be useful and beneficial, at the established quit-rents, though the Attorney and Solicitor-General of England had declared such patents void. Among others, Job Rothmaller and Thomas Cooper, having been accused of some illegal practices with respect to this matter, a petition was presented to the Assembly by thirty-nine inhabitants of Granville county in their vindication. When the Assembly examined into the matter, they ordered their messenger forthwith to take into custody Job Rothmaller and Thomas Cooper, for aiding, assisting, and superintending the deputy-surveyor in marking out tracks of land already surveyed, contrary to the quit rent act. But Cooper, being taken into custody, applied to Chief Justice Wright for a writ of *habeas corpus*, which was granted. The Assembly, however, sensible of the ill consequences that would attend such illegal practices, determined to put a stop to them by an act made on purpose. They complained to the Governor and Council against the Surveyor-General, for encouraging land-jobbers, and allowing such liberties as tended to create litigious disputes in the province, and to involve it in great confusion. In consequence of which, the Governor, to give an effectual check to such practices, prohibited St. John to survey lands to any person without an express warrant from him. The Surveyor-general, however, determined to make the most of his office, and having a considerable number to support him, represented both Governor and Council as persons disaffected to his Majesty's government, and enemies to the interest of the country. Being highly offended at the Assembly, he began to take great liberties without doors, and to turn some of their speeches into ridicule. Upon which an order was issued to take St. John also into custody; and then the Commons came to the following spirited resolutions: "That it is the undeniable privilege of this Assembly to commit such persons they may judge to deserve it: That the freedom of speech and debate ought not to be impeached or questioned in any court or place out of that house: That it is a contempt and violation of the privileges of that house, to call in question any of their commitments: That no writ of *habeas corpus* lies in favour of any person committed by that house, and that the messenger attending do yield no obedience to such; and that the Chief Justice be made acquainted with these resolutions." In consequence of which, Wright complained before the Governor and Council of these resolutions, as tending to the dissolution of all government, and charged the lower house with disallowing his Majesty's undoubted prerogative, and with renouncing obedience to his writs of *habeas corpus*. But the Council in general approved of their conduct, and were of opinion, that the Assembly of Carolina had that same privilege there, that the House of Commons had in England. In short, this affair created some trouble in the colony. For while a strong party, from motives of private interest, supported the Chief Justice; the Assembly resolved, "That he appeared to be prejudiced against the people, and was therefore unworthy of the office he held, and that it would tend to the tranquillity of the province immediately to suspend him."

In this situation was the colony about the end of the year 1733. Each planter, eager in the pursuit of large possessions of land, which were formerly neglected, because of little value, strenuously vied with his neighbour for a superiority of fortune, and seemed impatient of every restraint that hindered or cramped him in his favourite pursuit. Many favours and indulgences had already been granted them from the Crown, for promoting their success and prosperity, and for securing the province against external enemies. What farther favours they expected, we may learn from the following Memorial and Representation of the state of Carolina, transmitted to his Majesty, bearing date April 9th, 1734, and signed by the Governor, the President of the Council, and the Speaker of the Commons House of Assembly.

[Sidenote] State of the colony.

"Your Majesty's most dutiful subjects of this province, having often felt, with hearts full of gratitude, the many signal instances of your Majesty's peculiar favour and protection, to those distant parts of your dominions, and especially those late proofs of your Majesty's most gracious and benign care, so wisely calculated for the preservation of this your Majesty's frontier province on the continent of America, by your royal charter to the Trustees for establishing the colony of Georgia, and your great goodness so timely applied, for the promoting the settlement of the Swiss at Purisburgh; encouraged by such views of your Majesty's wise and paternal care, extended to your remotest subjects, and excited by the duty we owe to your most sacred Majesty, to be always watchful for the support and security of your Majesty's interest, especially at this very critical conjuncture, when the flame of a war breaking out in Europe may very speedily be lighted here, in this your Majesty's frontier province, which, in situation, is known to be of the utmost importance to the general trade and traffic in America: we, therefore, your Majesty's most faithful Governor, Council, and Commons, convened in your Majesty's province of South Carolina, crave leave with great humility to represent to your Majesty the present state and condition of this your province, and how greatly it stands in need of your Majesty's gracious and timely succour in case of a war, to assist our defence against the French and Spaniards, or any other enemies to your Majesty's dominions, as well as against the many nations of savages which so nearly threaten the safety of your Majesty's subjects.

"The province of South Carolina, and the new colony of Georgia, are the southern frontiers of all your Majesty's dominions on the continent of America; to the south and south-west of which is situated the strong castle of St. Augustine, garrisoned by four hundred Spaniards, who have several nations of Indians under their subjection, besides several other small settlements and garrisons, some of which are not eighty miles distant from the colony of Georgia. To the south-west and west of us the French have erected a considerable town, near Fort Thoulouse on the Moville river, and several other forts and garrisons, some not above three hundred miles distant from our settlements; and at New Orleans on the Mississippi river, since her late Majesty Queen Anne's war, they have exceedingly increased their strength and traffic, and have now many forts and garrisons on both sides of that great river for several hundred miles up the same; and since his most Christian Majesty has taken out of the Mississippi Company the government of that country into his own hands, the French natives in Canada come daily down in shoals to settle all along that river, where many regular forces have of late been sent over by the King to strengthen the garrisons in those places, and, according to our best and latest advices, they have five hundred men in pay, constantly employed as wood-rangers, to keep their neighbouring Indians in subjection, and to prevent the distant ones from disturbing the settlements; which management of the French has so well succeeded, that we are very well assured they have now wholly in their possession and under their influence, the several numerous nations of Indians that are situated near the Mississippi river, one of which, called the Choctaws, by estimation consists of about five thousand fighting men, and who were always deemed a very warlike nation, lies on this side the river, not above four hundred miles distant from our out-settlements, among whom, as well as several other nations of Indians, many French Europeans have been sent to settle, whom the priests and missionaries among them encourage to take Indian wives, and use divers other alluring methods to attach the Indians the better to the French alliance, by which means the French are become throughly acquainted with the Indian way, warring and living in the woods, and have now a great number of white men among them, able to perform a long march with an army of Indians upon any expedition.

"We further beg leave to inform your Majesty, that if the measures of France should provoke your Majesty to a state of hostility against it in Europe, we have great reason to expect an invasion will be here made upon your Majesty's subjects by the French and Indians from the Mississippi settlements. They have already paved a way for a design of that nature, by erecting a fort called the Albama fort, alias Fort Lewis, in the middle of the Upper Creek Indians, upon a navigable river leading to Mobile, which they have kept well garrisoned and mounted with fourteen pieces of cannon, and have lately been prevented from erecting a second nearer to us on that quarter. The Upper Creeks are a nation very bold, active and daring, consisting of about two thousand five hundred fighting men, (and not above one hundred and fifty miles distant from the Choctaws), whom, through we heretofore have traded with, claimed and held in our alliance, yet the French, on account of that fort and a superior ability to make them liberal presents, have been for some time striving to draw them over to their interest, and have succeeded with some of the towns of the Creeks; which, if they can be secured in your Majesty's interest, are the only nation which your Majesty's subjects here can depend upon as the best barrier against any attempts either of the French or their confederate Indians.

"We most humbly beg leave farther to inform your Majesty, that the French at Mobile perceiving that they could not gain the Indians to their interest without buying their deer-skins, (which is the only commodity the Indians have to purchase necessaries with), and the French not being able to dispose of those skins by reason of their having no vent for them in Old France, they have found means to encourage vessels from hence, New-York, and other places, (which are not prohibited by the acts of trade), to truck those skins with them for Indian trading goods, especially the British woollen manufactures, which the French dispose of to the Creeks and Choctaws, and other Indians, by which means the Indians are much more alienated from our interest, and on every occasion object to us that the French can supply them with strouds and blankets as well as the English, which would have the contrary effect if they were wholly supplied with those commodities by your Majesty's subjects trading with them. If a stop were therefore put to that pernicious trade with the French, the chief dependence of the Creek Indians would be on this government, and that of Georgia, to supply them with goods; by which means great part of the Choctaws, living next the Creeks, would see the advantage the Creek Indians enjoyed by having British woollen manufactures wholly from your Majesty's subjects, and thereby be invited in a short time to enter into a treaty of commerce with us, which they have lately made some offers for, and which, if effected, will soon lessen the interest of the French with those Indians, and by degrees attach them to that of your Majesty.

"The only expedient we can propose to recover and confirm that nation to your Majesty's interest, is by speedily making them presents to withdraw them from the French alliance, and by building some forts among them your Majesty may be put in such a situation, that on the first notice of hostilities with the French, your Majesty may be able at once to reduce the Albama fort, and we may then stand against the French and their Indians, which, if not timely prepared for before a war breaks out, we have too much reason to fear we may be soon over-run by the united strength of the French, the Creeks and Choctaws, with many other nations of their Indian allies: for, should the Creeks become wholly enemies, who are well acquainted with all our settlements, we probably should also be soon deserted by the Cherokees, and a few others, small tribes of Indians, who, for the sake of our booty, would readily join to make us a prey to the French and savages. Ever since the late Indian war, the offences given us then by the Creeks have made that nation very jealous of your Majesty's subjects of this province. We have therefore concerted measures with the honourable James Oglethorpe, Esq; who, being at the head of a new colony, will (we hope) be successful for your Majesty's interest among that people. He has already by presents attached the Lower Creeks to your Majesty, and has laudably undertaken to endeavour the fixing a garrison among the Upper Creeks, the expence of which is already in part provided for in this session of the General Assembly of this province. We hope therefore to prevent the French from encroaching farther on your Majesty's territories, until your Majesty is graciously pleased further to strengthen and secure the same.

"We find the Cherokee nation has lately become very insolent to your Majesty's subjects trading among them, notwithstanding the many favours the chiefs of that nation received from your Majesty in Great-Britain, besides a considerable expence which your Majesty's subjects of this province have been at in making them presents, which inclines us to believe that the French, by their Indians, have been tampering with them. We therefore beg leave to inform your Majesty, that the building and mounting some forts likewise among the Cherokees, and making them presents will be highly necessary to keep them steady in their duty to your Majesty, lest the French may prevail in seducing that nation, which they may the more readily be inclined to from the prospect of getting considerable plunder in slaves, cattle, &c. commodities which they very well know we have among us, several other forts will be indispensibly necessary, to be a cover to your Majesty's subjects settled backwards in this province, as also to those of the colony of Georgia, both which in length are very extensive; for though the trustees for establishing the colony of Georgia, by a particular scheme of good management, painfully conducted by the gentleman engaged here in that charitable enterprise, has put that small part of the colony, which he has not yet been able to establish, in a tenable condition, against the Spaniards of Florida which lie to the southward; yet the back exposition of those colonies to the vast number of French and Indians which border on the westward, must, in case of a war, cry greatly aloud for your Majesty's gracious and timely succour. The expense of our safety on such an occasion, we must, with all humility, acquaint your Majesty, either for men or money, can never be effected by your Majesty's subjects of this province, who, in conjunction with Georgia, do not in the whole amount to more than three thousand five hundred men, which compose the militia, and wholly consist of planters, tradesmen, and other men of business.

"Besides the many dangers which by land we are exposed to from so many enemies that lie on the back of us; we further beg leave to represent to your Majesty, the defenceless condition of our ports and harbours, where any enemies of your Majesty's dominions may very easily by sea invade us, there being no fortifications capable of making much resistance. Those in Charlestown harbour are now in a very shattered condition, occasioned by the late violent storms and hurricanes, which already cost this country a great deal of money, and now requires several thousands of pounds to repair the old and build new ones, to mount the ordnance which your Majesty was graciously pleased to send us, which, with great concern, we must inform your Majesty we have not yet been able to accomplish, being lately obliged, for the defence and support of this your Majesty's province and government, to raise, by a tax on the inhabitants, a supply of above forty thousand pounds paper currency *per annum*, which is a considerable deal more than a third part of all the currency among us; a charge which your Majesty's subjects of this province are but barely able to sustain. Since your Majesty's royal instruction to your Majesty's Governor here, an entire stop has been put to the duties which before accrued from European goods imported; and if a war should happen, or any thing extraordinary, to be farther expensive here, we should be under the utmost difficulties to provide additionally for the same, lest an increase of taxes with an apprehension of danger, should drive away many of our present inhabitants, as well as discourage others from coming here to settle for the defence and improvement of your Majesty's province, there being several daily moving with their families and effects to North Carolina, where there are no such fears and burdens.

"We must therefore beg leave to inform your Majesty, that, amidst our other perilous circumstances, we are subject to many intestine dangers from the great number of negroes that are now among us, who amount at least to twenty-two thousand persons, and are three to one of all your Majesty's white subjects in this province. Insurrections against us have been often attempted, and would at any time prove very fatal if the French should instigate them, by artfully giving them an expectation of freedom. In such a situation we most humbly crave leave to acquaint your Majesty, that even the present ordinary expences necessary for the care and support of this your Majesty's province and government, cannot be provided for by your Majesty's subjects of this province, without your Majesty's gracious pleasure to continue those laws for establishing the duty on negroes and other duties for seven years, and for appropriating the same, which now lie before your Majesty for your royal assent and approbation; and the further expences that will be requisite for the erecting some forts, and establishing garrisons in the several necessary places, so as to form a barrier for the security of this your Majesty's province, we most humbly submit to your Majesty.

"Your Majesty's subjects of this province, with fulness of zeal, duty and affection to your most gracious and sacred Majesty, are so highly sensible of the great importance of this province to the French, that we must conceive it more than probable, if a war should happen, they will use all endeavours to bring this country under their subjection; they would be thereby enabled to support their sugar islands with all sorts of provisions and lumber by an easy navigation, which to our great advantage is not so practicable from the present French colonies, besides the facility of gaining then to their interest most of the Indian trade on the northern continent; they might then easily unite the Canadees and Choctaws, with the many other nations of Indians which are now in their interest. And the several ports and harbours of Carolina and Georgia, which now enable your Majesty to be absolute master of the passage through the Gulf of Florida, and to impede, at your pleasure, the transportation home of the Spanish treasure, would then prove for many convenient harbours for your Majesty's enemies, by their privateers or ships of war to annoy a great part of the British trade to America, as well as that which is carried on through the Gulf from Jamaica; besides the loss which Great Britain must feel in so considerable a part of its navigation, as well as the exports of masts, pitch, tar, and turpentine, which, without any dependence on the northern parts of Europe, are from hence plentifully supplied for the use of the British shipping.

"This is the present state and condition of your Majesty's province of South Carolina, utterly incapable of finding funds sufficient for the defence of this wide frontier, and so destitute of white men, that even money itself cannot here raise a sufficient body of them.

"With all humility we therefore beg leave to lay ourselves at the feet of your Majesty, humbly imploring your Majesty's most gracious care in the extremities we should be reduced to on the breaking out of a war; and that your Majesty would be graciously pleased to extend your protection to us, as your Majesty, in your great wisdom, shall think proper."

[Sidenote] The regulations of the Trustees.

In the mean time the Trustees for Georgia had been employed in framing a plan of settlement and establishing such public regulations as they judged most proper for answering the great end of the corporation. In this general plan they considered each inhabitant both as a planter and a soldier who must be provided with arms and ammunition for defence, as well as with tools and utensils for cultivation. As the strength of the province was their chief object in view, they agreed to establish such tenures for holding lands in it as they judged most favourable for a military establishment. Each tract of land granted was considered as a military fief, for which the possessor was to appear in arms, and take the field, when called upon for the public defence. To prevent large tracts from falling in process of time into one hand, they agreed to grant their lands in tail male in preference to tail general. On the termination of the estate in tail male, the lands were to revert to the trust; and such lands thus reverting were to be granted again to such persons, as the common council of the trust should judge most advantageous for the colony; only the Trustees in such a case were to pay special regard to the daughters of such persons as had made improvements on their lots, especially when not already provided for by marriage. The wives of such persons as should survive them, were to be during their lives entitled to the mansion-house, and one-half of the lands improved by their husbands. No man was to be permitted to depart the province without licence. If any part of the lands granted by the Trustees, shall not by cultivated, cleared, and fenced round about with a worm fence, or pales, six feet high, within eighteen years from the date of the grant, such part was to revert to the trust, and the grant with respect to it to be void. All forfeitures for non-residence, high-treason, felonies, &c. were to the Trustees for the use and benefit of the colony. The use of negroes was to be absolutely prohibited, and also the importation of rum. None of the colonists were to be permitted to trade with Indians, but such as should obtain a special licence for that purpose.

[Sidenote] Their impolitical restrictions.

These were some of the fundamental regulations established by the Trustees of Georgia, and perhaps the imagination of man could scarcely have framed a system of rules worse adapted to the circumstances and situation of the poor settlers, and of more pernicious consequence to the prosperity of the province. Yet, although the Trustees were greatly mistaken, with respect to their plan of settlement, it must be acknowledged their views were generous. As the people sent out by them were the poor and unfortunate, who were to be provided with necessaries at their public store, they received their lands upon condition of cultivation, and by their personal residence, of defence. Silk and wine being the chief articles intended to be raised, they judged negroes were not requisite to these purposes. As the colony was designed to be a barrier to South Carolina, against the Spanish settlement at Augustine they imagined that negroes would rather weaken than strengthen it, and that such poor colonists would run into debt, and ruin themselves by purchasing them. Rum was judged pernicious to health, and ruinous to the infant settlement. A free trade with Indians was considered as a thing that might have a tendency to involve the people in quarrels and troubles with the powerful savages, and expose them to danger and destruction. Such were probably the motives which induced those humane and generous persons to impose such foolish and ridiculous restrictions on their colony. For by granting their small estates in tail male, they drove the settlers from Georgia, who soon found that abundance of lands could be obtained in America upon a larger scale, and on much better terms. By the prohibition of negroes, they rendered it impracticable in such a climate to make any impression on the thick forest, Europeans being utterly unqualified for the heavy task. By their discharging a trade with the West Indies, they not only deprived the colonists of an excellent and convenient market for their lumber, of which they had abundance on their lands, but also of rum, which, when mixed with a sufficient quantity of water, has been found in experience the cheapest, the most refreshing, and nourishing drink for workmen in such a soggy and burning climate. The Trustees, like other distant legislators, who framed their regulations upon principles of speculation, were liable to many errors and mistakes, and however good their design, their rules were found improper and impracticable. The Carolineans plainly perceived, that they would prove unsurmountable obstacles to the progress and prosperity of the colony, and therefore from motives of pity began to invite the poor Georgians to come over Savanna river, and settle in Carolina, being convinced that they could never succeed under such impolitic and oppressive restrictions.

[Sidenote] Two Colonies of Highlanders and Germans sent out.

Besides the large sums of money which the Trustees had expended for the settlement of Georgia, the Parliament had also granted during the two past years thirty-six thousand pounds towards carrying into execution the humane purpose of the corporation. But after the representation and memorial from the legislature of Carolina reached Britain, the nation considered Georgia to be of the utmost importance to the British settlements in America, and began to make still more vigorous efforts for its speedy population. The first embarkations of poor people from England, being collected from towns and cities, were found equally idle and useless members of society abroad, as they had been at home. An hardy and bold race of man, inured to rural labour and fatigue, they were persuaded would be much better adapted both for cultivation and defence. To find men possessed of these qualifications, the Trustees turned their eyes to Germany and the Highlands of Scotland, and resolved to send over a number of Scotch and German labourers to their infant province. When they published their terms at Inverness, an hundred and thirty Highlanders immediately accepted them, and were transported to Georgia. A town-ship on the river Alatamaha, which was considered as the boundary between the British and Spanish territories, was allotted for the Highlanders, on which dangerous situation they settled, and built a town, which they called New Inverness. About the same time an hundred and seventy Germans embarked with James Oglethorpe, and were fixed in another quarter; so that, in the space of three years, Georgia received above four hundred British subjects, and about an hundred and seventy foreigners. Afterwards several adventurers, both from Scotland and Germany, followed their countrymen, and added further strength to the province, and the Trustees flattered themselves with the hopes of soon seeing it in a promising condition.

[Sidenote] Thomas Broughton Lieut.-governor of Carolina.

The same year Carolina lost Robert Johnson, her favourite Governor, whose death was as much lamented by the people, as during his life he had been beloved and respected. The province having been much indebted to his wisdom, courage and abilities, to perpetuate his memory among them, and, in testimony of their esteem, a monument was erected in their church at the public expence. After his decease the government devolved on Thomas Broughton, a plain honest man, but little distinguished either for his knowledge or valour. As the welfare of the province depended greatly on its government, no man ought to be entrusted with such a charge but men of approved virtue and capacity. There is as much danger arising to a community from a feeble and contemptible government, as from an excess of power committed to its rulers. Weak and unexperienced hands hold the reins of government with awkwardness and difficulty, and being easily imposed upon, their authority sinks into contempt. At this time many of the leading men of the colony scrupled not to practise impositions, and being eagerly bent on engrossing lands, the Lieutenant-Governor freely granted them warrants; and the planters, provided they acquired large possessions, were not very scrupulous about the legality of the way and manner in which they were obtained.

[Sidenote] Oglethorpe fortifies Georgia.

James Oglethorpe having brought a number of great guns with him from England, now began to fortify Georgia, by erecting strong-holds on its frontiers, where he judged they might be useful for its safety and protection. At one place, which he called Augusta a fort was erected on the banks of Savanna river, which was excellently situated for protecting the Indian trade, and holding treaties of commerce and alliance with several of the savage nations. At another place, called Frederica, on an island nigh the mouth of the river Alatamaha, another fort, with four regular bastions, was erected, and several pieces of cannon were mounted on it. Ten miles nearer the sea a battery was raised, commanding the entrance into the sound, through which all ships of force must come that might be sent against Frederica. To keep little garrisons in these forts, to help the Trustees to defray the expences of such public works, ten thousand pounds were granted by the parliament of Great Britain.

[Sidenote] Which gives umbrage to the Spaniards.

While James Oglethorpe was thus busily employed in strengthening Georgia, he received a message from the Governor of Augustine, acquainting him that a Spanish Commissioner from Havanna had arrived there, in order to make certain demands of him, and would meet him at Frederica for that purpose. At the same time he had advice, that three companies of foot had came along with him to that Spanish settlement. A few days afterwards this Commissioner came to Georgia by sea, and Oglethorpe, unwilling to permit him to come to Frederica, dispatched a sloop to bring him into Jekyl Sound, where he intended to hold a conference with him. Here the Commissioner had the modesty to demand, that Oglethorpe and his people should immediately evacuate all the territories to the southward of St. Helena Sound, as they belonged to the King of Spain, who was determined to maintain his right to them; and if he refuted to comply with his demand, he had orders to proceed to Charlestown and lay the same before the Governor and Council of that province. Oglethorpe endeavoured to convince him that his Catholic Majesty had been misinformed with respect to those territories, but to no purpose; his instructions were peremptory, and the conference broke up without coming to any agreement. After which Oglethorpe embarked with all possible expedition, and sailed for England.

During his absence the strict law of the Trustees, respecting the rum trade, had like to have created a quarrel between the Carolineans and Georgians. The fortification at Augusta had induced some traders of Carolina to open stores at that place, so conveniently situated for commerce with Indian nations. For this purpose, land carriage being expensive, they intended to force their way by water with loaded boats up Savanna river to their stores at Augusta. But as they passed the town of Savanna, the magistrates rashly ordered the boats to be stopt, the packages to be opened, the casks of rum to be staved, and the people to be confined. Such injurious treatment was not to be suffered; the Carolineans determined to give a check to their insolence, and for that purpose deputed two persons, one from the Council and another from the Assembly, to demand of the Georgians by what authority they presumed to seize and destroy the effects of their traders, or to compel them to submit to their code of laws. The magistrates of Georgia, sensible of their error, made great concessions to the deputies, and treated them with the utmost civility and respect. The goods were instantly ordered to be returned, the people to be set at liberty, and all manner of satisfaction was given to the deputies they could have expected. Strict orders were sent to the agents of Georgia among Indians not to molest the traders from Carolina, but to give them all the assistance and protection in their power. The Carolineans, on the other hand, engaged not to smuggle any strong liquors among the settlers of Georgia, and the navigation on the river Savanna was declared equally open and free to both provinces.

[Sidenote] The brave Chickesaws defeat the French.

About the same time the French took the field against the Emperor; and the flames of war kindling between such powerful potentates, would, it was thought, inevitably spread, and involve all Europe in the quarrel. In case Great Britain should interfere in this matter; and declare in favour of the Emperor, orders were sent out to the Governors of Quebec and New Orleans to invade the weakest frontiers of the British settlements of America. For this purpose an army was formed in New France, and preparations were made for uniting the force of Canada and Louisiana to attack Carolina. But before this design was put in execution, advice came, that the clouds of war which threatened Europe were dispersed, and a general peace was restored, by the mediation of Britain and Holland. This put a stop to the motions of the main body in Canada; however, a detachment of two hundred French and four hundred Indians were sent down the Mississippi, to meet a party from New Orleans to cut off the Chickesaw Indians. This tribe were the firm allies of Britain, and the bravest nation of savages on the continent, but consisted only of between six and eight hundred gun-men. The French having encroached in their lands, and built some forts nigh them, had on that account drawn upon themselves their invincible enmity and resentment. The Chickesaws had long obstinately opposed their progress up the river Mississippi, and were now the chief obstacle that prevented a regular communication between Louisiana and Canada. The French determined to remove it, by extirpating this troublesome nation, and for this purpose fell down the river in boats to the place where they expected to meet their friends from New Orleans. But the party from the southward not coming up at the time appointed, and the Canadians thinking themselves strong enough for the enterprize, began the war by attacking the Chickesaw towns. Upon which the savages gathered together above three hundred warriors, gave the French battle in an open field, and, though with considerable loss, compleatly defeated them. Above forty Frenchmen and eight Indians were killed on the spot, and the rest were taken prisoners, among whom was their commander, and chief, brother to Mons. Bienville, Governor of New Orleans. Hard was the fate of the unfortunate prisoners, who for several days were kept almost perishing with hunger in the wilderness, and at last were tied to a stake, tortured, and burned to death. Another party of French from Mobile, in the same year, advanced against the Creeks, who were also unsuccessful, and obliged to retreat with considerable loss. Carolina rejoiced at those disasters, and began now more than ever to court the friendship and interest of these rude nations in their neighbourhood, considering them as the best barrier against their natural enemies.

[Sidenote] Religious state of the colony.

By this time the Episcopalian form of divine worship had gained ground in Carolina, and was more countenanced by the people than any other. That zeal for the right of private judgment had much abated, and those prejudices against the hierarchy, which the first emigrants carried from England with them, were now almost entirely worn off from the succeeding generation. To bring about this change, no doubt the well-timed zeal and extensive bounty of the society, incorporated for the propagation of the Gospel, had greatly contributed. At this time the corporation had no less than twelve missionaries in Carolina, each of whom shared of their bounty. Indeed, a mild church-government, together with able, virtuous, and prudent teachers, in time commonly give the establishment in every country a superiority over all sectaries. Spacious churches had been erected in the province, which were pretty well supplied with clergymen, who were paid from the public treasury, and countenanced by the civil authority, all which favoured the established church. The dissenters of Carolina were not only obliged to erect and uphold their churches, and maintain their clergy by private contributions, but also to contribute their share in the way of taxes, in proportion to their ability, equally with their neighbours; towards the maintenance of the poor, and the support of the establishment. This indeed many of them considered as a grievance, but having but few friends in the provincial assembly, no redress could be obtained for them. Besides, the establishment gave its adherents many advantageous privileges in point of power and authority over persons of other denominations. It gave them the best chance for being elected members of the legislature, and of course of being appointed to offices, both civil and military in their respective districts. Over youthful minds, fond of power, pomp and military parade, such advantages have great weight. Dissenters indeed had the free choice of their ministers, but even this is often the cause of division. When differences happen in a parish, the minority must yield, and therefore through private pique, discontent or resentment, they often conform to the establishment. It is always difficult, and often impossible for a minister to please all parties, especially where all claim an equal right to judge and chuse for themselves, and divisions and subdivisions seldom fail to ruin the power and influence of all sectaries. This was evidently the case in Carolina for many of the posterity of rigid Dissenters were now found firm adherents to the church of England, which had grown numerous on the ruins of the dissenting interest.

[Sidenote] The association of Presbyterians.

However, the emigrants from Scotland and Ireland, most of whom were Presbyterians, still composed a considerable party of the province, and kept up the Presbyterian form of worship in it. Archibald Stobo, of whom I have formerly taken notice, by great diligence and ability still preserved a number of followers. An association had been formed in favour of this mode of religious worship, by Messrs. Stobo, Fisher, and Witherspoon, three ministers of the church of Scotland, together with Joseph Stanyarn, and Joseph Blake, men of respectable characters and considerable fortunes. The Presbyterians had already erected churches at Charlestown, Wiltown, and in three of the maritime islands, for the use of the people adhering to that form of religious worship. As the inhabitants multiplied, several more in different parts of the province afterwards joined them, and built churches, particularly at Jacksonburgh, Indian Town, Port-Royal, and Williamsburgh. The first clergymen having received their ordination in the church of Scotland, the fundamental rules of the association were framed according to the forms, doctrines, and discipline of that establishment, to which they agreed to conform as closely as their local circumstances would admit. These ministers adopted this mode of religious worship, not only from a persuasion of its conformity to the primitive Apostolic form, but also from a conviction of its being, of all others, the most favourable to civil liberty, equality, and independence. Sensible that not only natural endowments, but also a competent measure of learning and acquired knowledge were necessary to qualify men for the sacred function, and enable them to discharge the duties of it with honour and success, they associated on purpose to prevent deluded mechanics, and illiterate novices from creeping into the pulpit, to the disgrace of the character, and the injury of religion. In different parts of the province, persons of this stamp had appeared, who cried down all establishments, both civil and religions, and seduced weak minds from the duties of allegiance, and all that the Presbytery could do was to prevent them from teaching under the sanction of their authority. But this association of Presbyterians having little countenance from government, and no name or authority in law, their success depended wholly on the superior knowledge, popular talents and exemplary life of their ministers. From time to time clergymen were afterwards sent out at the request of the people from Scotland and Ireland; and the colonists contributed to maintain them, till at length funds were established in trust by private legacies and donations, to be appropriated for the support of Presbyterian ministers, and the encouragement of that mode of religious worship and government.

[Sidenote] Remarks on paper-currency.

I have several times made remarks on the paper-currency of the province, which the planters were always for increasing, and the merchants and money lenders for sinking. The exchange of London, like a commercial thermometer, served to measure the rise or fall of paper-credit in Carolina; and the price of bills of exchange commonly ascertained the value of their current money. The permanent riches of the country consisted in lands, houses, and negroes; and the produce of the lands, improved by negroes, raw materials, provisions, and naval stores, were exchanged for what the province wanted from other countries. The attention of the mercantile part was chiefly employed about staple commodities; and as their great object was present profit it was natural for them to be governed by that great axiom in trade, whoever brings commodities cheapest and in the best order to market, must always meet with the greatest encouragement and success. The planters, on the other hand, attended to the balance of trade, which was turned in their favour, and concluded, that when the exports of any province exceeded its imports, whatever losses private persons might now and then sustain, yet that province upon the whole was growing rich. Let us suppose, what was indeed far from being the case, that Georgia so far advanced in improvement as to rival Carolina in raw materials, and exchangeable commodities, and to undersell her at the markets in Europe: This advantage could only arise from the superior quality of her lands, the cheapness of her labour, or her landed men being contented with smaller profits. In such a case it was the business of the Carolina merchants to lower the price of her commodities, in order to reap the same advantages with her neighbours; and this could only be done by reducing the quantity of paper-money in circulation. If gold and silver only past current in Georgia, which by general consent was the medium of commerce throughout the world, if she had a sufficient quantity of them to answer the purposes of trade, and no paper-currency had been permitted to pass current; in such case her commodities would bring their full value at the provincial market, and no more, according to the general standard of money in Europe. Supposing also that Carolina had a quantity of gold and silver in circulation, sufficient for the purposes of commerce, and that the planters, in order to raise the value of their produce, should issue paper-money equal to the quantity of gold and silver in circulation, the consequence would be, the price of labour, and of all articles of exportation would be doubled. But as the markets of Europe remained the same, and her commodities being of the same kind and quality with those of Georgia, they would not bring an higher price. Some persons must be losers, and in the fist instance this loss must fall on the mercantile interest, and moneyed men. Therefore this superabundance of paper-credit, on whose foundation the deluded province built its visionary fabric of great wealth, was not only useless, but prejudicial with respect to the community. Paper-money in such large quantities is the bane of commerce, a kind of fictitious wealth, making men by high founding language imagine they are worth thousands and millions, while a ship's load of it would not procure for the country a regiment of auxiliary troops in time of war, nor a suit of clothes at an European market in time of peace. Had America, from its first settlement, prohibited paper-money altogether, her staple commodities must have brought her, in the course of commerce, vast sums of gold and silver, which would have circulated through the continent, and answered all the purposes of trade both foreign and domestic. It is true the value of gold and silver is equally nominal, and rises and falls like the value of other articles of commerce, in proportion to the quantity in circulation. But as nations in general have fixed on these metals as the medium of trade, this has served to stamp a value on them, and render them the means not only of procuring every where the necessaries of life, but by supporting public credit, the chief means also of national protection.

However, some distinction in point of policy should perhaps be made between a colony in its infancy, and a nation already possessed of wealth, and in an advanced state of agriculture and commerce, especially while the former is united to, and under the protection of the latter. To a growing colony, such as Carolina, paper-credit, under certain limitations, was useful in several respects; especially as the gold and silver always left the country, when it answered the purpose of the merchant for remittance better than produce. This credit served to procure the planter strength of hands to clear and cultivate his fields, from which the real wealth of the province arose. But in an improved country such as England, supported by labourers, manufacturers and trade, large emissions of paper-money lessen the value of gold and silver, and both cause them to leave the country, and its produce and manufactures to come dearer to market. Adventurous planters in Carolina, eager to obtain a number of negroes, always stretched their credit with the traders to its utmost pitch; for as negroes on good lands cleared themselves in a few years, they by this means made an annual addition to their capital stock. After obtaining this credit, it then became their interest to maintain their superiority in assembly, and discharge their debt to the merchants in the easiest manner they could. The increase of paper-money always proved to them a considerable assistance, as it advanced the price of those commodities they brought to the market, by which they cancelled their debts with the merchants; so that however much this currency might depreciate, the loss occasioned by it from time to time fell not on the adventurous planters, but on the merchants and money-lenders, who were obliged to take it in payment of debts, or produce, which always arose in price in proportion to its depreciation.

In excuse for increasing provincial paper-money the planters always pled the exigencies of the public, such as warlike expeditions, raising fortifications, providing military stores, and maintaining garrisons; those no doubt rendered the measure sometimes necessary, and often reasonable, but private interest had also considerable weight in adopting it, and carrying it into execution. In the year 1737, a bill of exchange on London, for a hundred pounds sterling, sold for seven hundred and fifty pounds Carolina currency. Of this the merchants might complain, but from this period they had too little weight in the public councils to obtain any redress. The only resource left for them was to raise the price of negroes, and British articles of importation, according to the advanced price of produce, and bills of exchange. However, the exchange again fell to seven hundred *per cent.* at which standard it afterwards rested and remained.

[Sidenote] Small progress of Georgia.

By this time the poor colonists of Georgia, after trial, had become fully convinced of the impropriety and folly of the plan of settlement framed by the Trustees, which, however well intended, was ill adapted to their circumstances, and ruinous to the settlement. In the province of Carolina, which lay adjacent, the colonists discovered that there they could obtain lands not only on better terms, but also liberty to purchase negroes to assist in clearing and cultivating them. They found labour in the burning climate intolerable, and the dangers and hardships to which they were subjected unsurmountable. Instead of raising commodities for exportation, the Georgians, by the labour of several years, were not yet able to raise provisions sufficient to support themselves and families. Under each discouragements, numbers retired to the Carolina side of the river, where they had better prospects of success, and the magistrates observed the infant colony sinking into ruin, and likely to be totally deserted. The freeholders in and round Savanna assembled together, and drew up a state of their deplorable circumstances, and transmitted it to the Trustees, in which they represented their success in Georgia as a thing absolutely impossible, without the enjoyment of the same liberties and privileges with their neighbours in Carolina. In two respects they implored relief from the Trustees; they desired a fee-simple or free title to their lands, and liberty to import negroes under certain limitations, without which they declared they had neither encouragement to labour, nor ability to provide for their posterity. But the colony of Highlanders, instead of joining in this application, to a man remonstrated against the introduction of slaves. As they lay contiguous to the Spanish dominions, they were apprehensive that these enemies would entice their slaves from them in time of peace, and in time of war instigate them to rise against their masters. Besides, they considered perpetual slavery as shocking to human nature, and deemed the permission of it as a grievance, and which in some future day might also prove a scourge, and make many feel the smart of that oppression they so earnestly desired to introduce. For as the Spaniards had proclaimed freedom to them, they alledged that slaves would run away, and ruin poor planters; and at all events would disqualify them the more for defending the province against external enemies, while their families were exposed to barbarous domestics, provoked perhaps by harsh usage, or grown desperate through misery and oppression.

[Sidenote] Hardships of the first settlers.

Few persons who are acquainted with the country will wonder at the complaints of the poor settlers in Georgia; for if we consider the climate to which they were sent, and the labours and hardships they had to undergo, we may rather be astonished that any of them survived the first year after their arrival. When James Oglethorpe took possession of this wilderness, the whole was an immense thick forest, excepting savannas, which are natural plains where no trees grow, and a few Indian fields, where the savages planted maize for their subsistence. In the province there were the same wild animals, fishes, reptiles and insects, which were found in Carolina. The country in the maritime parts was likewise a spacious plain, covered with pine trees, where the lands were barren and sandy; and with narrow slips of oaks, hickory, cypress, cane, &c. where the lands were of a better quality.

Rains, thunder-storms, hurricanes, and whirlwinds, were equally frequent in the one province as in the other. Little difference could be perceived in the soil, which in both was barren or swampy; and the same diseases were common to both. The lands being covered with wood, through which the sea-breezes could not penetrate, there was little agitation in the air, which at some seasons was thick, heavy and foggy, and at others clear, close, and suffocating, both which are very pernicious to health. The air of the swampy land was pregnant with innumerable noxious qualities, insomuch that a more unwholesome climate was not perhaps to be found in the universe. The poor settlers considered this howling wilderness to which they were brought, to have been designed by nature rather for the habitation of wild beasts than human creatures. They found that diseases, or even misfortunes were in effect equally fatal: for though neither of them might prove mortal, yet either would disable them from living, and reduce them to a state in which they might more properly be said to perish than to die.

Nothing has retarded the progress and improvement of these southern settlements more than the inattention shewn to the natural productions of the soil, and the preference which has commonly been given to articles transplanted from Europe. Over the whole world different articles of produce are suited to different soils and climates. As Georgia lay so convenient for supplying the West Indies with maize, Indian pease, and potatoes, for which the demand was very great, perhaps the first planters could scarcely have turned their attention to more profitable articles, but without strength of hands little advantage could be reaped from them. It is true the West-India Islands would produce such articles, yet the planters would never cultivate them, while they could obtain them by purchase: the lands there suited other productions more valuable and advantageous. Abundance of stock, particularly hogs and black cattle, might have been raised in Georgia for the same market. Lumber was also in demand, and might have been rendered profitable to the province, but nothing could succeed there under the foolish restrictions of the Trustees. European grain, such as wheat, oats, barley, and rye, thrived very ill on the maritime parts; and even silk and wine were found upon trial by no means to answer their expectations. The bounties given for raising the latter were an encouragement to the settlers, but either no pains were taken to instruct the people in the proper methods of raising them, or the soil and climate were ill adapted for the purpose. The poor and ignorant planters applied themselves to those articles of husbandry to which probably they had been formerly accustomed, but which poorly rewarded them and left them, after all their toil, in a starved and miserable condition.

The complaints of the Georgians, however ignorant they might be, ought not to have been entirely disregarded by the Trustees. Experience suggested those inconveniencies and troubles from which they implored relief. The hints they gave certainly ought to have been improved towards correcting errors in the first plan of settlement, and framing another more favourable and advantageous. Such scattered thoughts of individuals sometimes afford wise men materials for forming just judgments, and improving towards the establishment of the best and most beneficial regulations. The people governed ought never to be excluded from the attention and regard of their Governors. The honour of the Trustees depended on the success and happiness of the settlers, and it was impossible for the people to succeed and be happy without those encouragements, liberties and privileges absolutely necessary to the first state of colonization. A free title to their land, liberty to chuse it, and then to manage it in such a manner as appeared to themselves most conducive to their interest, were the principal incentives to industry; and industry, well directed, is the grand source of opulence to every country.

It must be acknowledged, for the credit of the benevolent Trustees, that they sent out these emigrants to Georgia under several very favourable circumstances. They paid the expences of their passage, and furnished them with clothes, arms, ammunition, and instruments of husbandry. They gave them lands, and bought for some of them cows and hogs to begin their flock. They maintained their family during the first year of their occupancy, or until they should receive some return from their lands. So that if the planters were exposed to hazards from the climate, and obliged to undergo labour, they certainly entered on their task with several advantages. The taxes demanded, comparatively speaking, were a mere trifle. For their encouragement they wrought entirely for themselves, and for some time were favoured with a free and generous maintenance.

[Sidenote] An Irish colony planted.

By this time an account of the great privileges and indulgences granted by the crown for the encouragement of emigration to Carolina, had been published through Britain and Ireland, and many industrious people in different parts had resolved to take the benefit of his Majesty's bounty. Multitudes of labourers and husbandmen in Ireland, oppressed by landlords and bishops, and unable by their utmost diligence to procure a comfortable subsistence for their families, embarked for Carolina. The first colony of Irish people had lands granted them near Santee river, and formed the settlement called Williamsburgh township. But notwithstanding the bounty of the crown, these poor emigrants remained for several years in low and miserable circumstances. The rigours of the climate, joined to the want of precaution, so common to strangers, proved fatal to numbers of them. Having but scanty provisions in the first age of cultivation, vast numbers, by their heavy labour, being both debilitated in body and dejected in spirit, sickened and died in the woods. But as this township received frequent supplies from the same quarter, the Irish settlement, amidst every hardship, increased in number; and at length they applied to the merchants for negroes, who entrusted them with a few, by which means they were relieved from the severest part of the labour, then, by their great diligence and industry, spots of land were gradually cleared, which in the first place yielded them provisions, and in process of time became moderate and fruitful estates.

CHAPTER VIII

[Sidenote] Trade obstructed by the Spaniards of Mexico.

For several years before an open rupture took place between Great Britain and Spain, no good understanding subsisted between those two different courts, neither with respect to the privileges of navigation on the Mexican seas, nor to the limits between the provinces of Georgia and Florida. On one hand, the Spaniards pretended that they had an exclusive right to some latitudes in the bay of Mexico; and, on the other, though the matter had never been clearly ascertained by treaty, the British merchants claimed the privilege of cutting logwood on the bay of Campeachy. This liberty indeed had been tolerated on the part of Spain for several years, and the British merchants, from avaricious motives, had begun a traffic with the Spaniards, and supplied them with goods of English manufacture. To prevent this illicit trade, the Spaniards doubled the number of ships stationed in Mexico for guarding the coast, giving them orders to board and search every English vessel found in those seas, to seize on all that carried contraband commodities, and confine the sailors. At length not only smugglers, but fair traders were searched and detained, so that all commerce in those seas was entirely obstructed. The British merchants again and again complained to the ministry of depredations committed, and damages sustained; which indeed produced one remonstrance after another to the Spanish court; all which were answered only by evasive promises and delays. The Spaniards flattered the British minister, by telling him, they would enquire into the occasion of such grievances, and settle all differences by way of negotiation. Sir Robert Walpole, fond of pacific measures, and trusting to such proposals of accommodation, for several years suffered the grievances of the merchants to remain unredressed, and the trade of the nation to suffer great losses.

[Sidenote] William Bull Lieut.-governor.

In the year 1738, Samuel Horsley was appointed Governor of South Carolina, but he dying before he left England, the charge of the province devolved on William Bull, a man of good natural abilities, and well acquainted with the state of the province. The garrison at Augustine having received a considerable reinforcement, it therefore became the business of the people of Carolina, as well as those of Georgia, to watch the motions of their neighbours. As the Spaniards pretended a right to that province, they were pouring in troops into Augustine, which gave the British colonists some reason to apprehend they had resolved to assert their right by force of arms. William Bull despatched advice to England of the growing power of Spain in East Florida, and at the same time acquainted the Trustees, that such preparations were making there as evidently portended approaching hostilities. The British ministers were well acquainted with the state of Carolina, from a late representation transmitted by its provincial legislature. The Trustees for Georgia presented a memorial to the king, giving an account of the Spanish preparations, and the feeble and defenceless condition of Georgia, and imploring his Majesty's gracious assistance. In consequence of which, a regiment of six hundred effective men was ordered to be raised, with a view of sending them to Georgia. The King having made James Oglethorpe Major-General of all the forces of the two provinces, gave him the command of this regiment and ordered him out for the protection of the southern frontiers of the British dominions in America.

[Sidenote] Oglethorpe's regiment sent to Georgia.

About the middle of the same year, the Hector, and Blandford ships of war sailed, to convoy the transports which carried General Oglethorpe and his regiment to that province. Forty supernumeraries followed the General to supply the place of such officers or soldiers as might sicken and die by the change of the climate. Upon the arrival of this regiment, the people of Carolina and Georgia rejoiced, and testified their grateful sense of his Majesty's paternal care in the strongest terms. The Georgians, who had been for some time harassed with frequent alarms, now found themselves happily relieved, and placed in such circumstances as enabled them to bid defiance to the Spanish power. Parties of the regiment were sent to the different garrisons, and the expence the Trustees had formerly been at in maintaining them of course ceased. The General held his headquarters at Frederica, but raised forts on some other islands lying nearer the Spaniards, particularly in Cumberland and Jekyl islands, in which he also kept garrisons to watch the motions of his enemies.

[Sidenote] The Spaniards try in vain to seduce the Creeks.

While these hostile preparations were going on, it behoved General Oglethorpe to cultivate the firmest friendship with Indian nations, that they might be ready on every emergency to assist him. During his absence the Spaniards had made several attempts to seduce the Creeks, who were much attached to Oglethorpe, by telling them he was at Augustine, and promised them great presents in case they would pay him a visit at that place. Accordingly some of their leaders went down to see the beloved man, but not finding him there, they were highly offended, and resolved immediately to return to their nation. The Spanish Governor, in order to cover the fraud, or probably with a design of conveying those leaders out of the way, that they might the more easily corrupt their nation; told them, that the General lay sick on board of a ship in the harbour, where he would be extremely glad to see them. But the savages were jealous of some bad design, and refused to go, and even rejected their presents and offers of alliance. When they returned to their nation, they found an invitation from General Oglethorpe to all the chieftains to meet him at Frederica, which plainly discovered to them the insidious designs of the Spaniards, and helped not a little to increase his power and influence among them. A number of their head warriors immediately set out to meet him at the place appointed, where the General thanked them for their fidelity, made them many valuable presents, and renewed the treaty of friendship and alliance with them. At this congress the Creeks seemed better satisfied than usual, agreed to march a thousand men to the General's assistance whenever he should demand them, and invited him up to see their towns. But as he was then busy, he excused himself, by promising to visit them next summer, and accordingly dismissed them no less pleased with his kindness, than incensed against the Spaniards for their falsehood and deceit.

[Sidenote] Matters hastening to a rupture with Spain.

By this time the King of England had resolved to vindicate the honour of his crown, and maintain his right to those territories in Georgia, together with the freedom of commerce and navigation in the Mexican seas. The pacific system of Sir Robert Walpole had drawn upon him the displeasure of the nation, particularly of the mercantile part; and that amazing power and authority he had long maintained began to decline. The spirit of the nation was rouzed, insomuch that the administration could no longer wink at the insults, depredations, and cruelties of Spain. Instructions were sent to the British ambassador at the court of Madrid, to demand in the most absolute terms a compensation for the injuries of trade, which, upon calculation, amounted to two hundred thousand pounds sterling; and at the same time a squadron of ten ships of the line, under the command of Admiral Haddock, were sent to the Mediterranean sea. This produced an order from the Spanish Court to their ambassador, to allow the accounts of the British merchants, upon condition that the Spanish demand on the South-Sea Company be deducted: and that Oglethorpe be recalled from Georgia, and no more employed in that quarter, as he had there made great encroachments on his Catholic Majesty's dominions. These conditions were received at the court of Britain with that indignation which might have been expected from an injured and incensed nation. In answer to which the Spanish ambassador was given to understand, that the King of Great Britain was determined never to relinquish his right to a single foot of land in the province of Georgia; and that he must allow his subjects to make reprisals, since satisfaction for their losses in trade could in no other way be obtained. In this unsettled situation, however, matters remained for a little while between those two powerful potentates.

[Sidenote] Mutiny in Oglethorpe's camp.

In the mean time preparations were making both in Georgia and Florida, by raising fortifications on the borders of the two provinces, to hold each other at defiance. The British soldiers finding themselves subjected to a number of hardships in Georgia, to which they had not been accustomed in Britain, several of them were discontented and ungovernable. At length a plot was discovered in the camp for assassinating their general. Two companies of the regiment had been drawn from Gibraltar, some of whom could speak the Spanish language. While stationed on Cumberland island, the Spanish out-posts on the other side could approach so near as to converse with the British soldiers, one of whom had even been in the Spanish service, and not only understood their language, but also had so much of a Roman Catholic spirit as to harbour an aversion to Protestant heretics. The Spaniards had found means to corrupt this villain, who debauched the minds of several of his neighbours, insomuch that they united and formed a design first to murder General Oglethorpe, and then make their escape to Augustine. Accordingly, on a certain day a number of soldiers under arms came up to the General, and made some extraordinary demands; which being refused, they instantly cried out, one and all, and immediately one of them discharged his piece at him: and being only at the distance of a few paces, the ball whizzed over his shoulder, but the powder singed his clothes, and burnt his face. Another presented his piece, which flashed in the pan; a third drew his hanger and attempted to stab him, but the General parrying it off, an officer standing by run the ruffian through the body, and killed him on the spot. Upon which the mutineers ran, but were caught and laid in irons. A court-martial was called to try the ringleaders of this desperate conspiracy, some of whom were found guilty and condemned to be shot, in order to deter others from such dangerous attempts.

Nor was this the only concealed effort of Spanish policy, another of a more dangerous nature soon followed in Carolina, which might have been attended with much more bloody and fatal effects. At this time there were above forty thousand negroes in the province, a fierce, hardy and strong race, whose constitutions were adapted to the warm climate, whose nerves were braced with constant labour, and who could scarcely be supposed to be contented with that oppressive yoke under which they groaned. Long had liberty and protection been promised and proclaimed to them by the Spaniards at Augustine, nor were all the negroes in the province strangers to the proclamation. At different times Spanish emissaries had been found secretly tampering with them, and persuading them to fly from slavery to Florida, and several had made their escape to that settlement. Of these negro refugees the Governor of Florida had formed a regiment, appointing officers from among themselves, allowing them the same pay and clothing them in the same uniform with the regular Spanish soldiers. The most sensible part of the slaves in Carolina were not ignorant of this Spanish regiment, for whenever they run away from their masters, they constantly directed their course to this quarter. To no place could negro serjeants be sent for enlisting men where they could have a better prospect of success. Two Spaniards were caught in Georgia, and committed to jail, for enticing slaves to leave Carolina and join this regiment. Five negroes, who were cattle hunters at Indian Land, some of whom belonged to Captain McPherson, after wounding his son and killing another man, made their escape. Several more attempting to get away were taken, tried, and hanged at Charlestown.

[Sidenote] A negro insurrection in Carolina.

While Carolina was kept in a state of constant fear and agitation from this quarter, an insurrection openly broke out in the heart of the settlement which alarmed the whole province. A number of negroes having assembled together at Stono, first surprised and killed two young men in a warehouse, and then plundered it of guns and ammunition. Being thus provided with arms, they elected one of their number captain, and agreed to follow him, marching towards the south-west with colours flying and drums beating, like a disciplined company. They forcibly entered the house of Mr. Godfrey, and having murdered him, his wife, and children, they took all the arms he had in it, set fire to the house, and then proceeded towards Jacksonsburgh. In their way they plundered and burnt every house, among which were those of Sacheveral, Nash, and Spry, killing every white person they found in them, and compelling the negroes to join them. Governor Bull returning to Charlestown from the southward, met them, and, observing them armed, quickly rode out of their way. He spread the alarm, which soon reached the Presbyterian church at Wiltown, where Archibald Stobo was preaching to a numerous congregation of planters in that quarter. By a law of the province all planters were obliged to carry their arms to church, which at this critical juncture proved a very useful and necessary regulation. The women were left in church trembling with fear while the militia, under the command of Captain Bee, marched in quest of the negroes, who by this time had become formidable from the number that joined them. They had marched above twelve miles, and spread desolation through all the plantations in their way.

Having found rum in some houses, and drank freely of it, they halted in an open field, and began to sing and dance, by way of triumph. During these rejoicings the militia discovered them, and stationed themselves in different places around them, to prevent them from making their escape. The intoxication of several of the slaves favoured the assailants. One party advanced into the open field and attacked them, and, having killed some negroes, the remainder took to the woods, and were dispersed. Many ran back to their plantations, in hopes of escaping suspicion from the absence of their masters; but the greater part were taken and tried. Such as had been compelled to join them contrary to their inclination were pardoned, but all the chosen leaders and first insurgents suffered death.

All Carolina was struck with terror and consternation by this insurrection, in which above twenty persons were murdered before it was quelled, and had not the people in that quarter been fortunately collected together at church, it is probable many more would have suffered. Or had it become general, the whole colony must have fallen a sacrifice to their great power and indiscriminate fury. It was commonly believed, and not without reason, that the Spaniards were deeply concerned in promoting the mischief, and by their secret influence and intrigues with slaves had instigated them to this massacre. Having already four companies of negroes in their service, by penetrating into Carolina, and putting the province into confusion, they might no doubt have raised many more. But, to prevent farther attempts, Governor Bull sent an express to General Oglethorpe with advice of the insurrection, desiring him to double his vigilance in Georgia, and seize all straggling Spaniards and negroes. In consequence of which a proclamation was issued to stop all slaves found in that province, offering a reward for every one they might catch attempting to run off. At the same time a company of rangers were employed to patrole the frontiers, and block up all passages by which they might make their escape to Florida.

[Sidenote] A war with Spain.

In the mean time things were hastening to a rupture in Europe, and a war between England and Spain was thought unavoidable. The plenipotentiaries appointed for settling the boundaries between Georgia and Florida, and other differences and misunderstandings subsisting between the two crowns, had met at Pardo in convention, where preliminary articles were drawn up; but the conference ended to the satisfaction of neither party. Indeed the proposal of a negotiation, and the appointment of plenipotentiaries, gave universal offence to the people of Britain, who breathed nothing but war and vengeance against the proud and arrogant Spaniards. The merchants had lost all patience under their sufferings, and became clamorous for letters of reprisal, which at length they obtained. Public credit arose, and forwarded hostile preparations. All officers of the navy and army were ordered to their stations, and with the unanimous voice of the nation war was declared against Spain on the 23rd of October, 1739.

[Sidenote] A project for invading Florida.

While Admiral Vernon was sent to take the command of a squadron in the West-India station, with orders to act offensively against the Spanish dominions in that quarter, to divide their force, General Oglethorpe was ordered also to annoy the subjects of Spain in Florida by every method in his power. In consequence of which, the General immediately projected an expedition against the Spanish settlement at Augustine. His design he communicated by letter to Lieutenant Governor Bull, requesting the support and assistance of Carolina in the expedition. Mr. Bull laid his letter before the provincial assembly, recommending to them to raise a regiment, and give him all possible assistance in an enterprize of such interesting consequence. The assembly, sensible of the vast advantages that must accrue to them from getting rid of such troublesome neighbours, resolved that so soon as the General should communicate to them his plan of operations, together with a state of the assistance requisite, at the same time making it appear that there was a probability of success, they would most cheerfully assist him. The Carolineans, however, were apprehensive, that as that garrison had proved such a painful thorn in their side in time of peace, they would have more to dread from it in time of war; and although the colony had been much distressed by the small-pox and the yellow fever for two years past, which had cut off the hopes of many flourishing families; the people, nevertheless, lent a very favourable ear to the proposal, and earnestly wished to give all the assistance in their power towards dislodging an enemy so malicious and cruel.

[Sidenote] Measures concerted for this purpose.

In the mean time General Oglethorpe was industrious in picking up all the intelligence he could respecting the situation and strength of the garrison, and finding it in great straits for want of provisions, he urged the speedy execution of his project, with a view to surprise his enemy before a supply should arrive. He declared, that no personal toil or danger should discourage him from exerting himself towards freeing Carolina from such neighbours as had instigated their slaves to massacre them, and publicly protected them after such bloody attempts. To concert measures with the greater secrecy and expedition, he went to Charlestown himself, and laid before the legislature of Carolina an estimate of the force, arms, ammunition, and provisions, which he judged might be requisite for the expedition. In consequence of which, the Assembly voted one hundred and twenty thousand pounds, Carolina money, for the service of the war. A regiment, consisting of four hundred men, was raised, partly in Virginia and partly in North and South Carolina, with the greatest expedition, and the command was given to Colonel Vanderdussen. Indians were sent for from the different tribes in alliance with Britain. Vincent Price, commander of the ships of war on that station, agreed to assist with a naval force consisting of four ships of twenty guns each, and two sloops, which proved a great encouragement to the Carolineans, and induced them to enter with double vigour on military preparations. General Oglethorpe appointed the mouth of St. John's river, on the Florida shore, for the place of rendezvous, and having finished his preparations in Carolina, set out for Georgia to join his regiment, and make all ready for the expedition.

[Sidenote] General Oglethorpe marches against Florida.

On the 9th of May 1740, the General passed over to Florida with four hundred select men of his regiment, and a considerable party of Indians; and on the day following invested Diego, a small fort, about twenty-five miles from Augustine, which after a short resistance surrendered by capitulation. In this fort he left a garrison of sixty men, under the command of Lieutenant Dunbar, and returned to the place of general rendezvous, where he was joined by Colonel Vanderdussen, with the Carolina regiment, and a company of Highlanders, under the command of Captain M'Intosh. But by this time six Spanish half-galleys, with long brass nine pounders, and two sloops loaded with provisions, had got into the harbour at Augustine. A few days afterwards, the General marched with his whole force, consisting of above two thousand men, regulars, provincials and Indians, to Fort Moosa, situated within two miles of Augustine, which on his approach the Spanish garrison evacuated, and retired into the town. He immediately ordered the gates of this fort to be burnt, three breaches to be made in its walls, and then proceeded to reconnoitre the town and castle.

Notwithstanding the dispatch of the British army, the Spaniards, during their stay at Fort Diego, had collected all the cattle in the woods around them, and drove them into the town; and the General found, both from a view of the works, and the intelligence he had received from prisoners, that more difficulty would attend this enterprize than he at first expected. Indeed, if he intended a surprize, he ought not to have stopped at Fort Diego, for by that delay the enemy had notice of his approach, and time to gather their whole force, and put themselves in a posture of defence. The castle was built of soft stone, with four bastions; the curtain was sixty yards in length, the parapet nine feet thick; the rampart twenty feet high, casemated underneath for lodgings, arched over, and newly made bomb-proof. Fifty pieces of cannon were mounted, several of which were twenty-four pounders. Besides the castle, the town was entrenched with ten salient angles, on each of which some small cannon were mounted. The garrison consisted of seven hundred regulars, two troops of horse, four companies of armed negroes, besides the militia of the province, and Indians.

[Sidenote] Invests Augustine.

The General now plainly perceived that an attack by land upon the town, and an attempt to take the castle by storm would cost him dear before he could reduce the place, and therefore changed his plan of operations. With the assistance of the ships of war, which were now lying at anchor off Augustine-bar, he resolved to turn the siege into a blockade, and try to shut up every channel by which provisions could be conveyed to the garrison. For this purpose he left Colonel Palmer with ninety-five Highlanders, and forty-two Indians at Fort Moosa, with orders to scour the woods around the town, and intercept all supplies of cattle from the country by land. And, for the safety of his men, he at the same time ordered him to encamp every night in a different place, to keep strict watch around his camp, and by all means avoid coming to any action. This small party was the whole force the General left for guarding the land side. Then he sent Colonel Vanderdussen, with the Carolina regiment, over a small creek, to take possession of a neck of land called Point Quartel, above a mile distant from the castle, with orders to erect a battery upon it; while he himself, with his regiment, and the greatest part of the Indians, embarked in boats, and landed on the island of Anastatia. In this island the Spaniards had a small party of men stationed for a guard, who immediately fled to town, and as it lay opposite to the castle, from this place, the General resolved to bombard the town. Captain Pierce stationed one of his ships to guard the passage, by way of the Motanzas, and with the others blocked up the mouth of the harbour, so that the Spaniards were cut off from all supplies by sea. On the island of Anastatia batteries were soon erected, and several cannon mounted by the assistance of the active and enterprising sailors. Having made these dispositions, General Oglethorpe then summoned the Spanish Governor to a surrender; but the haughty Don, secure in his strong hold, sent him for answer, that he would be glad to shake hands with him in his castle.

This insulting answer excited the highest degree of wrath and indignation in the General's mind, and made him resolve to exert himself to the utmost for humbling his pride. The opportunity of surprizing the place being now lost, he had no other secure method left but to attack it at the distance in which he then stood. For this purpose he opened his batteries against the castle, and at the same time threw a number of shells into the town. The fire was returned with equal spirit both from the Spanish fort and from six half-gallies in the harbour, but so great was the distance, that though they continued the cannonade for several days, little execution was done on either side. Captain Warren, a brave naval officer, perceiving that all efforts in this way for demolishing the castle were vain and ineffectual, proposed to destroy the Spanish gallies in the harbour, by an attack in the night, and offered to go himself and head the attempt. A council of war was held to consider of and concert a plan for that service; but, upon sounding the bar, it was found it would admit no large ship to the attack, and with small ones it was judged rash and impracticable, the gallies being covered by the cannon of the castle, and therefore that design was dropt.

[Sidenote] Raises the siege.

In the mean time the Spanish commander observing the besiegers embarrassed, and their operations beginning to relax, sent out a detachment of three hundred men against Colonel Palmer, who surprised him at Fort Moosa, and, while most of his party lay asleep, cut them almost entirely to pieces. A few that accidentally escaped, went over in a small boat to the Carolina regiment at Point Quartel. Some of the Chickesaw Indians coming from that fort having met with a Spaniard, cut off his head, agreeable to their savage manner of waging war, and presented it to the General in his camp: but he rejected it with abhorrence, calling them barbarous dogs, and bidding them begone. At this disdainful behaviour, however, the Chickesaws were offended, declaring, that if they had carried the head of an Englishman to the French, they would not have treated them so: and perhaps the General discovered more humanity than good policy by it, for these Indians, who knew none of the European customs and refinements in war, soon after deserted him. About the same time the vessel stationed at the Metanzas being ordered off, some small ships from the Havanna with provisions, and a reinforcement of men, got into Augustine, by that narrow channel, to the relief of the garrison. A party of Creeks having surprised one of their small boats, brought four Spanish prisoners to the General, who informed him, that the garrison had received seven hundred men, and a large supply of provisions. Then all prospects of starving the enemy being lost, the army began to despair of forcing the place to surrender. The Carolinean troops, enfeebled by the heat, dispirited by sickness, and fatigued by fruitless efforts, marched away in large bodies. The navy being short of provisions, and the usual season of hurricanes approaching, the commander judged it imprudent to hazard his Majesty's ships, by remaining longer on that coast. Last of all, the General himself, sick of a fever, and his regiment worn out with fatigue, and rendered unfit for action by a flux, with sorrow and regret followed, and reached Frederica about the 10th of July 1740.

Thus ended the unsuccessful expedition against Augustine, to the great disappointment of both Georgia and Carolina. Many heavy reflections were afterwards thrown out against General Oglethorpe for his conduct during the whole enterprize. Perhaps the only chance of success he had from the beginning was by surprising this garrison in the night by some sudden attempt. He was blamed for remaining so long at fort Diego, by which means the enemy had full intelligence of his approach, and time to prepare for receiving him. He was charged with timidity afterwards, in making no bold attempt on the town. It was said, that the officer who means to act on the offensive, where difficulties must be surmounted, ought to display some courage; and that too much timidity in war is often as culpable as too much temerity. Great caution he indeed used for saving his men, for excepting those who fell by the sword in fort Moosa, he lost more men by sickness than by the hands of the enemy. Though the disaster of Colonel Palmer, in which many brave Highlanders were massacred, was perhaps occasioned chiefly by want of vigilance and a disobedience of orders, yet many were of opinion, that it was too hazardous to have left so small a party on the main land, exposed to sallies from a superior enemy, and entirely cut off from all possibility of support and assistance from the main body. In short, the Carolineans called in question the General's military judgment and skill in many respects; and protested that he had spent the time in barren deliberations, harassed the men with unnecessary marches, allowed them not a sufficient quantity of provisions, and poisoned them with breakish water. He, on the other hand, declared he had no confidence in the firmness and courage of the provincials; for that they refused obedience to his orders, and at last abandoned his camp, and retreated to Carolina. The truth was, so strongly fortified was the place, both by nature and art, that probably the attempt must have failed, though it had been conducted by the ablest officer, and executed by the best disciplined troops. The miscarriage, however, was particularly ruinous to Carolina, having not only subjected the province to a great expence, but also left it in a worse situation than it was before the attempt.

[Sidenote] A great fire at Charlestown.

The same year stands distinguished in the annals of Carolina, not only for this unsuccessful expedition against the Spaniards, but also for a desolating fire, which in November following broke out in the capital, and laid the half of it in ruins. This fire began about two o'clock in the afternoon, and burnt with unquenchable violence until eight at night. The houses being built of wood, and the wind blowing hard at north-west, the flames spread with astonishing rapidity. From Broad-street, where the fire kindled, to Granville's Bastion, almost every house was at one time in flames, and exhibited an awful and striking scene. The vast quantities of deerskins, rum, pitch, tar, turpentine and powder, in the different stores, served to increase the horror, and the more speedily to spread the desolation. Amidst the cries and shrieks of women and children, and the bursting forth of flames in different quarters, occasioned by the violent wind, which carried the burning shingles to a great distance, the men were put into confusion, and so anxious were they about the safety of their families, that they could not be prevailed upon to unite their efforts for extinguishing the fire. The sailors from the men of war, and ships in the harbour were the most active and adventurous hands engaged in the service. But such was the violence of the flames, that it baffled all the art and power of man, and burnt until the calmness of the evening closed the dreadful scene. Three hundred of the best and most convenient buildings in the town were consumed, which, together with lots of goods, and provincial commodities, amounted to a prodigious sum. Happily few lives were lost, but the lamentations of ruined families were heard in every quarter. In short, from a flourishing condition the town was reduced in the space of six hours to the lowest and most deplorable state. All those inhabitants whose houses escaped the flames, went around and kindly invited their unfortunate neighbours to them, so that two and three families were lodged in places built only for the accommodation of one. After the legislature met, to take the miserable state of the people under consideration, they agreed to make application to the British parliament for relief. The British parliament voted twenty thousand pounds sterling, to be distributed among the sufferers at Charlestown, which relief was equally seasonable and useful on the one side, as it was generous and noble on the other. No time should obliterate the impressions of such benevolent actions. This gift certainly deserved to be wrote on the table of every heart, in the most indelible characters. For all men must acknowledge, that it merited the warmest returns of gratitude, not only from the unfortunate objects of such bounty, but from the whole province.

[Sidenote] A petition in favour of the rice trade.

While the war between Great Britain and Spain continued, a bill was brought into parliament to prevent the exportation of rice, among other articles of provision, to France or Spain, with a view to distress these enemies as much as possible. In consequence of which, a representation to the following effect, in behalf of the province of Carolina, and the merchants concerned in that trade, was presented to the House of Commons while the bill was depending before them, praying that the article of rice might be excepted out of the bill, and endeavouring to prove, that the prohibiting its importation would be highly detrimental to Great Britain, and in no respect to her enemies: "The inhabitants of South Carolina have not any manufactures of their own, but are supplied from Great Britain with all their clothing, and the other manufactures by them consumed, to the amount of one hundred and fifty thousand pounds sterling a-year. The only commodity of consequence produced in South Carolina is rice, and they reckon it as much their staple commodity as sugar is to Barbadoes and Jamaica, or tobacco to Virginia and Maryland; so that if any stop be put to the exportation of rice from South Carolina to Europe, it will not only render the planters there incapable of paying their debts, but also reduce the government of that province to such difficulties for want of money, as at this present precarious time may render the whole colony an easy prey to their neighbours the Indians and Spaniards, and also to those yet more dangerous enemies their own negroes, who are ready to revolt on the first opportunity, and are eight times as many in number as there are white men able to bear arms, and the danger in this respect is greater since the unhappy expedition to Augustine.

"From the year 1729, when his Majesty purchased South Carolina, the trade of it hath so increased, that their annual exports and imports of late have been double the value of what they were in the said year; and their exports of rice in particular have increased in a greater proportion: for, from the year 1720 to 1729, being ten years, both included, the whole export of rice was 264,488 barrels, making 44,081 tons. From the 1730 to 1739, being also ten years, the whole export of rice was 499,525 barrels, making 99,905 tons; so that the export of the latter ten years exceeded the former by 235,037 barrels, or 55,824 tons: and of the vast quantities of rice thus exported, scarcely one fifteenth part is consumed either in Great Britain or in any part of the British dominions; so that the produce of the other fourteen parts is clear gain to the nation; whereas almost all the sugar, and one fourth part of the tobacco, exported from the British colonies, are consumed by the people of Great Britain, or by British subjects; from whence it is evident, that the national gain arising from rice is several times as great in proportion, as the national gain arising from either sugar or tobacco.

"This year, *viz.* 1740, in particular, we shall export from South Carolina above ninety thousand barrels of rice, of which quantity there will not be three thousand barrels used here, so that the clear national gain upon that export will be very great; for at the lowest computation, of twenty-five shillings sterling *per* barrel, the eighty-seven thousand barrels exported will amount in value to one hundred and eight thousand seven hundred and fifty pounds, at the first hand; whereto there must be added the charge of freight, *&c.* from South Carolina to Europe, which amount to more than the first cost of the rice, and are also gain to Great Britain; so that the least gain upon this article for the present year will be two hundred and twenty thousand pounds, over and above the naval advantage of annually employing more than one hundred and sixty ships of one hundred tons each."

"Rice being an enumerated commodity, it cannot be exported from South Carolina without giving bond for double the value that the same shall be landed in Great Britain, or in some of the British plantations, excepting to the southward of Cape Finisterre, which last was permitted by a law made in the year 1729; and the motive for such permission was, that the rice might arrive more seasonably and in better condition at market. We have hereunto added an account of the several quantities of rice which have been exported from South Carolina to the different European markets since the said law was made; and it will thereby appear, that we have not in those ten years been able to find sale for any considerable quantity of rice in Spain; for in all that time we have not sold above three thousand five hundred and seventy barrels to the Spaniards, making only three hundred and fifty-seven barrels annually upon a medium; nor can we in the time to come expect any alteration in favour of our rice trade there, because the Spaniards are supplied with an inferior sort of rice from Turkey, &c. equally agreeable to them and a great deal cheaper than ours; the truth whereof appears by the rice taken in a ship called the Baltic Merchant and carried into St. Sebastians, where it was sold at a price so much under the market rate here, or in Holland, as to encourage the sending of it thence to Holland and Hamburgh.

"In France the importation of Carolina rice without licence is prohibited; and though during the last and present years there hath, by permission, been some consumption of it there, yet the whole did not exceed nine thousand barrels, and they have received from Turkey so much rice of the present year's growth, as to make that commodity five shillings *per* 100 *lb.* cheaper at Marseilles than here, and even at Dunkirk it is one shilling and sixpence *per* 100 *lb.* cheaper than here; so that there is not any prospect of a demand for Carolina rice in France, even if liberty could be obtained for sending the same to any port of that kingdom.

"Germany and Holland are the countries where we find the best market for our rice, and there the greater part of it is consumed; so that the present intended embargo, or prohibitory law, cannot have any other effect, in relation to rice, than that of preventing our allies from using what our enemies do not want, nor we ourselves consume more than a twentieth part of, and which is of so perishable a nature, that even in a cold climate it doth not keep above a year without decaying, and in a warm climate it perishes entirely. The great consumption of rice in Germany and Holland is during the winter season, when pease and all kinds of pulse, &c. are scarce; and the rice intended for those markets ought to be brought there before the frost begins, time enough to be carried up the rivers; so that preventing the exportation only a few days may be attended with this had consequence, that by the frost the winter sale may be lost.

"And as we have now, *viz.* since November 11th, above ten thousand barrels of old rice arrived, so we may in a few weeks expect double that quantity, besides the new crop now shipping off from Carolina; the stopping of all which, in a country where there is not any sale for it, instead of permitting the same to be carried to the only places of consumption, must soon reduce the price thereof to so low a rate, that the merchants who have purchased that rice will not be able to sell it for the prime cost, much less will they be able to recover the money they have paid for duty, freight, and other charges thereon, which amount to double the first cost: for the rice that an hundred pounds sterling will purchase in South Carolina, costs the importer two hundred more in British duties, freight, and other charges[1]."

[1] An Account of Rice exported in Ten Years after the Province was purchased for the King.

Barrels. To Portugal, - - - -
- - - 83,379 To Gibraltar, - - - -
- - 958 To Spain, - - - - - - - -
3,570 To France, - - - - - - - -
9,500 To Great Britain,
Ireland, and the British
Plantations, - - - 30,000 To
Holland, Hamburgh and
Bremen, including 7000
barrels to Sweden and
Denmark, - - - - - - - 372,118
— — —- Total quantity exported in
those ten years, - -- 499,525

"Thus it appears, that by prohibiting the exportation of rice from this kingdom, the merchants who have purchased the vast quantities before mentioned will not only lose the money it cost them, but twice as much more in duties, freight, and other charges, by their having a perishable commodity embargoed in a country where it is not used. Or if, instead of laying the prohibition here, it be laid in South Carolina; that province, the planters there, and the merchants who deal with them, must all be involved in ruin; the province, for want of means to support the expense of government; the planters, for want of the means to pay their debts and provide future supplies; and the merchants, by not only losing those debts, but twice as much more in the freight, duties, and other charges, upon rice which they cannot sell. So that, in either case, a very profitable colony, and the merchants concerned in the trade of it, would be ruined for the present, if not totally lost to this kingdom, by prohibiting the exportation of rice; and all this without doing any national good in another way, for such prohibition could not in any shape distress our enemies. It is therefore humbly hoped, that rice will be excepted out of the bill now before the honourable House of Commons."

As this representation contains a distinct account of the produce and trade of the province, and shews its usefulness and importance to Great Britain, we judged it worthy of the particular attention of our readers, and therefore have inserted it. With respect to the internal dangers arising from the savage nature and vast number of the slaves, mentioned in this and a former state of the province, we shall now make some remarks, in which we will be naturally led to consider their miserable condition, and the harsh treatment to which slavery necessarily subjects them.

[Sidenote] Remarks on the treatment of slaves.

That slavery has been practiced by many of the most civilized nations in the world, is indeed a truth evident from the history of them. In war the conquerors were supposed to have a right to the life of their captives, insomuch that they might kill, torture or enslave them, as they thought proper. Yet, though war may be justifiable on the principles of self-preservation and defence, it is no easy matter to vindicate the conqueror's right to murder or enslave a disarmed enemy. Slavery in general, like several other enormities, ought to be ascribed to the corruption and avarice of men, rather than to any principles of nature and humanity, which evidently testify against it; and that vindication which is drawn from the custom and practice of ancient nations in favour of such an institution, is equally applicable to many other enormities which are a shame and disgrace to human nature. Helpless children have been exposed to the fury of wild beasts; pride and ambition have spread their desolations far and wide; but such practices are not therefore humane and just. That many nations have encouraged slavery, and that the remains of it are still observable among the freest of them, are argument which none will plead for their honour and credit. That species of servitude which still remains in Britain among the labourers in the coal mines, &c. is very different from that to which the natives of Africa are subjected in the western world; because such labourers voluntarily enter on such servitude, they acquire wages as their reward, and both their persons and properties are under the protection of the laws of the realm.

Upon the slightest reflection all men must confess, that those Africans, whom the powers of Europe have conspired to enslave, are by nature equally free and independent, equally susceptible of pain and pleasure, equally averse from bondage and misery, as Europeans themselves. Like all rude nations, they have a strong attachment to their native country, and to those friends and relations with whom they spent the early years of life. By this trade being torn from those nearest connections, and transported to a distant land, it is no easy thing to describe the uneasiness and pain they must endure from such violence and banishment. During the passage being loaded with irons, and cooped up in a ship, oppressed with the most gloomy apprehensions, many of them sicken and die through fear and regret. The provisions made for the voyage by the merchants and masters of ships, who consult their worldly interest more than the dictates of humanity, we may be sure are neither of the best kind, nor distributed among them in the most plentiful manner. After their arrival they are sold and delivered over to the colonists, to whose temper, language and manners they are utter strangers; where their situation for some time, in case of harsh usage, is little better than that of the dumb beasts, having no language but groans in which they can express their pains, nor any friend to pity or relieve them. Some destroy themselves through despair, and from a persuasion they fondly entertain, that, after death, they will return to their beloved friends and native country.

[Sidenote] The hardships of their situation.

After the sale the purchasers become vested with the absolute property of them, according to the laws, usages, and customs of the trade, and whatever hardships are thereby imposed on those foreigners, the planters are so far excusable, having the sanction of the supreme legislature for the purchase they make. The laws of England, from necessity or expediency, have permitted such labourers to be imported among them; and therefore, on their part, the purchase, however injurious, cannot be illegal. Having acquired this kind of property, it then lies with the colonists to frame laws and regulations for the future management of their slaves. In doing this, absolute obedience and non-resistance are fundamental principles established for the government of them, and enforced by the severest penalties. All laws framed with respect to them, give their masters such authority over them as is under few limitations. Their power of correction may be said to be only not allowed to extend to death. However severely beat and abused, no negro can bring an action against his owner, or appear as an evidence against white men, in any court of law or justice. Their natural rights as human creatures are entirely disregarded, and punishments are commonly inflicted according to the will of their master, however cruel and barbarous his disposition may be. A common place of correction is instituted, to which they are sent to receive such a number of stripes as their owners shall order, and such blunders have been committed in giving and executing those orders, that the innocent sometimes have suffered along with the guilty. In short, such is their miserable condition, that they are exposed defenceless to the insolence, caprice, and passions of owners, obliged to labour all their life without any prospect of reward, or any hope of an end of their toil until the day of their death. At the decease of their masters they descend, like other estates of inheritance, to the heir at law, and sometimes to thoughtless and giddy youth, habituated from their earliest days to treat them like brutes. At other times, no doubt, they are more fortunate, but their condition of life evidently subjects them to harsh usage even from the best of masters, and we leave the world to judge what they have to expect from the worst.

Indeed it must be acknowledged, in justice to the planters of Carolina in general, that they treat their slaves with as much, and perhaps more tenderness, than those of any British colony where slavery exists; yet a disinterested stranger must observe, even among the best of masters, several instances of cruelty and negligence in the manner of managing their slaves. Comparatively speaking, they are well clothed and fed in that province, which while they continue in health fits and qualifies them for their task. When they happen to fall sick, they are carefully attended by a physician; in which respect their condition is better than that of the poorest class of labourers in Europe. But in the West Indies, we have been told, they are both covered with rags and have a scanty portion of provisions allowed them, in which case urgent necessity and pinching hunger must often urge them to pilfer, and commit many injuries to which otherwise they would have no inclination, and for which they incur severe punishment. In cases of violence and murder committed on these wretched creatures, it is next to impossible to have the delinquents brought to punishment; for either the grand jury refuse to find the bill, or the petty jury bring in the verdict not guilty. When they are tempted to fly to the woods to shun severe labour or punishment then they may be hunted down or shot as wild beasts. When whipped to death, the murderer, after all, is only subjected to an inconsiderable fine, or a short imprisonment, by the provincial laws. It is impossible that the Author of nature ever intended human beings for such a wretched fate; for surely he who gave life, gave also an undoubted right to the means of self-preservation and happiness, and all the common rights and privileges of nature.

But there is another circumstance which renders their case still more wretched and deplorable. Good masters and mistresses, whose humanity and a sense of interest will not permit them to treat their negroes in a harsh manner, do not always reside at their plantations. Many planters have several settlements at considerable distances from the place where they usually live, which they visit perhaps only three or four times in a year. In their absence the charge of negroes is given to overseers, many of whom are ignorant and cruel, and all totally disinterested in the welfare of their charge. In such a case it can scarcely be expected that justice will be equally dispensed, or punishments properly inflicted. The negroes, however, ly entirely at the mercy of such men, and such monsters they sometimes are, as can inflict misery in sport, and hear the groans extorted from nature with laughter and triumph. All slaves under their care must yield absolute obedience to their orders, however unreasonable and difficult, or suffer punishment for their disobedience. It would rouze the anguish and indignation of a humane person to stand by while a puny overseer chastises those slaves, and behold with what piercing stripes he furrows the back of an able negro, whose greatness of soul will not suffer him to complain, and whose strength could crush his tormentor to atoms. The unmerciful whip with which they are chastised is made of cow-skin, hardened, twisted, and tapering, which brings the blood with every blow, and leaves a scar on their naked back which they carry with them to their grave. At the arbitrary will of such managers, many of them with hearts of adamant, this unfortunate race are brought to the post of correction, often no doubt through malice and wantonness, often for the most trifling offences, and sometimes, O horrid! when entirely innocent. Can it be deemed wonderful, that such unhappy creatures should now and then be tempted to assert the rights of nature? Must not such harsh usage often fire them with desires of liberty and vengeance? What can be expected but that they should sometimes give those oppressors grounds of fear, who have subjected them to such intolerable hardships.

But from those labourers in the field the colonials have perhaps less danger to dread, than from the number of tradesmen and mechanics in towns, and domestic slaves. Many negroes discover great capacities, and an amazing aptness for learning trades, where dangerous tools are used; and many owners, from motives of profit and advantage, breed them to be coopers, carpenters, bricklayers, smiths, and other trades. Out of mere ostentation the colonists also keep a number of them about their families, who attend their tables, and hear their conversation, which very often turns upon their own various arts, plots, and assassinations. From such open and imprudent conversation those domestics may no doubt take dangerous hints, which, on a fair opportunity, may be applied to their owners hurt. They have also easy access to fire arms, which gives them a double advantage for mischief. When they are of a passionate and revengeful disposition, such domestic slaves seldom want an opportunity of striking a sudden blow, and avenging themselves, in case of ill usage, by killing or poisoning their owners. Such crimes have often been committed in the colonies, and punished; and there is reason to believe they have also frequently happened, when they have passed undiscovered. Prudence and self-preservation strongly dictate to the Carolineans the necessity of guarding against those dangers which arise from domestic slaves, many of whom are idle, cunning and deceitful.

[Sidenote] Oppressed with ignorance and superstition.

In other respects the policy of the colonists, with respect to the management and treatment of slaves is extremely defective. The hardships to which their bodies are exposed, would be much more tolerable and justifiable, were any provision made for civilizing and improving their minds. But how grievous their circumstances when we consider, that, together with their bodily toil and misery, they are also kept in heathen ignorance and darkness, destitute of the means of instruction, and excluded in a manner from the pale of the Christian church. Humanity places every rational creature upon a level, and gives all an equal title those rights of nature, which are essential to life and happiness. Christianity breathes a spirit of benevolence, gentleness, and compassion for mankind in general, of what nation or complexion soever they be. As government has tolerated and established slavery in the plantations, the supreme charge of these creatures may be regarded rather as a national than a provincial concern. Being members of a great empire, living under its supreme care and jurisdiction, and contributing to the increase of trade and commerce, to the improvement and opulence of the British dominions, they are unquestionably entitled to a share of national benevolence and Christian charity. An institution for their religious instruction was an object of such usefulness and importance, that it merited the attention of the supreme legislature; and the expence of a few superb and perhaps empty churches in England, would certainly have been better employed in erecting some neat buildings in the plantations for this beneficial purpose. To such an institution the merchants of Britain, especially those who owe a great part of their opulence to the labours of Africans, and whose plea for the trade was the bringing them within the pale of the Christian church, ought certainly to have contributed in the most liberal manner. The profits of the trade, abstracting from other considerations, could well admit of it; but every principle of compassion for the ignorant, the poor, and the unfortunate, powerfully dictates the same duty, the neglect of which, to every impartial judge, must appear in a very inexcusable and criminal light. Masters of slaves under the French and Spanish jurisdictions, are obliged by law to allow them time for instruction, and to bring them up in the knowledge and practice of the Catholic religion. Is it not a reproach to the subjects of Britain, who profess to be the freest and most civilized people upon earth, that no provision is made for this purpose, and that they suffer so many thousands of these creatures, residing in the British dominions, to live and die the slaves of ignorance and superstition? How can they expect the blessing of heaven on the riches flowing from their foreign plantations, when they are at no pains to introduce those objects of their care to the knowledge of the true God, and to make them partakers of the benefits and hopes of Christianity.

The advantages of religion, like the other gifts of heaven, ought to be free and common as the air we breathe to every human creature, capable of making a proper use and improvement of them. To the honour of the society for the propagation of the Gospel it must indeed be acknowledged, that they have made some efforts for the conversion and instruction of those heathens. Not many years ago they had no less than twelve missionaries in Carolina, who had instructions to give all the assistance in their power for this laudable purpose, and to each of whom they allowed fifty pounds a-year, over and above their provincial salaries. But it is well known, that the fruit of their labours has been very small and inconsiderable. Such feeble exertions were no ways equal to the extent of the work required, nor to the greatness of the end proposed. Whether their small success ought to be ascribed to the rude and untractable dispositions of the negroes, to the discouragements and obstructions thrown in the way by their owners, or to the negligence and indolence of the missionaries themselves we cannot pretend to determine. Perhaps we may venture to assert, that it has been more or less owing to all these different causes. One thing is very certain, that the negroes of that country, a few only excepted, are to this day as great strangers to Christianity, and as much under the influence of Pagan darkness, idolatry and superstition, as they were at their first arrival from Africa.

But, though neglected by the British nation, they are entitled to a share of the common privileges of humanity and Christianity, from their provincial owners. It is their duty and interest to use slaves with tenderness and compassion, and render them as happy and contented as their situation will admit. Were they to allow them certain portions of time from their labours of body for the improvement of their mind, and open the way for, and provide the means of instruction, would not kind usage be productive of many beneficial effects? The loss of labour none but avaricious wretches would grudge, and the day of rest allotted for man and beast since the beginning of the world, and properly improved for that purpose, might of itself be attended with good consequences; whereas, to encourage them to labour on that day for themselves, is not only robbing them of the opportunities of instruction, but abusing the Sunday, by making it to them the most laborious day of the week. It would strike a stranger with astonishment and indignation, to hear the excuses planters make for this criminal neglect. Some will tell you they are beings of an inferior rank, and little exalted above brute creatures; that they have no souls, and therefore no concern need be taken about their salvation. Others affirm, that they would become more expert in vice by being taught, and greater knaves by being made Christians. But such advocates for heathen ignorance and barbarism merit no serious notice, being enemies to all improvements in human nature, and all the benefits resulting to society from civilization and Christianity. Certain it is, the inhabitants of Africa have the same faculties with those of Europe. Their minds are equally capable of cultivation, equally susceptible of the impressions of religion. Ridiculous is it to imagine, that the black tincture of their skin, or the barbarous state in which they were there found, can make any material alteration. Though fortune has put the former under the power of the latter, and assigned them the portion of perpetual labour to procure the mere luxuries of life for other men; yet, if such a traffic be reasonable and just, there is no crime negroes can commit that may not be defended and justified upon the same principles. If Europe, to obtain sugar, rum, rice, and tobacco, has a right to enslave Africa; surely Africa, if she had the power, has a much better right to rob Europe of those commodities, the fruits of her children's labour. Every argument that can be brought in support of the institution of slavery, tends to the subversion of justice and morality in the world. The best treatment possible from the colonists cannot compensate for so great a loss. Freedom, in its meanest circumstances, is infinitely preferable to slavery, though it were in golden fetters, and accompanied with the greatest splendour, ease, and abundance.

If then the greatest advantages are not a sufficient compensation for the loss of liberty, what shall we think of those who deny them the smallest? But one would imagine that, exclusive of every other motive, personal safety would even induce the colonists to provide for them those advantages which would render them as easy and contented as possible with their condition. Were they duly impressed with a sense of their duty to God and man; were they taught the common rules of honesty, justice, and truth; were their dispositions to humility, submission, and obedience, cultivated and improved; would not such advantages place them more on a level with hired servants, who pay a ready and cheerful obedience to their masters? Were they favoured with the privileges of Christianity, would they not be more faithful and diligent, and better reconciled to their servile condition? Besides, Christianity has a tendency to tame fierce and wild tempers. It is not an easy thing to display the great and extensive influence which the fear of God, and the expectation of a future account, would have upon their minds: Christianity enforces the obligations of morality, and produces a more regular and uniform obedience to its laws. A due sense of the divine presence, the hopes of his approbation, and the fears of his displeasure, are motives that operate powerfully with the human mind, and in fact would prove stronger barriers against trespasses, murders, plots, and conspiracies, than any number of stripes from the hands of men, or even the terrors of certain death. Whereas, to keep the minds of human creatures under clouds of darkness, neither disciplined by reason, nor regulated by religion, is a reproach to the name of Protestants, especially in a land of Christian light and liberty. Sundays and holidays are indeed allowed the negroes in Carolina, the former cannot consistent with the laws be denied them; the latter, as they are commonly spent are nuisances to the province. Holidays there are days of idleness, riot, wantonness and excess; in which the slaves assemble together in alarming crowds, for the purposes of dancing, feasting and merriment. At such seasons the inhabitants have the greatest reason to dread mischief from them; when let loose from their usual employments, they have fair opportunities of hatching plots and conspiracies, and of executing them with greater facility, from the intemperance of their owners and overseers.

After all, it must be confessed, that the freemen of Carolina themselves were for many years in a destitute condition with respect to religious instruction; partly owing to their own poverty and the unhealthiness of the climate, and partly owing to troubles and divisions subsisting among them during the proprietary government. At that time the first object of their concern would no doubt be to provide for themselves and their children: but since the province has been taken under the royal care, their circumstances in every respect have changed for the better, insomuch that they are not only able to provide instruction for themselves and families, but also to extend the benefit to those living in a state of servitude among them. Now they are arrived to such an easy and flourishing situation, as renders their neglect entirely without excuse. The instruction of negroes would no doubt be a difficult, but by no means an impracticable undertaking, and the more difficult the end, the more praise and merit would be due to those who should effectually accomplish it. Even the Catholics of Spain pitied the miserable condition of negroes living among the protestant colonies, and to induce them to revolt, proffered them the advantages of liberty and religion at Augustine. Is it not a shame to a Protestant nation to keep such a number of human creatures so long among them, beings of the same nature, subjects of the same government, who have souls to be saved, and capable of being eternally happy or miserable in a future world, not only in a miserable state of slavery, but also of pagan darkness and superstition. What could be expected from creatures thus doomed to endless labour, and deprived of the natural rights of humanity and the privileges of Christianity, but that they should snatch at the least glimmering hopes and prospects of a better state, and give their task-masters reason to dread, that they would lay hold of some opportunity of forcing their way to it. This inexcusable negligence with respect to them may be considered of itself as no small source of danger to the colonists, as the hazard is greater from savage and ferocious, than mild and civilized dispositions, and, as the restraints of terror and temporal punishments are less constant and powerful than those of conscience and religion. The political and commercial connection subsisting between the mother country and the colonies, makes the charge of negroes, in reason and justice, to fall equally upon both. And whatever other men may think, we are of opinion, that an institution for their instruction was an object of the highest consequence, and that, by all the laws of God and man, that nation which brought this unfortunate race into such a situation, was bound to consult both their temporal and eternal felicity.

[Sidenote] James Glen governor.

About this time James Glen received a commission from his majesty, investing him with the government of South Carolina, and at the same time was appointed Colonel of a new regiment of foot to be raised in the province. He was a man of considerable knowledge, courteous, and polite; exceedingly fond of military parade and ostentation, which commonly have great force on ordinary minds, and by these means he maintained his dignity and importance in the eyes of the people. All governors invested with extensive powers ought to be well acquainted with the common and civil laws of their country; and every wise prince will guard against nominating weak or wicked persons to an high office, which affords them many opportunities of exercising their power to the prejudice of the people. When men are promoted to the government of provinces on account of their abilities and merit, and not through the interest of friends, then we may expect to see public affairs wisely managed, authority revered, and every man sitting secure under his vine, and enjoying the fruits of his industry with contentment and satisfaction. But when such offices are bestowed on ignorant or needy persons, because they happen to be favourites of some powerful and clamorous Lord at court, without any view to the interest and happiness of the people, then avarice and oppression commonly prevail on one hand, and murmur and discontent on the other. The appointment of Governor Glen was so far proper, as he possessed those qualifications which rendered his government respectable, and the people living under it for several years happy and contented. His council, consisting of twelve men, were appointed also by the King, under his sign manual. The assembly of representatives consisted of forty-four members, and were elected every third year by the freeholders of sixteen parishes. The court of chancery was composed of the Governor and Council, to which court belonged a master of chancery and a register. There was a court of vice-admiralty, the Judge, Register, and Marshal of which were appointed by the Lords Commissioners of the Admiralty in England. The Court of King's Bench consisted of a Chief Justice appointed by the King, who sat with some assistant justices of the province; and the same judges constituted the Court of Common Pleas. There were likewise an Attorney-General, a Clerk, and Provost-Marshal. The Secretary of the province, who was also Register, the Surveyor-general of the lands, and the Receiver-general of the quit-rents, were all appointed by the Crown. The Comptroller of the customs, and three Collectors, at the ports of Charlestown, Port-Royal, and Georgetown, were appointed by the Commissioners of the Customs in England. The provincial Treasurer was appointed by the General Assembly. The clergy were elected by the freeholders of the parish. All Justices of the peace, and officers of the militia, were appointed by the Governor in Council. This is the nature of the provincial government and constitution, and in this way were the principal officers of each branch appointed or elected, under the royal establishment.

[Sidenote] Ld. Carteret's property divided from that of the Crown.

About the same time John Lord Carteret (now Earl of Granville) applied by petition to his Majesty, praying that the eighth part of the lands and soil granted by King Charles, and referred to him by the act of parliament establishing an agreement with the other seven Lords Proprietors for the surrender of their title and interest to his Majesty, might be set apart and allotted to him and his heirs for ever, and proposing to appoint persons to divide the same; at the same time offering to resign to the King his share of, and interest in the government, and to convey, release and confirm to his Majesty, and his heirs, the other seven parts of the province. This petition being referred to the Lords Commissioners of trade and plantations, they reported, that it would be for his Majesty's service that Lord Carteret's property should be separated from that of his Majesty, and that the method proposed by his Lordship would be the most proper and effectual for the purpose. Accordingly five commissioners were appointed on the part of the King, and five on that of Lord Carteret for separating his Lordship's share, and making it one entire district by itself. The territory allotted him was divided on the north-east by the line which separated North Carolina from Virginia; on the east by the Atlantic ocean; on the south by a point on the sea-shore, in latitude thirty-five degrees and thirty-four minutes; and, agreeable to the charter, westward from these points on the sea-shore it extended, in a line parallel to the boundary line of Virginia, to the Pacific

Ocean. Not long afterwards, a grant of the eighth part of Carolina, together with all yearly rents and profits arising from it, passed the great seal, to John Lord Carteret and his heirs. But the power of making laws, calling and holding assemblies, erecting courts of justice, appointing judges and justices, pardoning criminals, granting titles of honour, making ports and havens, taking customs or duties on goods, executing the martial law, exercising the royal rights of a county palatine, or any other prerogatives relating to the administrations of government, were all excepted out of the grant. Lord Carteret was to hold this estate upon condition of yielding and paying to his Majesty and his heirs and successors, the annual-rent of one pound thirteen shillings and fourpence, on the feast of All-Saints, for ever, and also one fourth part of all the gold and silver ore found within this eighth part of the territory so separated and granted him.

[Sidenote] The country much exposed to invasion.

As Carolina abounds with navigable rivers, while it enjoys many advantages for commerce and trade, it is also much exposed to foreign invasions. The tide on that coast flows from six to ten feet perpendicular, and makes its way up into the flat country by a variety of channels. All vessels that draw not above seventeen feet water, may safely pass over the bar of Charlestown, which at spring-tides will admit ships that draw eighteen feet. This bar lies in thirty-two degrees and forty minutes north latitude, and seventy-eight degrees and forty-five minutes west longitude from London. Its situation is variable, owing to a sandy foundation and the rapid flux and reflux of the sea. The channel leading to George-town is twelve or thirteen feet deep, and likewise those of North and South Edisto rivers, and will admit all ships that draw not above ten or eleven feet of water. At Stono there is also a large creek, which admits vessels of the same draught of water; but Sewee and Santee rivers, and many others of less note, are for smaller craft which draw seven, eight, or nine feet. The channel up to Port Royal harbour is deep enough for the largest ships that sail on the sea; and the whole royal navy of England may ride with safety in it. Nature has evidently ordained this place for trade and commerce, by the many advantages with which she hath favoured it. It lies in thirty-two degrees and five minutes north latitude, and in longitude seventy-nine degrees five minutes. Its situation renders it an excellent station for a squadron of ships in time of war, as the run from it is short to the windward islands, but especially as it lies so convenient for distressing the immense trade coming through the Gulf of Florida. From this harbour ships may run out to the Gulf stream in one day, and return with equal ease the next, so that it would be very difficult to escape a sufficient number of cruisers stationed at Beaufort. The harbour is also defended by a small fort, built of tappy, which is a kind of cement composed of oyster-shells beat small, and mixed with lime and water, which when dry becomes hard and durable. The fort has two demi-bastions to the river, and one bastion to the land, with a gate and ditch, mounting sixteen heavy cannon, and containing barracks for an hundred men.

Several leagues to the southward of Port-Royal, Savanna river empties itself into the ocean, which is also navigable for ships that draw not above fourteen feet water. At the southern boundary of Georgia the great river Alatamaha falls into the Atlantic sea, about sixteen leagues north-east of Augustine, which lies in twenty-nine degrees fifty minutes. This river admits ships of large burden as far as Frederica, a small town built by General Oglethorpe, on an eminence in Simon's Island. The island on the west end is washed by a branch of the river Alatamaha, before it empties itself into the sea at Jekyl sound. At Frederica the river forms a kind of bay. The fort General Oglethorpe erected here for the defence of Georgia had several eighteen pounders mounted on it and commanded the river both upwards and downwards. It was built of tappy, with four bastions, surrounded by a quadrangular rampart, and a palisadoed ditch, which included also the King's stores, and two large buildings of brick and timber. The town was surrounded with a rampart, in the form of a pentagon, with flankers of the same thickness with that at the fort, and a dry ditch. On this rampart several pieces of ordnance were also mounted. In this situation General Oglethorpe had pitched his camp, which was divided into streets, distinguished by the names of the several Captains of his regiment. Their little huts were built of wood, and constructed for holding each four or five men. At some distance from Frederica was the colony of Highlanders, situated on the same river, a wild and intrepid race, living in a state of rural freedom and independence. Their settlement being near the frontiers, afforded them abundance of scope for the exercise of their warlike temper; and having received one severe blow from the garrison at Augustine, they seemed to long for an opportunity of revenging the massacre of their beloved friends.

[Sidenote] The Spaniards invade Georgia.

The time was fast approaching for giving them what they desired. For although the territory granted by the second charter to the proprietors at Carolina extended far to the south-west of the river Alatamaha, the Spaniards had never relinquished their pretended claim to the province of Georgia. Their ambassador at the British court had even declared that his Catholic Majesty would as soon part with Madrid as his claim to that territory. The squadron commanded by Admiral Vernon had for some time occupied their attention in the West Indies so much, that they could spare none of their forces to maintain their supposed right. But no sooner had the greatest part of the British fleet left those seas, and returned to England, than they immediately turned their eyes to Georgia, and began to make preparations for dislodging the English settlers in that province. Finding that threats could not terrify General Oglethorpe to compliance with their demands, an armament was prepared at the Havanna to go against him, and expel him by force of arms from their frontiers. With this view two thousand forces, commanded by Don Antonio de Rodondo, embarked at the Havanna, under the convoy of a strong squadron, and arrived at Augustine in May 1742.

But before this formidable fleet and armament had reached Augustine, they were observed by Captain Haymer, of the Flamborough man of war, who was cruising on that coast; and advice was immediately sent to General Oglethorpe of their arrival in Florida. Georgia now began to tremble in her turn. The General sent intelligence to Governor Glen at Carolina, requesting him to collect all the forces he could with the greatest expedition, and send them to his assistance; and at the same time to dispatch a sloop to the West Indies, to acquaint Admiral Vernon with the intended invasion.

Carolina by this time had found great advantage from the settlement of Georgia, which had proved an excellent barrier to that province, against the incursions of Spaniards and Spanish Indians. The southern parts being rendered secure by the regiment of General Oglethorpe in Georgia, the lands backward of Port-Royal had become much in demand, and risen four times their former value. But though the Carolineans were equally interested with their neighbours in the defence of Georgia, having little confidence in General Oglethorpe's military abilities, since his unsuccessful expedition against Augustine, the planters, struck with terror, especially those on the southern parts, deserted their habitations, and flocked to Charlestown with their families and effects. The inhabitants of Charlestown, many of whom being prejudiced against the man, declared against sending him any assistance, and determined rather to fortify their town, and stand upon their own grounds in a posture of defence. In this resolution, however, it is plain they acted from bad motives, in leaving that officer to stand alone against such a superior force. At such an emergency, good policy evidently required the firmest union, and the utmost exertion of the force of both colonies; for so soon as General Oglethorpe should be crushed, the reduction of Georgia would open to the common enemy an easy access into the bowels of Carolina, and render the force of both provinces, thus divided, unequal to the public defence.

In the mean time General Oglethorpe was making all possible preparations at Frederica for a vigorous stand. Message after message was sent to his Indian allies, who were greatly attached to him, and crowded to his camp. A company of Highlanders joined him on the first notice; and seemed joyful at the opportunity of retorting Spanish vengeance on their own heads. With his regiment, and a few rangers, Highlanders, and Indians, the General fixed his head quarters at Frederica, never doubting of a reinforcement from Carolina, and expecting their arrival every day; but in the mean time determined, in case he should be attacked, to sell his life as dear as possible in defence of the province.

About the end of June, 1742, the Spanish fleet, amounting to thirty-two sail; and carrying above three thousand men, under the command of Don Manuel de Monteano, came to anchor off Simons's bar. Here they continued for some time sounding the channel, and after finding a depth of water sufficient to admit their ships, they came in with the tide of flood into Jekyl sound. General Oglethorpe, who was at Simons's fort, fired at them as they passed the sound, which the Spaniards returned from their ships, and proceeded up the river Alatamaha, out of the reach of his guns. There the enemy having hoisted a red flag at the mizen top-mast-head of the largest ship, landed their forces upon the island, and erected a battery, with twenty eighteen pounders mounted on it. Among their land forces they had a fine company of artillery, under the command of Don Antonio de Rodondo, and a regiment of negroes. The negro commanders were clothed in lace, bore the same rank with white officers, and with equal freedom and familiarity walked and conversed with their commander and chief. Such an example might justly have alarmed Carolina. For should the enemy penetrate into that province, where there were such numbers of negroes, they would soon have acquired such a force, as must have rendered all opposition fruitless and ineffectual.

General Oglethorpe having found that he could not stop the progress of the enemy up the river, and judging his situation at Fort Simons too dangerous, nailed up the guns, burst the bombs and coehorns, destroyed the stores, and retreated to his head quarters at Frederica. So great was the force of the enemy, that he plainly perceived that nothing remained for him to achieve, with his handful of men, and therefore resolved to use his utmost vigilance, and to act only on the defensive. On all sides he sent out scouting parties to watch the motions of the Spaniards, while the main body were employed in working at the fortifications, making them as strong as circumstances would admit. Day and night he kept his Indian allies ranging through the woods, to harass the outposts of the enemy, who at length brought in five Spanish prisoners, who informed him of their number and force, and that the Governor of Augustine was commander in chief of the expedition. The General, still expecting a reinforcement from Carolina, used all his address in planning measures for gaining time, and preventing the garrison from sinking into despair. For this purpose he sent out the Highland company also to assist the Indians, and obstruct as much as possible the approach of the enemy till he should obtain assistance and relief. His provisions for the garrison were neither good nor plentiful, and his great distance from all settlements, together with the enemy keeping the command of the river, cut off entirely all prospects of a supply. To prolong the defence, however, he concealed every discouraging circumstance from his little army, which, besides Indians, did not amount to more than seven hundred men; and to animate them to perseverance, exposed himself to the same hardships and fatigues with the meanest soldier in his garrison.

[Sidenote] A stratagem to get rid of the enemy.

While Oglethorpe remained in this situation, the enemy made several attempts to pierce through the woods, with a view to attack the fort; but met with such opposition from deep morasses, and dark thickets, lined with fierce Indians, and wild Highlanders, that they honestly confessed that the devil himself could not pass through them to Frederica. Don Manuel de Monteano, however, had no other prospect left, and these difficulties must either be surmounted, or the design dropt; and therefore one party after another was sent out to explore the thickets, and to take possession of every advantageous post to be found in them. In two skirmishes with the Highlanders and Indians, the enemy had one captain, and two lieutenants killed, with above one hundred men taken prisoners. After which the Spanish commander changed his plan of operations, and keeping his men under cover of his cannon, proceeded with some gallies up the river with the tide of flood, to reconnoitre the fort, and draw the General's attention to another quarter. To this place Oglethorpe sent a party of Indians, with orders to lie in ambuscade in the woods, and endeavour to prevent their landing. About the same time an English prisoner escaped from the Spanish camp, and brought advice to General Oglethorpe of a difference subsisting in it, in so much that the forces from Cuba, and those from Augustine encamped in separate places. Upon which the General resolved to attempt a surprise on one of the Spanish camps, and taking the advantage of his knowledge of the woods, marched out in the night with three hundred chosen men, the Highland company, and some rangers. Having advanced within two miles of the enemy's camp, he halted, and went forward with a small party to take a view of the posture of the enemy. But while he wanted above all things to conceal his approach, a Frenchman fired his musket, run off and alarmed the enemy. Upon which Oglethorpe finding his design defeated, retreated to Frederica, and being apprehensive that the deserter would discover his weakness, began to study by what device he might most effectually defeat the credit of his informations. For this purpose he wrote a letter, addressing it to the deserter, in which he desired him to acquaint the Spaniards with the defenceless state of Frederica, and how easy and practicable it would be to cut him and his small garrison to pieces. He begged him, as his spy, to bring them forward to the attack, and assure them of success; but if he could not prevail with them to make that attempt, to use all his art and influence to persuade them to stay at least three days more at Fort Simons, for within that time, according to the advice he had just received from Carolina, he would have a reinforcement of two thousand land-forces, and six British ships of war, with which he doubted not he would be able to give a good account of the Spanish invaders. He intreated the deserter to urge them to stay, and above all things cautioned him against mentioning a single word of Vernon coming against Augustine, assuring him, that for such services he should be amply rewarded by his Britannic Majesty. This letter he gave to one of the Spanish prisoners, who for the sake of liberty and a small reward, promised to deliver it to the French deserter; but, instead of that, as Oglethorpe expected, he delivered it to the commander and chief of the Spanish army.

[Sidenote] The Spaniards retreat to Augustine.

Various were the speculations and conjectures which this letter occasioned in the Spanish camp, and the commander, among others, was not a little perplexed what to infer from it. In the first place he ordered the French deserter to be put in irons, to prevent his escape, and then called a council of war, to consider what was most proper to be done in consequence of intelligence, so puzzling and alarming. Some officers were of opinion, that the letter was intended to deceive, and to prevent them from attacking Frederica; others thought that the things mentioned in it appeared so feasible, that there were good grounds to believe, the English General wished them to take place, and therefore gave their voice for consulting the safety of Augustine, and dropping a plan of conquest attended with so many difficulties, and which, in the issue, might perhaps hazard the loss of both army and fleet, if not of the whole province of Florida. While the Spanish leaders were employed in these deliberations, and much embarrassed, fortunately three ships of force, which the Governor of South Carolina had sent out, appeared at some distance on the coast. This corresponding with the letter, convinced the Spanish commander of its real intent, and struck such a panic into the army, that they immediately set fire to their fort, and in great hurry and confusion embarked, leaving behind them several cannon, and a quantity of provisions and military stores. The wind being contrary, the English ships could not, during that day, beat up to the mouth of the river, and before next morning the invaders got past them, and escaped to Augustine.

In this manner was the province of Georgia delivered, when brought to the very brink of destruction by a formidable enemy. Fifteen days had Don Manuel de Monteano been on the small island on which Frederica was situated, without gaining the smallest advantage over an handful of men, and in different skirmishes lost some of his bravest troops. What number of men Oglethorpe lost we have not been able to learn, but it must have been very inconsiderable. In this resolute defence of the country he displayed both military skill and personal courage, and an equal degree of praise was due to him from the Carolineans as from the Georgians. It is not improbable that the Spaniards had Carolina chiefly in their eye, and had meditated an attack where rich plunder could have been obtained, and where, by an accession of slaves, they might have increased their force in proportion to their progress. Never did the Carolineans make so bad a figure in defence of their country. When union, activity and dispatch were so requisite, they ingloriously stood at a distance, and suffering private pique to prevail over public spirit, seemed determined to risk the safety of their country, rather than General Oglethorpe, by their help, should gain the smallest degree of honour and reputation. Money, indeed, they voted for the service, and at length sent some ships, but, by coming so late, they proved useful rather from the fortunate co-operation of an accidental cause, than from the zeal and public spirit of the people. The Georgians with justice blamed their more powerful neighbours, who, by keeping at a distance in the day of danger, had almost hazarded the loss of both provinces. Had the enemy pursued their operations with vigour and courage, the province of Georgia must have fallen a prey to the invaders, and Carolina had every thing to dread in consequence of the conquest. Upon the return of the Spanish troops to the Havanna, the commander was imprisoned, and ordered to take his trial for his conduct during this expedition, the result of which proved so shameful and ignominious to the Spanish arms. Though the enemy threatened to renew the invasion, yet we do not find that after this repulse they made any attempts by force of arms to gain possession of Georgia.

[Sidenote] Ill treatment of General Oglethorpe.

The Carolineans having had little or no share of the glory gained by this brave defence, were also divided in their opinions with respect to the conduct of General Oglethorpe. While one party acknowledged his signal services, and poured out the highest encomiums on his wisdom and courage; another shamefully censured his conduct, and meanly detracted from his merit. None took any notice of his services, except the inhabitants in and about Port-Royal, who addressed him in the following manner: "We the inhabitants of the southern parts of Carolina beg leave to congratulate your Excellency on your late wonderful success over your and our inveterate enemies the Spaniards, who so lately invaded Georgia, in such a numerous and formidable body, to the great terror of his Majesty's subjects in these southern parts. It was very certain, had the Spaniards succeeded in those attempts against your Excellency, they would also have entirely destroyed us, laid our province waste and desolate, and filled our habitations with blood and slaughter; so that his Majesty must have lost the fine and spacious harbour of Port-Royal, where the largest ships of the British nation may remain in security on any occasion. We are very sensible of the great protection and safety we have long enjoyed, by your Excellency being to the southwards of us, and keeping your armed sloops cruising on the coast, which has secured our trade and fortunes more than all the ships of war ever stationed at Charlestown; but more by your late resolution in frustrating the attempts of the Spaniards, when nothing could have saved us from utter ruin, next to the Providence of Almighty God, but your Excellency's singular conduct, and the bravery of the troops under your command. We think it our duty to pray God to protect your Excellency, and send you success in all your undertakings for his Majesty's service; and we assure your Excellency, that there is not a man of us but would most willingly have ventured his all, in support of your Excellency and your gallant troops, had we been assisted, and put in a condition to have been of service to you; and that we always looked upon our interest to be so united to that of the colony of Georgia, that had your Excellency been cut off, we must have fallen of course."

But while the inhabitants in and about Port-Royal were thus addressing General Oglethorpe, reports were circulating in Charlestown to his prejudice, insomuch that both his honour and honesty were called in question. Such malicious rumours had even reached London, and occasioned some of his bills to return to America protested. Lieutenant-Colonel William Cook, who owed his preferment to the General's particular friendship and generosity, and who, on pretence of sickness, had left Georgia before this invasion, had filed no less than nineteen articles of complaint against him, summoning several officers and soldiers from Georgia to prove the charge. As the General had, in fact, stretched his credit, exhausted his strength, and risqued his life for the defence of Carolina in its frontier colony, such a recompence must have been equally provoking, as it was unmerited. We are apt to believe, that such injurious treatment could not have arisen from the wiser and better part of the inhabitants, and therefore must be solely ascribed to some envious and malicious spirits, who are to be found in all communities.

Envy cannot bear the blaze of superior virtue, and malice rejoices in the stains which even falsehood throws on a distinguished character; and such is the extensive freedom of the British form of government that every one, even the meanest, may step forth as an enemy to great abilities and an unblemished reputation. The charges of envy and malice, Oglethorpe might have treated with contempt; but to vindicate himself against the rude attacks of an inferior officer, he thought himself at this time bound in honour to return to England.

[Sidenote] His character cleared, and conduct vindicated.

Soon after his arrival a court-martial of general officers was called, who sat two days at the Horse Guards, examining one by one the various articles of complaint lodged against him. After the most mature examination, the board adjudged the charge to be false, malicious, and groundless, and reported the same to his Majesty. In consequence of which Lieutenant-Colonel Cook was dismissed from the service, and declared incapable of serving his Majesty in any military capacity whatever. By this means the character of General Oglethorpe was divested of those dark stains with which it had been overclouded, and began to appear to the world in its true and favourable light. Carolina owed this benefactor her friendship and love. Georgia was indebted to him for both her existence and protection. Indeed his generous services for both colonies deserved to be deeply imprinted on the memory of every inhabitant and the benefits resulting from them to be remembered to the latest age with joy and gratitude.

After this period General Oglethorpe never returned to the province of Georgia, but upon all occasions discovered in England an uncommon zeal for its prosperity and improvement. From its first settlement the colony had hitherto been under a military government, executed by the General and such officers as he thought proper to nominate and appoint. But now the Trustees thought proper to establish a kind of civil government, and committed the charge of it to a president and four assistants, who were to act agreeable to the instructions they should receive from them, and to be accountable to that corporation for their public conduct. William Stephens was made chief magistrate, and Thomas Jones, Henry Parker, John Fallowfield, and Samuel Mercer, were appointed assistants. They were instructed to hold four general courts at Savanna every year, for regulating public affairs, and determining all differences relating to private property. No public money could be disposed of but by a warrant under the seal of the President and major part of the Assistants in council assembled, who were enjoined to send monthly accounts to England of money expended, and of the particular services to which it was applied. All officers of militia were continued, for the purpose of holding musters, and keeping the men properly trained for military services; and Oglethorpe's regiment was left in the colony for its defence.

By this time the Trustees had transported to Georgia, at different times, above one thousand five hundred men, women and children. As the colony was intended as a barrier to Carolina, by their charter the Trustees were at first laid under several restraints with respect to the method of granting lands, as well as the settlers with respect to the terms of holding and disposing of them. Now it was found expedient to relieve both the former and latter from those foolish and impolitic restrictions. Under the care of General Oglethorpe the infant province had surmounted many difficulties, yet still it promised a poor recompense to Britain for the vast sums of money expended for its protection. The indigent emigrants, especially those from England, having little acquaintance with husbandry, and less inclination to labour, made bad settlers; and as greater privileges were allowed them on the Carolina side of the river, they were easily decoyed away to that colony. The Highlanders and Germans indeed, being more frugal and industrious, succeeded better, but hitherto had made very small progress, owing partly to wars with the Spaniards, and to severe hardships attending all kinds of culture in such an unhealthy climate and woody country. The staple commodities intended to be raised in Georgia were silk and wine, which were indeed very profitable articles; but so small was the improvement made in them, that they had hitherto turned out to little account. The most industrious and successful settlers could as yet scarcely provide for their families, and the unfortunate, the sick, and indolent part, remained in a starved and miserable condition.

[Sidenote] The Carolineans petition for three independent companies.

Soon after the departure of General Oglethorpe, the Carolineans petitioned the King, praying that three independent companies, consisting each of an hundred men, might be raised in the colonies, paid by Great Britain, and stationed in Carolina, to be entirely under the command of the Governor and Council of that province. This petition was referred to the Lords of his Majesty's Privy-council, and a time appointed for considering, whether the present state of Carolina was such as rendered this additional charge to the nation proper and necessary. Two reasons were assigned by the colonists for the necessity of this military force: the first was, to preserve peace and security at home; the second, to protect the colony against foreign invasions. They alledged, that as the country was overstocked with negroes, such a military force was requisite to overawe them, and prevent insurrections; and as the coast was so extensive, and the ports lay exposed to every French and Spanish plunderer that might at any time invade the province, their security against such attempts was of the highest consequence to the nation. But though they afterwards obtained some independent companies, those reasons, at this time, did not appear to the Privy-council of weight sufficient to induce them to give their advice for this military establishment. It was their opinion, that it belonged to the provincial legislature to make proper laws for limiting the importation of negroes, and regulating and restraining them when imported; rather than put the mother country to the expence of keeping a standing force in the province to overawe them: that Georgia, and the Indians on the Apalachian hills, were a barrier against foreign enemies on the western frontiers: that Fort Johnson, and the fortifications in Charlestown, were a sufficient protection for that port; besides, that as the entrance over the bar was so difficult to strangers, before a foreign enemy could land five hundred men in that town, half the militia in the province might be collected for its defence. Georgetown and Port-Royal indeed were exposed, but the inhabitants being both few in number and poor, it could not be worth the pains and risque of a single privateer to look into those harbours. For which reasons it was judged, that Carolina could be in little danger till a foreign enemy had possession of Georgia; and therefore it was agreed to maintain Oglethorpe's regiment in that settlement complete; and give orders to the commandant to send detachments to the forts in James's Island, Port-Royal, and such other places where their service might be thought useful and necessary to the provincial safety and defence.

[Sidenote] The colony's advantages from Britain.

Many are the advantages Carolina has derived from its political and commercial connection with Britain. Its growing and flourishing state the colony owes almost entirely to the mother-country, without the protection and indulgence of which, the people had little or no encouragement to be industrious. Britain first furnished a number of bold and enterprising settlers, who carried with them the knowledge, arts, and improvements of a civilized nation. This may be said to be the chief favour for which Carolina stands indebted to the parent state during the proprietary government. But since the province has been taken under the royal care, it has been nursed and protected by a rich and powerful nation. Its government has been stable, private property secure, and the privileges and liberties of the people have been extensive. Lands the planters obtained from the King at a cheap rate. To cultivate them the mother-country furnished them with labourers upon credit. Each person had entire liberty to manage his affairs for his own profit and advantage, and having no tythes, and very trifling taxes to pay, reaped almost the whole fruits of his industry. The best and most extensive market was allowed to the commodities he produced, and his staples increased in value in proportion to the quantity raised, and the demand for them in Europe. All British manufactures he obtained at an easy rate, and drawbacks were allowed on articles of foreign manufacture, that they might be brought the cheaper to the American market. In consequence of which frugal planters, every three or four years, doubled their capital, and their progress towards independence and opulence was rapid. Indeed, the colonists had many reasons for gratitude, and none for fear, except what arose from their immoderate haste to be rich, and from purchasing such numbers of slaves, as exposed them to danger and destruction.

The plan of settling townships, especially as it came accompanied with the royal bounty, had proved beneficial in many respects. It encouraged multitudes of poor oppressed people in Ireland, Holland and Germany to emigrate, by which means the province received a number of frugal and industrious settlers. As many of them came from manufacturing towns in Europe, it might have been expected that they would naturally have pursued those occupations to which they had been bred, and in which their chief skill consisted. But this was by no means the case; for, excepting a few of them that took up their residence in Charlestown, they procured lands, applied to pasturage and agriculture, and by raising hemp, wheat and maize in the interior parts of the country, and curing hams, bacon, and beef, they supplied the market with abundance of provision, while at the same time they found that they had taken the shortest way of arriving at easy and independent circumstances.

[Sidenote] Its advantage and importance to Britain.

Indeed while such vast territories in Carolina remained unoccupied, it was neither for the interest of the province, nor that of the mother-country, to employ any hands in manufactures. So long as labour bestowed on lands was most profitable, no prudent colonist would direct his attention or strength to any other employment, especially as the mother-country could supply him with all kinds of manufactures at a much cheaper rate than he could make them. The surplus part of British commodities and manufactures for which there was no vent in Britain, found in Carolina a good market, and in return brought the English merchant such articles as were in demand at home, by which means the advantages were mutual and reciprocal. The exclusive privilege of supplying this market encouraged labour in England, and augmented the annual income of the nation. From the monopoly of this trade with America, which was always increasing, Britain derived many substantial advantages. These colonies consumed all her superfluities which lay upon hand, and enlarged her commerce, which, without such a market, must have been confined to its ancient narrow channel. In the year 1744, two hundred and thirty vessels were loaded at the port of Charlestown, so that the national value of the province was not only considerable in respect of the large quantity of goods it consumed, but also in respect to the naval strength it promoted. Fifteen hundred seamen at least found employment in the trade of this province, and, besides other advantages, the profits of freight must make a considerable addition to the account in favour of Britain.

Nor is there the smallest reason to expect that manufactures will be encouraged in Carolina, while landed property can be obtained on such easy terms. The cooper, the carpenter, the brick-layer, the shipbuilder, and every other artificer and tradesman, after having laboured for a few years at their respective employments, and purchased a few negroes, commonly retreat to the country, and settle tracts of uncultivated land. While they labour at their trades, they find themselves dependent on their employers; this is one reason for their wishing at least to be their own masters; and though the wages allowed them are high, yet the means of subsistence in towns are also dear, and therefore they long to be in the same situation with their neighbours, who derive an easy subsistence from a plantation, which they cultivate at pleasure, and are answerable to no master for their conduct. Even the merchant becomes weary of attending the store, and risking his flock on the stormy seas, or in the hands of men where it is often exposed to equal hazards, and therefore collects it as soon as possible, and settles a plantation. Upon this plantation he sets himself down, and being both landlord and farmer, immediately finds himself an independent man. Having his capital in lands and negroes around him, and his affairs collected within a narrow circle, he can manage and improve them as he thinks fit. He soon obtains plenty of the necessaries of life from his plantation; nor need he want any of its conveniencies and luxuries. The greatest difficulties he has to surmount arise from the marshy soil, and unhealthy climate, which often cut men off in the midst of their days. Indeed in this respect Carolina is the reverse of most countries in Europe, where the rural life, when compared with that of the town, is commonly healthy and delightful.

CHAPTER IX

[Sidenote] All commotions and oppressions in Europe favourable to America.

The war between England and France still raged in Europe, and being carried on under many disadvantages on the side of the allied army, was almost as unsuccessful as their enemies could have desired. The battle of Fontenoy was obstinate and bloody, and many thousands were left on the field on the side of the vanquished. The victorious army had little reason for boasting, having likewise bought their victory very dear. Though bad success attended the British arms on the continent at this time, yet that evil being considered as remote, the people seemed only to feel it as affecting the honour of the nation, which by some fortunate change might retrieve the glory of its arms; but a plot of a more interesting nature was discovered, which added greatly to the national perplexity and distress. A civil war broke out within the bowels of the kingdom, the object of which was nothing less than the recovery of the British crown from the house of Brunswick. Charles Edward Stuart, the young pretender, stimulated by the fire of youth, encouraged by the deceitful promises of France, and invited by a discontented party of the Scotch nation, had landed in North Britain to head the rash enterprise. Multitudes of bold and deluded Highlanders, and several Lowlanders, who owed their misfortunes to their firm adherence to that family, joined his army. He became formidable both by the numbers that followed him, and the success that at first attended his arms. But at length, after having struck a terror into the nation, he was routed at Culloden field, and his party were either dispersed, or made prisoners of war.

What to make of the prisoners of war became a matter of public deliberation. To punish all, without distinction, would have been unjustifiable cruelty in any government, especially where so many were young, ignorant, and misled: to pardon all, on the other hand, would discover unreasonable weakness, and dangerous lenity. The prisoners had nothing to plead but the clemency of the King, and the tenderness of the British constitution. Examples of justice were necessary to deter men from the like attempts; but it was agreed to temper justice with mercy, in order to convince the nation of the gentleness of that constitution, which made not only a distinction between the innocent and guilty, but even among the guilty themselves, between those who were more, and those who were less criminal. The King ordered a general pardon to pass the Great Seal, in which he extended mercy to the ignorant, and misled among the rebels, which pardon comprehended nineteen out of twenty, who drew lots for this purpose, were exempted from trial, and transported to the British plantations. Among other settlements in America, the southern provinces had a share of these bold and hardy Caledonians, who afterwards proved excellent and industrious settlers.

As every family of labourers is an acquisition to a growing colony, such as Carolina, where lands are plenty, and hands only wanted to improve them; to encourage emigration, a door was opened there to Protestants of every nation. The poor and distressed subjects of the British dominions, and those of Germany and Holland, were easily induced to leave oppression, and transport themselves and families to that province. Lands free of quit-rents, for the first ten years, were allotted to men, women, and children. Utensils for cultivation, and hogs and cows to begin their stock, they purchased with their bounty-money. The like bounty was allowed to all servants after the expiration of the term of their servitude. From this period Carolina was found to be an excellent refuge to the poor, the unfortunate, and oppressed. The population and prosperity of her colonies engrossed the attention of the mother-country. His Majesty's bounty served to alleviate the hardships inseparable from the first years of cultivation, and landed property animated the poor emigrants to industry and perseverance. The different townships yearly increased in numbers. Every one upon his arrival obtained his grant of land, and sat down on his freehold with no taxes, or very trifling ones, no tythes, no poor rates, with full liberty of hunting and fishing, and many other advantages and privileges he never knew in Europe. It is true the unhealthiness of the climate was a great bar to his progress, and proved fatal to many of these first settlers; but to such as surmounted this obstacle, every year brought new profits, and opened more advantageous prospects. All who escaped the dangers of the climate, if they could not be called rich during their own life, by improving their little freeholds, they commonly left their children in easy or opulent circumstances. Even in the first age being free, contented, and accountable to man for their labour and management, their condition in many respects was preferable to that of the poorest class of labourers in Europe. In all improved countries, where commerce and manufactures have been long established, and luxury prevails, the poorest ranks of citizens are always oppressed and miserable. Indeed this must necessarily be the case, otherwise trade and manufactures, which flourish principally by the low price of labour and provisions, must decay. In Carolina, though exposed to more troubles and hardships for a few years, such industrious people had better opportunities than in Europe for advancing to an easy and independent state. Hence it happened that few emigrants ever returned to their native country; on the contrary, the success and prosperity of the most fortunate, brought many adventurers and relations after them. Their love to their former friends, and their natural partiality for their countrymen, induced the old planters to receive the new settlers joyfully, and even to assist and relieve them. Having each his own property and possession, this independence produced mutual respect and beneficence, and such general harmony and industry reigned among them, that those townships, formerly a desolate wilderness, now stocked with diligent labourers, promised soon to become fruitful fields.

[Sidenote] Cultivation attended with salutary effects.

It has been observed, that in proportion as the lands have been cleared and improved, and scope given for a more free circulation of air, the climate has likewise become more salubrious and pleasant. This change was more remarkable in the heart of the country than in the maritime parts, where the best plantations of rice are, and where water is carefully preserved to overflow the fields; yet even in those places cultivation has been attended with salutary effects. Time and experience had now taught the planters, that, during the autumnal months, their living among the low rice plantations subjected them to many disorders, from which the inhabitants of the capital were entirely exempted. This induced the richer part to retreat to town during this unhealthy season. Those who were less able to bear the expences of this retreat, and had learned to guard against the inconveniencies of the climate, sometimes escaped; but laborious strangers suffered much during these autumnal months. Accustomed as they were in Europe to toil through the heat of the day, and expose themselves in all weathers, they followed the same practices in Carolina, where the climate would by no means admit of such liberties. Apprehensive of no ill consequences from such exposure, they began their improvement with vigour and resolution, and persevered until the hot climate and heavy toil exhausted their spirits, and brought home to them the unwelcome intimations of danger.

[Sidenote] Mean heat in Carolina.

In the months of July, August, and September, the heat in the shaded air, from noon to three o'clock, is often between ninety and an hundred degrees; and as such extreme heat is of short duration, being commonly productive of thunder-showers, it becomes on that account the more dangerous. I have seen the mercury in Fahrenheit's thermometer arise in the shade to ninety-six in the hottest, and fall to sixteen in the coolest season of the year; others have observed it as high as an hundred, and as low as ten; which range between the extreme heat of summer and cold in winter is prodigious, and must have a great effect upon the constitution of all, even of those who are best guarded against the climate; what then must be the situation of such as are exposed to the open air and burning sky in all seasons? The mean diurnal heat of the different seasons has been, upon the most careful observation, fixed at sixty-four in spring, seventy-nine in summer, seventy-two in autumn, and fifty-two in winter; and the mean nocturnal heat in those seasons at fifty-six degrees in spring, seventy-five in summer, sixty-eight in autumn, and forty-six in winter.

[Sidenote] The diseases of the country.

As this climate differs so much from that of Britain, Ireland, and Germany, and every where has great influence on the human constitution, no wonder that many of these settlers should sicken and die by the change, during the first state of colonization. In the hot season the human body is relaxed by perpetual perspiration, and becomes feeble and sickly, especially during the dog-days, when the air is one while suffocating and sultry, and another moist and foggy. Exhausted of fluids, it is perhaps not at all, or very improperly, supplied. Hence intermittent, nervous, putrid and bilious fevers, are common in the country, and prove fatal to many of its inhabitants. Young children are very subject to the worm-fever, which cuts off multitudes of them. The dry belly-ache, which is a dreadful disorder, is no stranger to the climate. An irruption, commonly called the Prickly Heat, often breaks out during the summer, which is attended with troublesome itching and stinging pains; but this disease being common, and not dangerous, is little regarded; and if proper caution be used to prevent it from striking suddenly inward, is thought to be attended even with salutary effects. In the spring and winter pleurisies and peripneumonies are common, often obstinate, and frequently fatal diseases. So changeable is the weather, that the spirits in the thermometer will often rise or fall twenty, twenty-five, and thirty degrees, in the space of twenty four hours, which must make havock of the human constitution. In autumn there is sometimes a difference of twenty degrees between the heat of the day and that of the night, and in winter a greater difference between the heat of the morning and that of noon-day. We leave it to physicians more particularly to describe the various disorders incident to this climate, together with the causes of them; but if violent heat and continual perspiration in summer, noxious vapours and sudden changes in autumn, piercing cold nights, and hot noon-days in winter, affect the human constitution, the inhabitants of Carolina, especially in the maritime parts, have all these and many more changes and hardships during the year to undergo. Not only man, but every animal, is strongly affected by the sultry heat of summer. Horses and cows retire to the shade, and there, though harassed with insects, they stand and profusely sweat through the violence of the day. Hogs and dogs are also much distressed with it. Poultry and wild fowls droop their wings, hang out their tongues, and, with open throats, pant for breath. The planter who consults his health is not only cautious in his dress and diet, but rises early for the business of the field, and transacts it before ten o'clock, and then retreats to the house or shade during the melting heat of the day, until the coolness of the evening again invites him to the field. Such is his feebleness of body and languor of spirit at noon, that the greatest pleasure of life consists in being entirely at rest. Even during the night he is often restless and depressed, insomuch that refreshing sleep is kept a stranger to his eyes. If unfortunately the poor labourer is taken sick in such weather, perhaps far removed from, or unable to employ, a physician, how great must be his hazard. In towns this heat is still rendered more intolerable by the glowing reflection from houses, and the burning sand in the streets. But how it is possible for cooks, blacksmiths, and other tradesmen, to work at the side of a fire, as many in the province do during such a season, we must leave to the world to judge.

[Sidenote] Climate favourable to the culture of indigo.

This hot weather, however, has been found favourable to the culture of indigo, which at this time was introduced into Carolina, and has since proved one of its chief articles of commerce. About the year 1745 a fortunate discovery was made, that this plant grew spontaneously in the province, and was found almost every where among the wild weeds of the forest. As the soil naturally yielded a weed which furnished the world with so useful and valuable a dye, it loudly called for cultivation and improvement. For this purpose some indigo seed was imported from the French West Indies, where it had been cultivated with great success, and yielded the planters immense profit. At first the seed was planted by way of experiment, and it was found to answer the most sanguine expectations. In consequence of which several planters turned their attention to the culture of indigo and studied the art of extracting the dye from it. Every trial brought them fresh encouragement. In the year 1747 a considerable quantity of it was sent to England, which induced the merchants trading to Carolina to petition parliament for a bounty on Carolina indigo. The parliament, upon examination, found that it was one of the most beneficial articles of French commerce, that their West India islands supplied all the markets of Europe; and that Britain alone consumed annually six hundred thousand weight of French indigo, which, at five shillings a pound, cost the nation the prodigious sum of one hundred and fifty thousand pounds sterling. It was demonstrated by the merchants, that this vast expence might be saved, by encouraging the cultivation of indigo in Carolina, and commonly believed that in time the colony might bring it to such perfection, as to rival the French at the markets of Europe. This petition of the merchants was soon followed by another from the planters and inhabitants of Carolina, and others to the same effect from the clothiers, dyers, and traders of different towns in Britain. It was proved, that the demand for indigo annually increased, and it could never he expected that the planters in the West Indies would turn their hands to it, while the culture of sugar canes proved more profitable. Accordingly, an act of parliament passed, about the beginning of the year 1748, for allowing a bounty of sixpence *per* pound on all indigo raised in the British American plantations, and imported directly into Britain from the place of its growth. In consequence of which act the planters applied themselves with double vigour and spirit to that article, and seemed to vie with each other who should bring the best kind and greatest quantity of it to the market. Some years indeed elapsed before they learned the nice art of making it as well as the French, whom long practice and experience had taught it to perfection; but every year they acquired greater skill and knowledge in preparing it, and received incredible profit as the reward of their labours. While many of them doubled their capital every three or four years by planting indigo, they in process of time brought it to such a degree of perfection, as not only to supply the mother-country, but also to undersel the French at several European markets.

[Sidenote] The manner of cultivating and making indigo.

Here it may not be improper to give the reader some account of the manner in which the people of Carolina cultivate this plant, and extract the dye from it. As we pretend to little knowledge of this matter ourselves, we shall give the following rules and directions of an ingenious person, who practised them for several years with great success. "As both the quantity and quality of indigo greatly depend on the cultivation of the plant, it is proper to observe, that it seems to thrive best in a rich, light soil, unmixed with clay or sand. The ground to be planted should be plowed, or turned up with hoes, some time in December, that the frost may render it rich and mellow. It must also be well harrowed, and cleansed from all grass, roots, and stumps of trees, to facilitate the hoeing after the weed appears above ground. The next thing to be considered is the choice of the seed, in which the planters should be very nice; there is great variety of it, and from every sort good indigo may be made; but none answers so well in this colony as the true Guatimala, which if good is a small oblong black seed, very bright and full, and when rubbed in the hand will appear as if finely polished.

"In Carolina we generally begin to plant about the beginning of April, in the following manner: The ground being well prepared, furrows are made with a drill-plow, or hoe, two inches deep, and eighteen inches distant from each other, to receive the seed, which is sown regularly, and not very thick, after which it is lightly covered with earth. A bushel of seed will sow four English acres. If the weather proves warm and serene, the plant will appear above ground in ten or four-teen days. After the plant appears, the ground, though not grassy, should be hoed to loosen the earth about it, which otherwise would much hinder its growth. In good seasons it grows very fast, and must all the while be kept perfectly clean of weeds. Whenever the plant is in full bloom it must be cut down, without paying any regard to its height, as its leaves are then thick and full of juice, and this commonly happens in about four months after planting. But, previous to the season for cutting, a complete set of vats of the following dimensions, for every twenty acres of weed, must be provided, and kept in good order. The steeper or vat in which the weed is first put to ferment, must be sixteen feet square in the clear, and two and a half feet deep; the second vat or battery twelve feet long, ten feet wide, and four and a half feet deep from the top of the plate. These vats should be made of the best cypress or yellow-pine plank, two and a half inches thick, well fastened to the joints and studs with seven-inch spikes, and then caulked, to prevent their leaking. Vats thus made will last in Carolina, notwithstanding the excessive heat, at least seven years. When every thing is ready, the weed must be cut and laid regularly in the steeper with the stalk upward, which will hasten the fermentation; then long rails must be laid the length of the vat, at eighteen inches distance from one another, and wedged down to the weed, to prevent its buoying up when the water is pumped into the steeper. For this purpose the softest water answers best, and the quantity of it necessary must be just sufficient to cover all the weed. In this situation it is left to ferment, which will begin sooner or later in proportion to the heat of the weather, and the ripeness of the plant, but for the most part takes twelve or fifteen hours. After the water is loaded with the salts and substance of the weed, it must be let out of the steeper into the battery, there to be beat; in order to perform which operation, many different machines have been invented: but for this purpose any instrument that will agitate the water with great violence may be used. When the water has been violently agitated for fifteen or twenty minutes in the battery, by taking a little of the liquor up in a plate it will appear full of small grain or curdled; then you are to let in a quantity of lime-water kept in a vat for the purpose, to augment and precipitate the faeculae, still continuing to stir and beat vehemently the indigo water, till it becomes of a strong purple colour, and the grain hardly perceptible. Then it must be left to settle, which it will do in eight or ten hours. After which the water must be gently drawn out of the battery through plug-holes contrived for that purpose, so that the faeculae may remain at the bottom of the vat. It must then be taken up, and carefully strained through a horse-hair sieve, to render the indigo perfectly clean, and put into bags made of Osnaburghs, eighteen inches long, and twelve wide, and suspended for six hours, to drain the water out of it. After which the mouths of these bags being well fastened, it must be put into a press to be entirely freed from any remains of water, which would otherwise greatly hurt the quality of the indigo. The press commonly used for this purpose is a box of five feet in length, two and a half wide, and two deep, with holes at one end to let out the water. In this box the bags must be laid, one upon another, until it is full, upon which a plank must be laid, fitted to go within the box, and upon all a sufficient number of weights to squeeze out the water entirely by a constant and gradual pressure, so that the indigo may become a fine stiff paste; which is then taken out and cut into small pieces, each about two inches square, and laid out to dry. A house made of logs must be prepared on purpose for drying it, and so constructed that it may receive all the advantages of an open and free air, without being exposed to the sun, which is very pernicious to the dye. For here indigo placed in the sun, in a few hours will be burnt up to a perfect cinder. While the indigo remains in the drying house, it must be carefully turned three or four times in a day, to prevent its rotting. Flies should likewise be carefully kept from it, which at this season of the year are hatched in millions, and infest an indigo plantation like a plague. After all, great care must also be taken, that the indigo be sufficiently dry before it is packed, lest after it is headed up in barrels it should sweat, which will certainly spoil and rot it."

In this manner indigo is cultivated and prepared in Carolina, and the richest land in the heart of the country is found to answer best for it. The maritime islands, however, which are commonly sandy, are not unfavourable for this production, especially those that contain spots of land covered with oak, and hickory trees. It is one of those rank weeds which in a few years will exhaust the strength and fertility of the best lands in the world. It is commonly cut in the West Indies six and seven times in the year, but in Carolina no more than two or three times before the frost begins. Our planters have been blamed by the English merchants for paying too much attention to the quantity, and too little to the quality of their indigo, hence the West-India indigo brings an higher price at the market. He that prefers the quality to the quantity, is very careful to cut the plant at the proper season, that is, when the weed begins to bloom; for the more luxuriant and tender the plant, the more beautiful the indigo. While it is curing, indigo has an offensive and disagreeable smell, and as the dregs of the weed are full of salts, and make excellent manure, therefore they should be immediately buried under ground when brought out of the steeper. It is commonly observed, that all creatures about an indigo plantation are starved, whereas, about a rice one, which abounds with provisions for man and beast, they thrive and flourish. The season for making indigo in Carolina ends with the first frosty weather, which puts a stop to fermentation, and then double labour is not only requisite for beating it, but when prepared it is commonly good for nothing.

[Sidenote] The common methods of judging of its quality.

The planters bring their indigo to market about the end of the year, and frequently earlier. The merchant judges of its quality by breaking it, and observing the closeness of its grain, and its brilliant copper, or violet blue colour. The weight in some measure proves its quality, for heavy indigo of every colour is always bad. Good indigo almost entirely consumes away in the fire, the bad leaves a quantity of ashes. In water also pure and fine indigo entirely melts and dissolves, but the heterogeneous and solid parts of the bad sink to the bottom like sand. From this period it became a staple to Carolina, and proved equally profitable as the mines of Mexico or Peru. To the mother country it was no less beneficial, in excluding the French indigo entirely from her market, and promoting her manufactures, and trade. I shall afterwards take notice of the rapid progress made in the cultivation of this article; particularly with respect to the quantity produced and yearly shipped to Britain, to supply the markets in Europe.

[Sidenote] Nova Scotia settled.

The great bounty and indulgence of Britain towards her American colonies increased with their progress in cultivation, and favour after favour was extended to them. Filled with the prospect of opening an excellent market for her manufactures, and enlarging her commerce and navigation, in which her strength in a great measure consisted, these colonies were become the chief objects of her care, and new ones were planted for the protection of the old. At this time the peace of Aix la Chapelle left a number of brave sailors and soldiers without employment. Good policy required that they should be rendered useful to the nation, and at the same time furnished with employment for their own subsistence. Acadia, which was ceded to Britain by the treaty of peace, changed its name to Nova Scotia, and was capable of producing every species of naval stores. The sea there abounded with excellent fish, which might furnish employment for a number of sailors, and be made an useful and advantageous branch of trade. But the excellent natural harbours which the country afforded, of all other things proved the greatest inducement for establishing a colony in it, the possession of which would not only promote trade in the time of peace, but also prove a safe station for British fleets in time of war. Besides, for the sake of commercial advantage, it was judged proper to confine the settlements in America as much as possible to the sea-coast. The parliament therefore determined to send out a colony to Nova Scotia, and, to forward the settlement, voted forty thousand pounds. The following advantageous terms were held forth to the people by government, and a number of adventurers agreed to accept them. Fifty acres of land were to be allowed to every soldier and sailor, two hundred to every ensign, three hundred to every lieutenant, four hundred and sixty to every captain, and six hundred to all officers of higher rank; together with thirty for every servant they should carry along with them. No quit-rents were to be demanded for the first ten years. They were also to be furnished with instruments for fishing and agriculture, to have their passage free, and provisions found them for the first year after their arrival. Three thousand seven hundred and sixty adventurers embarked for America on these favourable terms, and settled at Halifax, which place was fixed on as the seat of government, and fortified. The Acadians, the former inhabitants of the country, were allowed peaceably to remain in it, and having sworn never to bear arms against their countrymen, submitted to the English government, and passed under the denomination of French neutrals. The greatest difficulty which the new settlers of Nova Scotia had to surmount at this time arose from the Micmac Indians, who held that territory from nature, and for some time obstinately defended their right to their ancient possessions; and it was not without considerable loss that the British subjects at length, by force of arms, drove them away from those territories.

[Sidenote] The great care of Britain for these colonies.

Nor did this new settlement engross the whole attention and liberality of the parent state; the province of Georgia also every year shared plentifully from the same hands. Indeed the bounty of the mother country was extensive as her dominions, and, like the sun, cherished and invigorated every object on which it shone. All the colonies might have been sensible of her constant attention to their safety and prosperity, and had great reason to acknowledge themselves under the strongest obligations to her goodness. If she expected a future recompense by the channel of commerce, which is for the most part mutually advantageous, it was no more than she had justly merited. The colonists, we allow, carried with them the rights and liberties of the subjects of Britain, and they owed in return the duties of obedience to her laws and subjection to her government. The privileges and duties of subjects in all states have been reciprocal, and as the mother country had incurred great expence for the establishment and support of these foreign settlements; as she had multiplied her burdens for their defence and improvement; surely such protection and kindness laid a foundation for the firmest union, and the most dutiful returns of allegiance and gratitude.

[Sidenote] Low state of Georgia.

However, the province of Georgia, notwithstanding all that Britain had done for its population and improvement, still remained in a poor and languishing condition. Its settlers consisted of two sorts of people; first, of indigent subjects and foreigners, whom the Trustees transported and maintained; secondly, of men of some substance, whom flattering descriptions of the province had induced voluntarily to emigrate to it. After the peace Oglethorpe's regiment being disbanded, a number of soldiers accepted the encouragement offered them by government, and took up their residence in Georgia. All those adventurers who had brought some substance along with them, having by this time exhausted their small stock in fruitless experiments, were reduced to indigence, so that emigrants from Britain, foreigners, and soldiers, were all on a level in point of poverty. From the impolitic restrictions of the Trustees, these settlers had no prospects during life but those of hardship and poverty, and of consequence, at their decease, of bequeathing a number of orphans to the care of Providence. Nor was the trade of the province in a better situation than its agriculture. The want of credit was an unsurmountable obstacle to its progress in every respect. Formerly the inhabitants in and about Savanna had transmitted to the Trustees a representation of their grievous circumstances, and obtained from them some partial relief. But now, chagrined with disappointments, and dispirited by the severities of the climate, they could view the design of the Trustees in no other light than that of having decoyed them into misery. Even though they had been favoured with credit, and had proved successful, which was far from being their case; as the tenure of their freehold was restricted to heirs male, their eldest son could only reap the benefit of their toil, and the rest must depend on his bounty, or be left wholly to the charge of that Being who feeds the fowls of the air. They considered their younger children and daughters as equally entitled to paternal regard, and could not brook their holding lands under such a tenure, as excluded them from the rights and privileges of other colonists. They saw numbers daily leaving the province through mere necessity, and frankly told the Trustees, that nothing could prevent it from being totally deserted, but the same encouragements with their more fortunate neighbours in Carolina.

[Sidenote: Complaint of the people.]

That the Trustees might have a just view of their condition, the Georgians stated before them their grievances, and renewed their application for redress. They judged that the British constitution, zealous for the rights and liberties of mankind, could not permit subjects who had voluntarily risked their lives, and spent their substance on the public faith, to effect a settlement in the most dangerous frontiers of the British empire, to be deprived of the common privileges of all colonists. They complained that the land-holders in Georgia were prohibited from selling or leasing their possessions; that a tract containing fifty acres of the best lands was too small an allowance for the maintenance of a family, and much more so when they were refused the freedom to chuse it; that a much higher quit-rent was exacted from them than was paid for the best lands in America; that the importation of negroes was prohibited, and white people were utterly unequal to the labours requisite; that the public money granted yearly by parliament, for the relief of settlers and the improvement of the province, was misapplied, and therefore the wise purposes for which it was granted were by no means answered. That these inconveniencies and hardships kept them in a state of poverty and misery, and that the chief cause of all their calamities was the strict adherence of the Trustees to their chimerical and impracticable scheme of settlement, by which the people were refused the obvious means of subsistence, and cut off from all prospects of success.

We have already observed, that the laws and regulations even of the wisest men, founded on principles of speculation, have often proved to be foreign and impracticable. The Trustees had an example of this in the fundamental constitutions of John Locke. Instead of prescribing narrower limits to the industry and ambition of the Georgians, they ought to have learned wisdom from the case of the Proprietors of Carolina, and enlarged their plan with respect to both liberty and property. By such indulgence alone they could encourage emigrations, and animate the inhabitants to diligence and perseverance. The lands in Georgia, especially such as were first occupied, were sandy and barren; the hardships of clearing and cultivating them were great, the climate was unfavourable for labourers, and dangerous to European constitutions. The greater the difficulties were with which the settlers had to struggle, the more encouragement was requisite to surmount them. The plan of settlement ought to have arisen from the nature of the climate, country, and soil, and the circumstances of the settlers, and been the result of experience and not of speculation.

Hitherto Georgia had not only made small improvement in agriculture and trade, but her government was feeble and contemptible. At this time, by the avarice and ambition of a single family, the whole colony was brought to the very brink of destruction. As the concerns of these settlements are closely connected and interwoven with the affairs of Indian nations, it is impossible to attain proper views of the circumstances and situation of the people, without frequently taking notice of the relation in which they stood to their savage neighbours. A considerable branch of provincial commerce, as well as the safety of the colonists, depended on their friendship with Indians; and, to avoid all danger from their savage temper, no small share of prudence and courage was often requisite. This will appear more obvious from the following occurrence, which, because it is somewhat remarkable, we shall the more circumstantially relate.

[Sidenote] Troubles excited by Thomas Bosomworth.

I have already observed, that during the time General Oglethorpe had the direction of public affairs in Georgia, he had, from maxims of policy, treated an Indian woman, called Mary, with particular kindness and generosity. Finding that she had great influence among the Creeks, and understood their language, he made use of her as an interpreter, in order the more easily to form treaties of alliance with them, allowing her for her services an hundred pounds sterling a-year. This woman Thomas Bosomworth, who was chaplain to Oglethorpe's regiment, had married, and among the rest had accepted a track of land from the crown, and settled in the province. Finding that his wife laid claim to some islands on the sea-coast, which, by treaty, had been allotted the Indians as part of their hunting lands; to stock them he had purchased cattle from the planters of Carolina, from whom he obtained credit to a considerable amount. However, this plan not proving so successful as the proud and ambitious clergyman expected, he took to audacious methods of supporting his credit, and acquiring a fortune. His wife pretended to be descended in a maternal line from an Indian king, who held from nature the territories of the Creeks, and Bosomworth now persuaded her to assert her right to them, as superior not only to that of the Trustees, but also to that of the King. Accordingly Mary immediately assumed the title of an independent empress, disavowing all subjection or allegiance to the King of Great Britain, otherwise than by way of treaty and alliance, such as one independent sovereign might make with another. A meeting of all the Creeks was summoned, to whom Mary made a speech, setting forth the justice of her claim, and the great injury done to her and them by taking possession of their ancient territories, and stirring them up to defend their property by force of arms. The Indians immediately took fire, and to a man declared they would stand by her to the last drop of their blood in defence of their lands. In consequence of which Mary, with a large body of savages at her back, set out for Savanna, to demand a formal surrender of them from the president of the province. A messenger was despatched before hand, to acquaint him that Mary had assumed her right of sovereignty over the whole territories of the upper and lower Creeks, and to demand that all lands belonging to them be instantly relinquished; for as she was the hereditary and rightful queen of both nations, and could command every man of them to follow her, in case of refusal, she had determined to extirpate the settlement.

The president and council, alarmed at her high pretensions and bold threats, and sensible of her great power and influence with the savages, were not a little embarrassed what steps to take for the public safety. They determined to use soft and healing measures until an opportunity might offer of privately laying hold of her, and shipping her off to England. But, in the mean time, orders were sent to all the captains of the militia, to hold themselves in readiness to march to Savanna at an hour's warning. The town was put in the best posture of defence, but the whole militia in it amounted to no more than one hundred and seventy men, able to bear arms. A messenger was sent to Mary at the head of the Creeks, while several miles distant from town, to know whether she was serious in such wild pretensions, and to try to persuade her to dismiss her followers, and drop her audacious design. But finding her inflexible and resolute, the president resolved to put on a bold countenance, and receive the savages with firmness and resolution. The militia was ordered under arms, to overawe them as much as possible, and as the Indians entered the town, Captain Jones, at the head of his company of horse, stopped them, and demanded whether they came with hostile or friendly intentions? But receiving no satisfactory answer, he told them they must there ground their arms, for he had orders not to suffer a man of them armed to set his foot within the town. The savages with great reluctance submitted, and accordingly Thomas Bosomworth, in his canonical robes, with his queen by his side, followed by the various chiefs according to their rank, marched into town, making a formidable appearance. All the inhabitants were struck with terror at the sight of the fierce and mighty host. When they advanced to the parade, they found the militia drawn up under arms to receive them, who saluted them with fifteen cannon, and conducted them to the president's house. There Thomas and Adam Bosomworth being ordered to withdraw, the Indian chiefs, in a friendly manner, were called upon to declare their intention of visiting the town in so large a body, without being sent for by any person in lawful authority. The warriors, as they had been previously instructed, answered, that Mary was to speak for them, and that they would abide by her words. They had heard, they said, that she was to be sent like a captive over the great waters, and they were come to know on what account they were to lose their queen. They assured the president they intended no harm, and begged their arms might be restored; and, after consulting with Bosomworth and his wife, they would return and settle all public affairs. To please them their muskets were accordingly given back, but strict orders were issued to allow them no ammunition, until the council should see more clearly into their dark designs.

On the day following, the Indians having had some private conferences with their queen, began to be very surly, and to run in a mad and tumultuous manner up and down the streets, seemingly bent on some mischief. All the men being obliged to mount guard, the women were terrified to remain by themselves in their houses, expecting every moment to be murdered or scalped. During this confusion, a false rumour was spread, that they had cut off the president's head with a tomahawk, which so exasperated the inhabitants, that it was with difficulty the officers could prevent them from firing on the savages. To save a town from destruction, never was greater prudence requisite. Orders were given to the militia to lay hold of Bosomworth, and carry him out of the way into close confinement. Upon which Mary became outrageous and frantic, and insolently threatened vengeance against the magistrates and whole colony. She ordered every man of them to depart from her territories, and at their peril to refuse. She cursed General Oglethorpe and his fraudulent treaties, and, furiously stamping with her feet upon the ground, swore by her Maker that the whole earth on which she trode was her own. To prevent bribery, which she knew to have great weight with her warriors, she kept the leading men constantly in her eye, and would not suffer them to speak a word respecting public affairs but in her presence.

The president finding that no peaceable agreement could be made with the Indians while under the baleful eye and influence of their pretended queen privately laid hold of her, and put her under confinement with her husband. This step was necessary, before any terms of negotiation could be proposed. Having secured the chief promoters of the conspiracy, he then employed men acquainted with the Indian tongue to entertain the warriors in the most friendly and hospitable manner, and explain to them the wicked designs of Bosomworth and his wife. Accordingly a feast was prepared for all the chief leaders; at which they were informed, that Mr. Bosomworth had involved himself in debt, and wanted not only their lands, but also a large share of the royal bounty, to satisfy his creditors in Carolina: that the King's presents were only intended for Indians, on account of their useful services and firm attachment to him during the former wars: that the lands adjoining the town were reserved for them to encamp upon, when they should come to visit their beloved friends at Savanna, and the three maritime islands to hunt upon, when they should come to bathe in the salt waters: that neither Mary nor her husband had any right to those lands, which were the common property of the Creek nations: that the great King had ordered the president to defend their right to them, and expected that all his subjects, both white and red, would live together like brethren; in short that he would suffer no man or woman to molest or injure them, and had ordered these words to be left on record, that their children might know them when they were dead and gone.

Such policy produced the desired effect, and many of the chieftains being convinced that Bosomworth had deceived them, declared they would trust him no more. Even Malatchee, the leader of the Lower Creeks, and a relation to their pretended empress, seemed satisfied, and was not a little pleased to hear, that the great King had sent them some valuable present. Being asked why he acknowledged Mary as the Empress of the great nation of Creeks, and resigned his power and possessions to a despicable old woman, while all Georgia owned him as a chief of the nation, and the president and council were now to give him many rich clothes and medals for his services? He replied, that the whole nation acknowledged her as their Queen, and none could distribute the royal presents but one of her family. The president by this answer perceiving more clearly the design of the family of Bosomworth, to lessen their influence, and shew the Indians that he had power to divide the royal bounty among the chiefs, determined to do it immediately, and dismiss them, and the hardships the inhabitants underwent, in keeping guard night and day for the defence of the town.

In the mean time Malatchee, whom the Indians compared to the wind, because of his fickle and variable temper, having, at his own request, obtained access to Bosomworth and his wife, was again seduced and drawn over to support their chimerical claim. While the Indians were gathered together to receive their respective shares of the royal bounty; he stood up in the midst of them, and with a frowning countenance, and in violent agitation of spirit, delivered a speech fraught with the most dangerous insinuations. He protested, that Mary possessed that country before General Oglethorpe; and that all the lands belonged to her as Queen, and head of the Creeks; that it was by her permission Englishmen were at first allowed to set their foot on them; that they still held them of her as the original proprietor; that her words were the voice of the whole nation, consisting of above three thousand warriors, and at her command every one of them would take up the hatchet in defence of her right; and then pulling out a paper out of his pocket, he delivered it to the president in confirmation of what he had said. This was evidently the production of Bosomworth, and served to discover in the plainest manner, his ambitious views and wicked intrigues. The preamble was filled with the names of Indians, called kings, of all the towns of the Upper and Lower Creeks, none of whom, however, were present, excepting two. The substance of it corresponded with Malatchee's speech; styling Mary the rightful princess and chief of their nation, descended in a maternal line from the emperor, and invested with full power and authority from them to settle and finally determine all public affairs and causes, relating to lands and other things, with King George and his beloved men on both sides of the sea, and whatever should be said or done by her, they would abide by, as if said or done by themselves.

After reading this paper in council, the whole board were struck with astonishment; and Malatchee, perceiving their uneasiness, begged to have it again, declaring he did not know it to be a bad talk, and promising he would return it immediately to the person from whom he had received it. To remove all impression made on the minds of the Indians by Malatchee's speech, and convince them of the deceitful and dangerous tendency of this confederacy into which Bosomworth and his wife had betrayed them, had now become a matter of the highest consequence; happy was it for the province this was a thing neither difficult nor impracticable; for as ignorant savages are easily misled on the one hand, so, on the other, it was equally easy to convince them of their error. Accordingly, having gathered the Indians together for this purpose, the president addressed them to the following effect. "Friends and brothers, when Mr. Oglethorpe and his people first arrived in Georgia, they found Mary, then the wife of John Musgrove, living in a small hut at Yamacraw, having a licence from the Governor of South Carolina to trade with Indians. She then appeared to be in a poor ragged condition, and was neglected and despised by the Creeks. But Mr. Oglethorpe finding that she could speak both the English and Creek languages, employed her as an interpreter, richly clothed her, and made her the woman of the consequence she now appears. The people of Georgia always respected her until she married Thomas Bosomworth, but from that time she has proved a liar and a deceiver. In fact, she was no relation of Malatchee, but the daughter of an Indian woman of no note, by a white man. General Oglethorpe did not treat with her for the lands of Georgia, she having none of her own, but with the old and wise leaders of the Creek nation, who voluntarily surrendered their territories to the King. The Indians at that time having much waste land, that was useless to themselves, parted with a share of it to their friends, and were glad that white people had settled among them to supply their wants. He told them that the present bad humour of the Creeks had been artfully infused into them by Mary, at the instigation of her husband, who owed four hundred pounds sterling in Carolina for cattle; that he demanded a third part of the royal bounty, in order to rob the naked Indians of their right; that he had quarrelled with the president and council of Georgia for refusing to answer his exorbitant demands, and therefore had filled the heads of Indians with wild fancies and groundless jealousies, in order to breed mischief, and induce them to break their alliances with their best friends, who alone were able to supply their wants, and defend them against all their enemies." Here the Indians desired him to stop, and put an end to the contest, declaring that their eyes were now opened, and they saw through his insidious design. But though he intended to break the chain of friendship, they were determined to hold it fast, and therefore begged that all might immediatly smoke the pipe of peace. Accordingly pipes and rum were brought, and the whole congress, joining hand in hand, drank and smoked together in friendship, every one wishing that their hearts might be united in like manner as their hands. Then all the royal presents, except ammunition, with which is was judged imprudent to trust them until they were at some distance from town, were brought and distributed among them. The most disaffected were purchased with the largest presents. Even Malatchee himself seemed fully contented with his share, and the savages in general perceiving the poverty and insignificance of the family of Bosomworth, and their total inability to supply their wants, determined to break off all connection with them for ever.

While the president and council flattered themselves that all differences were amicably compromised, and were rejoicing in the re-establishment of their former friendly intercourse with the Creeks, Mary, drunk with liquor, and disappointed in her views, came rushing in among them like a fury, and told the president that these were her people, that he had no business with them, and he should soon be convinced of it to his cost. The president calmly advised her to keep to her lodgings, and forbear to poison the minds of Indians, otherwise he would order her again into close confinement. Upon which turning about to Malatchee in great rage, she told him what the president had said, who instantly started from his seat, laid hold of his arms, and then calling upon the rest to follow his example, dared any man to touch his queen. The whole house was filled in a moment with tumult and uproar. Every Indian having his tomahawk in his hand, the president and council expected nothing but instant death. During this confusion Captain Jones, who commanded the guard, very seasonably interposed, and ordered the Indians immediately to deliver up their arms. Such courage was not only necessary to overawe them, but at the same time great prudence was also requisite, to avoid coming to extremities with them. With reluctance the Indians submitted, and Mary was conveyed to a private room, where a guard was set over her, and all further intercourse with savages denied her during their stay in Savanna. Then her husband was sent for, in order to reason with him and convince him of the folly of his chimerical pretensions, and of the dangerous consequences that might result from persisting in them. But no sooner did he appear before the president and council, than he began to abuse them to their face. In spite of every argument used to persuade him to submission, he remained obstinate and contumacious, and protested he would stand forth in vindication of his wife's right to the last extremity, and that the province of Georgia should soon feel the weight of her vengeance. Finding that fair means were fruitless and ineffectual, the council then determined to remove him also out of the way of the savages, and to humble him by force. After having secured the two leaders, it only then remained to persuade the Indians peaceably to leave the town, and return to their settlements. Captain Ellick, a young warrior, who had distinguished himself in discovering to his tribe the base intrigues of Bosomworth, being afraid to accompany Malatchee and his followers, thought fit to set out among the first: the rest followed him in different parties, and the inhabitants, wearied out with constant watching, and harassed with frequent alarms, were at length happily relieved.

[Sidenote] With difficulty settled.

By this time Adam Bosomworth, another brother of the family, who was agent for Indian affairs in Carolina, had arrived from that province, and being made acquainted with what had passed in Georgia, was filled with shame and indignation. He found his ambitious brother, not contented with the common allowance of land granted by the crown, aspiring after sovereignty, and attempting to obtain by force one of the largest landed estates in the world. His plot was artfully contrived, and had it been executed with equal courage, fatal must the consequence have been. Had he taken possession of the provincial magazine on his arrival at Savanna, and supplied the Creeks with ammunition, the militia must soon have been overpowered, and every family must of course have fallen a sacrifice to the indiscriminate vengeance of savages. Happily, by the interposition of his brother, all differences were peaceably compromised. Thomas Bosomworth at length having returned to sober reflection, began to repent of his folly, and to ask pardon of the magistrates and people. He wrote to the president, acquainting him that he was now deeply sensible of his duty as a subject, and of the respect he owed to civil authority, and could no longer justify the conduct of his wife; but hoped that her present remorse, and past services to the province, would entirely blot out the remembrance of her unguarded expressions and rash design. He appealed to the letters of General Oglethorpe for her former irreproachable conduct, and steady friendship to the settlement, and hoped her good behaviour for the future would atone for her past offences, and reinstate her in the public favour. For his own part, he acknowledged her title to be groundless, and for ever relinquished all claim to the lands of the province. The colonists generously forgave and forgot all that had past; and public tranquillity being re-established, new settlers applied for lands as usual, without meeting any more obstacles from the idle claims of Indian queens and chieftains.

[Sidenote] The charter surrendered to the King.

The Trustees of Georgia finding that the province languished under their care, and weary of the complaints of the people, in the year 1752 surrendered their charter to the King, and it was made a royal government.

In consequence of which his Majesty appointed John Reynolds, an officer of the navy, Governor of the province, and a legislature similar to that of the other royal governments in America was established in it. Great had been the expence which the mother country had already incurred, besides private benefactions, for supporting this colony; and small had been the returns yet made by it. The vestiges of cultivation were scarcely perceptible in the forest, and in England all commerce with it was neglected and despised. At this time the whole annual exports of Georgia did not amount to ten thousand pounds sterling. Though the people were now favoured with the same liberties and privileges enjoyed by their neighbours under the royal care, yet several years more elapsed before the value of the lands in Georgia was known, and that spirit of industry broke out in it which afterwards diffused its happy influence over the country.

[Sidenote] George Whitfield's settlement.

In the annals of Georgia the famous George Whitfield may not be unworthy of some notice, especially as the world through which he wandered has heard so much of his Orphan-house built in that province. Actuated by religious motives, this wanderer several times passed the Atlantic to convert the Americans, whom he addressed in such a manner as if they had been all equal strangers to the privileges and benefits of religion with the original inhabitants of the forest. However, his zeal never led him beyond the maritime parts of America, through which he travelled, spreading what he called the true evangelical faith among the most populous towns and villages. One would have imagined that the heathens, or at least those who were most destitute of the means of instruction, would have been the primary and most proper objects of his zeal and compassion; but this was far from being the case. However, wherever he went in America, as in Britain, he had multitudes of followers. When he first visited Charlestown, Alexander Garden, a man of some sense and erudition, who was the episcopal clergyman of that place, to put the people upon their guard, took occasion to point out to them the pernicious tendency of Whitfield's wild doctrines and irregular manner of life. He represented him as a religious impostor or quack, who had an excellent knack of setting off to advantage his poisonous tenets. On the other hand, Whitfield, who had been accustomed to bear reproach and face opposition, recriminated with double acrimony and greater success. While Alexander Garden, to keep his flock from straying after this strange pastor, expatiated on the words of Scripture, "Those that have turned the world upside down are come hither also." Whitfield, with all the force of comic humour and wit for which he was so much distinguished, by way of reply, enlarged on these words, "Alexander the coppersmith hath done me much evil, the Lord reward him according to his works." In short, the pulpit was perverted by both into the mean purposes of spite and malevolence, and every one catching a share of the infection, spoke of the clergymen as they were differently affected.

[Sidenote] Whitfield's Orphan-house.

In Georgia Whitfield having obtained a track of land from the Trustees, erected a wooden house two stories high, the dimensions of which were seventy feet by forty, upon a sandy beach nigh the sea-shore. This house, which he called the Orphan-House, he began to build about the year 1740, and afterwards finished it at a great expense. It was intended to be a lodging for poor children, where they were to be clothed and fed by charitable contributions, and and trained up in the knowledge and practice of the Christian religion. The design, beyond doubt, was humane and laudable; but, perhaps, had he travelled over the whole earth, he could scarcely have found out a spot of ground upon it more improper for the purpose. The whole province of Georgia could not furnish him with a track of land of the same extent more barren and unprofitable. To this house poor children were to be sent from at least a healthy country, to be supported partly by charity, and partly by the produce of this land cultivated by negroes. Nor was the climate better suited to the purpose than the soil, for it is certain, before the unwholesome marshes around the house were fertilized, the influences of both air and water must have conspired to the children's destruction.

However, Whitfield having formed his chimerical project, determined to accomplish it, and, instead of bring discouraged by obstacles and difficulties, gloried in despising them. He wandered through the British empire, persuaded the ignorant and credulous part of the world of the excellence of his design, and obtained from them money, clothes, and books, to forward his undertaking, and supply his poor orphans in Georgia. About thirty years after this wooden house was finished it was burned to the ground; during which time, if I am well informed, few or none of the children educated in it have proved either useful members of society, or exemplary in respect to religion. Some say the fire was occasioned by a foul chimney, and others by a flash of lightning; but whatever was the cause, it burnt with such violence that little of either the furniture or library escaped the flames. When I saw the ruins of this fabric, I could not help reflecting on that great abuse of the fruits of charity too prevalent in the world. That money which was sunk here had been collected chiefly from the poorest class of mankind. Most of those bibles which were here burnt had been extorted from indigent and credulous persons, who perhaps had not money to purchase more for themselves. Happy was it for the zealous founder of this institution, that he did not live to see the ruin of his works. After his death he was brought from New-England, above eight hundred miles, and buried at this Orphan-house. In his last will he left Lady Huntingdon sole executrix, who has now converted the lands and negroes belonging to the poor benefactors of Great Britain and her dominions, to the support of clergymen of the same irregular stamp with the deceased, but void of his shining talents, and it is become a seminary of dissension and sedition.

[Sidenote] Sketch of his character.

As George Whitfield appeared in such different lights in the successive stages of life, it is no easy matter to delineate his character without an uncommon mixture and vast variety of colours. He was in the British empire not unlike one of those strange and erratic meteors which appear now and then in the system of nature. In his youth, as he often confessed and lamented, he was gay, giddy and profligate; so fondly attached to the stage, that he joined a company of strolling actors and vagabonds, and spent a part of his life in that capacity. At this period it is probable he learned that grimace, buffoonery and gesticulation which he afterwards displayed from the pulpit. From an abandoned and licentious course of life he was converted; and, what is no uncommon thing, from one extreme he run into the other, and became a most zealous and indefatigable teacher of religion. Having studied some time at Oxford, he received ordination in the church of England; yet he submitted to none of the regulations of that or any other church, but became a preacher in churches, meeting-houses, halls, fields, in all places, and to all denominations, without exception. Though little distinguished for genius or learning, yet he possessed a lively imagination, much humour, and had acquired considerable knowledge of human nature and the manners of the world. His pretensions to humanity and benevolence were great, yet he would swell with venom, like a snake, against opposition and contradiction. His reading was inconsiderable, and mankind being the object of his study, he could, when he pleased, raise the passions, and touch the tone of the human heart to great perfection. By this affecting eloquence and address he impressed on the minds of many, especially of the more soft and delicate sex, such a strong sense of sin and guilt as often plunged them into dejection and despair. As his custom was to frequent those larger cities and towns, that are commonly best supplied with the means of instruction, it would appear that the love of fame and popular applause was his leading passion; yet in candour it must be acknowledged, that he always discovered a warm zeal for the honour of God and the happiness of men. While he was almost worshipped by the vulgar, men of superior rank and erudition found him the polite gentleman, and the facetious and jocular companion. Though he loved good cheer, and frequented the houses of the rich or more hospitable people of America, yet he was an enemy to all manner of excess and intemperance. While his vagrant temper led him from place to place, his natural discernment enabled him to form no bad judgment of the characters and manners of men wherever he went. Though he appeared a friend to no established church, yet good policy winked at all his irregularities, as he every where proved a steady friend to monarchy and the civil constitution. He knew well how to keep up the curiosity of the multitude, and his roving manner stamped a kind of novelty on his instructions. When exposed to the taunts of the scoffer, and the ridicule of the flagitious, he remained firm to his purpose, and could even retort these weapons with astonishing ease and dexterity, and render vice abashed under the lash of his satire and wit. Sometimes, indeed, he made little scruple of consigning over to damnation such as differed from him or despised him; yet he was not entirely devoid of liberality of sentiment. To habitual sinners his address was for the most part applicable and powerful, and with equal ease could alarm the secure, and confirm the unsteady. Though, in prayer, he commonly addressed the second person of the Trinity in a familiar and fulsome style, and in his sermons used many ridiculous forms of speech, and told many of his own wonderful works, yet these seemed only shades to set off to greater advantage the lustre of his good qualities. In short, though it is acknowledged he had many oddities and failings, and was too much the slave of party and vain-glory, yet in justice it cannot be denied, that religion in America owed not a little to the zeal, diligence, and oratory, of this extraordinary man.

Having said so much with respect to the character which Mr. Whitfield bore in America, if we view the effects of his example and manner of life in that country, he will appear to us in a less favourable light. His great ambition was to be the founder of a new sect, regulated entirely by popular fancy and caprice, depending on the gifts of nature, regardless of the improvements of education and all ecclesiastical laws and institutions. Accordingly, after him a servile race of ignorant and despicable imitators sprung up, and wandered from place to place, spreading doctrines subversive of all public order and peace. We acknowledge the propriety and justice of allowing every reasonable indulgence to men in matters of religion. The laws of toleration being part of our happy constitution, it lies with men to learn their duty from them, and claim protection under them. But after a church has been erected and established by the most skilful architects, and for ages received the approbation of the wisest and best men, it serves only to create endless confusion to be making alterations and additions to gratify the fancy of every Gothic pretender to that art. Though Whitfield was in fact a friend to civil government, yet his followers on that continent have been distinguished for the contrary character, and have for the most part discovered an aversion to our constitution both of church and state. Toleration to men who remain peaceable subjects to the state is reasonable; but dissention, when it grows lawless and headstrong, is dangerous, and summons men in general to take shelter under the constitution, that the salutary laws of our country may be executed by its united strength. No man ought to claim any lordship over the conscience; but when the consciences of obstinate sectaries become civil nuisances, and destructive of public tranquillity, they ought to be restrained by legal authority. For certainly human laws, if they have not the primary, have, or ought to have, a secondary power to restrain the irregular and wild excesses of men in religious as well as in civil matters.

[Sidenote] A congress with Creeks.

About the year 1752 the flames of war broke out among some Indian nations, which threatened to involve the province of Carolina in the calamity. The Creeks having quarrelled with their neighbours for permitting some Indians to pass through their country to wage war against them, by way of revenge had killed some Cherokees nigh the gates of Charlestown. A British trader to the Chickesaw nation had likewise been scalped by a party of warriors belonging to the same nation. Governor Glen, in order to demand satisfaction for these outrages, sent a messenger to the Creeks, requesting a conference at Charlestown with their leading men. The Creeks returned for answer, that they were willing to meet him, but as the path had not been open and safe for some time, they could not enter the settlement without a guard to escort them. Upon which the Governor sent fifty horsemen, who met them at the confines of their territories, and convoyed Malatchee, with above an hundred of his warriors, to Charlestown.

[Sidenote] The governor's speech to them.

As they arrived on Sunday the Governor did not summon his council until the day following, to hold a congress with them. At this meeting a number of gentlemen were present, whom curiosity had drawn together to see the warriors and hear their speeches. When they entered the council-chamber the Governor arose and took them by the hand, signifying that he was glad to see them, and then addressed them to the following effect: "Being tied together by the most solemn treaties, I call you by the beloved names of friends and brothers. In the name of the great King George I have sent for you, on business of the greatest consequence to your nation. I would have received you yesterday on your arrival, but it was a beloved day, dedicated to repose and the concerns of a future life. I am sorry to hear that you have taken up the hatchet, which I flattered myself had been for ever buried. It is my desire to have the chain brightened and renewed, not only between you and the English, but also between you and other Indian nations. You are all our friends, and I could wish that all Indians in friendship with us were also friends one with another. You have complained to me of the

Cherokees permitting the northern Indians to come through their country to war against you, and supplying them with provisions and ammunition for that purpose. The Cherokees, on the other hand, alledge, that it is not in their power to prevent them, and declare, that while their people happen to be out hunting those northern Indians come in to their towns well armed, and in such numbers that they are not able to resist them.

"I propose that a treaty of friendship and peace be concluded first with the English, and then with the Cherokees, in such a manner as may render it durable. Some of your people have from smaller crimes proceeded to greater. First, they waylaid the Cherokees, and killed one of them in the midst of our settlements; then they came to Charlestown, where some Cherokees at the same time happened to be, and though I cautioned them, and they promised to do no mischief, yet the next day they assaulted and murdered several of them nigh the gates of this town. For these outrages I have sent for you, to demand satisfaction; and also for the murder committed in one of your towns, for which satisfaction was made by the death of another person, and not of the murderer. For the future, I acquaint you, that nothing will be deemed as satisfaction for the lives of our people, but the lives of these persons themselves who shall be guilty of the murder. The English never make treaties of friendship but with the greatest deliberation, and when made observe them with the strictest punctuality. They are, at the same time vigilant, and will not suffer other nations to infringe the smallest article of such treaties. It would tend to the happiness of your people were you equally careful to watch against the beginnings of evil; for sometimes a small spark, if not attended to, may kindle a great fire; and a slight sore, if suffered to spread, may endanger the whole body. Therefore, I have sent for you to prevent farther mischief, and I hope you come disposed to give satisfaction for the outrages already committed, and to promise and agree to maintain peace and friendship with your neighbours for the future."

[Sidenote: Malatchee's answer.] This speech delivered to the Indians was interpreted by Lachlan McGilvray, an Indian trader, who understood their language. After which Malatchee, the king of the Lower Creek nation, stood forth, and with a solemnity and dignity of manner that astonished all present, in answer, addressed the Governor to the following effect: "I never had the honour to see the great King George, nor to hear his talk—But you are in his place—I have heard yours, and I like it well—Your sentiments are agreeable to my own—The great King wisely judged, that the best way of maintaining friendship between white and red people was by trade and commerce: —He knew we are poor, and want many things, and that skins are all we have to give in exchange for what we want—I have ordered my people to bring you some as a present, and, in the name of our nation, I lay them at your Excellency's feet—You have sent for us—we are come to hear what you have to say—But I did not expect to hear our whole nation accused for the faults of a few private men—Our head-men neither knew nor approved of the mischief done—We imagined our young men had gone a-hunting as usual—When we heard what had happened at Charlestown, I knew you would send and demand satisfaction—When your agent came and told me what satisfaction you required, I owned the justice of it—But it was not adviseable for me alone to grant it—It was prudent to consult with our beloved men, and have their advice in a matter of such importance—We met—we found that the behaviour of some of our people had been bad—We found that blood had been spilt at your gates—We thought it just that satisfaction should he made—We turned our thoughts to find out the chief persons concerned; (for a man will sometimes employ another to commit a crime he does not chuse to be guilty of himself) —We found the Acorn Whistler was the chief contriver and promoter of the mischief—We agreed that he was the man that ought to suffer—Some of his relations, who are here present, then said he deserved death, and voted for it—Accordingly he was put to death—He was a very great warrior, and had many friends and relations in different parts of the country—We thought it prudent to conceal for some time the true reason of his death, which was known only to the head men that concerted it—We did this for fear some of his friends in the heat of fury would take revenge on some of your traders—At a general meeting all matters were explained—The reasons of his death were made known—His relations approved of all that was done.—Satisfaction being made, I say no more about that matter—I hope our friendship with the English will continue as heretofore.

"As to the injuries done to the Cherokees, which you spoke of, we are sorry for them—We acknowledge our young men do many things they ought not to do, and very often act like madmen—But it is well known I and the other head warriors did all we could to oblige them to make restitution—I rode from town to town with Mr. Bosomworth and his wife to assist them in this matter—Most of the things taken have been restored—When this was over, another accident happened which created fresh troubles—A Chickesaw who lived in our nation; in a drunken fit shot a white man—I knew you would demand satisfaction—I thought it best to give it before it was asked—The murder was committed at a great distance from me—I mounted my horse and rode through the towns with your agent—I took the head men of every town along with me—We went to the place and demanded satisfaction—It was given—The blood of the Indian was spilt for the blood of a white man—The uncle of the murderer purchased his life, and voluntarily killed himself in his stead—Now I have done—I am glad to see you face to face to settle those matters—it is good to renew treaties of friendship—I shall always be glad to call you friends and brothers."

This speech throws no small light on the judicial proceedings of barbarous nations, and shews that human nature in its rudest state possesses a strong sense of right and wrong. Although Indians have little property, yet here we behold their chief magistrate protecting what they have, and, in cases of robbery, acknowledging the necessity of making restitution. They indeed chiefly injure one another in their persons or reputations, and in all cases of murder the guilty are brought to trial and condemned to death by the general consent of the nation. Even the friends and relations of the murderer here voted for his death. But what is more remarkable, they give us an instance of an atonement made, and justice satisfied, by the substitution of an innocent man in place of the guilty. An uncle voluntarily and generously offers to die in the place of his nephew, the savages accept of the offer, and in consequence of his death declare that satisfaction is made. Next to personal defence, the Indian guards his character and reputation; for as it is only from the general opinion his nation entertains of his wisdom, justice and valour, that he can expect to arrive at rank and distinction, he is exceedingly watchful against doing any thing for which he may incur public blame or disgrace. In this answer to Governor Glen, Malatchee discovers considerable talents as a public speaker, and appears to be insensible neither to his own dignity and freedom, not to the honour and independence of his nation. Genius and liberty are the gifts of heaven; the former is universal as that space over which it has scope to range, the latter inspires confidence, and gives a natural confidence to our words and actions.

During the months of June, July, and August, 1752, the weather in Carolina was warmer than any of the inhabitants then alive had ever felt it, and the mercury in the shade often arose above the nintieth, and at one time was observed at the hundred and first degree of the thermometer; and, at the same time, when exposed to the sun, and suspended at the distance of five feet from the ground, it arose above the hundred and twentieth division. By this excessive heat the air becomes greatly rarified, and a violent hurricane commonly comes and restores the balance in the atmosphere. In such a case the wind usually proceeds from the north-east, directly opposite to the point from which it had long blown before. Those storms indeed seldom happen except in seasons when there has been little thunder, when the weather has been long exceeding dry and intolerably hot, and though they occasion damages to some individuals, there is reason to believe that they are wisely ordered, and productive upon the whole of good and salutary effects. Among the close and dark recesses of the woods the air stagnates, and requires some violent storm to clear it of putrid effluvia, and render it fit for respiration. At the same time the earth emits vapours which in a few days causes the finest polished metals to rust. To penetrate through the thick forest, and restore the air to a salubrious state, hurricanes may be useful and necessary. And as such storms have been observed to be productive of good effects, the want of them for many years together may be deemed a great misfortune by the inhabitants, especially such as are exposed to the noon-day heat, to the heavy fogs that fall every morning and evening, and all the severities of the climate.

It is not improbable that the maritime parts of Carolina have been forsaken by the sea. Though you dig ever so deep in those places you find no stones or rocks, but every where sand or beds of shells. As a small decrease of water will leave so flat a country entirely bare, so a small increase will again cover it. The coast is not only very level, but the dangerous hurricanes commonly proceed from the north-east; and as the stream of the Gulf of Florida flows rapidly towards the same point, this large body of water, when obstructed by the tempest, recurs upon the shore, and overflows the country.

[Sidenote] A hurricane at Charlestown.

In the month of September, 1752, a dreadful hurricane happened at Charlestown. In the night before, it was observed by the inhabitants that the wind at north-east began to blow hard, and continued increasing in violence till next morning. Then the sky appeared wild and cloudy, and it began to drizzle and rain. About nine o'clock the flood came rolling in with great impetuosity, and in a little time rose ten feet above high water mark at the highest tides. As usual in such cases, the town was overflown, and the streets were covered with boats, boards, and wrecks of houses and ships. Before eleven all the ships in the harbour were driven ashore, and sloops and schooners were dashing against the houses of Bay-Street, in which great quantities of goods were damaged and destroyed. Except the Hornet man of war, which by cutting away her masts, rode out the storm, no vessel escaped being damaged or wrecked. The tremor and consternation which seized the inhabitants may be more easily conceived than expressed. Finding themselves in the midst of a tempestuous sea, and expecting the tide to flow till one o'clock, its usual hour, at eleven they retired to the upper stories of their houses, and there remained despairing of life. At this critical time Providence however mercifully interposed, and surprised them with a sudden and unexpected deliverance. Soon after eleven the wind shifted, in consequence of which the waters fell five feet in the space of ten minutes. By this happy change the Gulf stream, stemmed by the violent blast, had freedom to run in its usual course, and the town was saved from imminent danger and destruction. Had the water continued to rise, and the tide to flow until its usual hour, every inhabitant of Charlestown must have perished. Almost all the tiled and slated houses were uncovered, several persons were hurt, and some were drowned. The fortifications and wharfs were almost entirely demolished: the provisions in the field, in the maritime parts, were destroyed, and numbers of cattle and hogs perished in the waters. The pest-house in Sullivan's island, built of wood, with fifteen persons in it, was carried several miles up Cooper river, and nine out of the fifteen were drowned. In short, such is the low situation of Charlestown, that it is subject to be destroyed at any time by such an inundation, and the frequent warnings the people have had may justly fill them with a deep sense of their dependent condition, and with constant gratitude to Providence for their preservation.

[Sidenote] The advantages of poor settlers in the province.

We have seen the hardships under which the Carolineans laboured from the hot climate and low situation of the province, it may not be improper to take a view of those advantages afforded them which served to animate them amidst such difficulties to industry and perseverance. In that growing colony, where there are vast quantities of land unoccupied, the poorest class of people have many opportunities and advantages, from which they are entirely excluded in countries fully peopled and highly improved. During the first years of occupancy they are indeed exposed to many dangers in providing for themselves and families an habitation for a shelter against the rigours of the climate, and in clearing fields for raising the necessaries of life. But when they have the good fortune to surmount the hardships of the first years of cultivation, the inconveniencies gradually decrease in proportion to their improvements. The merchants being favoured with credit from Britain, are enabled to extend it to the swarm of labourers in the country. The planters having established their characters for honesty and industry, obtain hands to assist them in the harder tasks of clearing and cultivation. Their wealth consists in the increase of their slaves, stock and improvements. Having abundance of waste land, they can extend their culture in proportion to their capital. They live almost entirely on the produce of their estates, and consequently spend but a small part of their annual income. The surplus is yearly added to the capital, and they enlarge their prospects in proportion to their wealth and strength. At market if there be a great demand for the commodities they raise, this is an additional advantage, and renders their progress rapid beyond their most sanguine expectations; they labour, and they receive more and more encouragement to persevere, until they advance to an easy and comfortable state. It has been observed, on the other hand, that few or none of those emigrants that brought much property along with them have ever succeeded in that country.

[Sidenote] The advantages of money lenders.

Or, if the poor emigrant be an artificer, and chuses to follow his trade, the high price of labour is no less encouraging. By the indulgence of the merchants, or by the security of a friend, he obtains credit for a few negroes. He learns them his trade, and a few good tradesmen, well employed, are equal to a small estate. Having got some hands, instead of a labourer he becomes an undertaker, and enters into contract with his employer, to erect his house; to build his ship; to furnish his plantations with shoes, or the capital with bricks. In a little time he acquires some money, and, like several others in the city whose yearly gain exceeds what is requisite for the support of themselves and families, lays it out on interest. Ten and eight *per cent.* being given for money, proved a great temptation, and induced many, who were averse from the trouble of settling plantations, or were unable to bestow that attention to them which they demanded, to take this method of increasing their fortune. If the moneylender followed his employment in the capital, or reserved in his hands a sufficiency for family use, and allowed the interest to be added yearly to the capital stock, his fortune increased fast, and soon became considerable. Several persons preferred this method of accumulating riches to that of cultivation, especially those whom age or infirmity had rendered unfit for action and fatigue.

Notwithstanding the extensive credit commonly allowed the planting interest by the merchants, the number of borrowers always exceeded that of the lenders of money. Having vast extent of territory, the planters were eager to obtain numbers of labourers, which raised the demand for money, and kept up the high rate of interest. The interest of money in every country is for the most part according to the demand, and the demand according to the profits made by the use of it. The profits must always be great where men can afford to take money at the rate of eight and ten *per cent.* and allow it to remain in their hands upon compound interest. In Carolina labourers on good lands cleared their first cost and charges in a few years, and therefore great was the demand for money in order to procure them.

[Sidenote] And of the borrowers.

Let us next take a view of those advantages in favour of the borrower of money. His landed estate he obtained from the Crown. The quit-rents and taxes were trifling and inconsiderable. Being both landlord and farmer he had perfect liberty to manage and improve his plantation as he pleased, and was accountable to none but himself for any of the fruits of his industry. His estate furnished him with game and fish, which he had freedom to kill and use at pleasure. In the woods his cattle, hogs and horses grazed at their ease, attended perhaps only by a negro boy. If his sheep did not thrive well, he had calves, hogs and poultry in abundance for the use of his family. All his able labourers he could turn to the field, and exert his strength in railing his staple commodity. The low country being every where interspersed with navigable rivers and creeks, the expence of conveying his rice to the market, which otherwise would have been intolerable, was thereby rendered easy. Having provisions from his estate to support his family and labourers, he applies his whole staple commodities for the purposes of answering the demands of the merchant and moneylender. He expects that his annual produce will not only answer those demands against him, but also bring an addition to his capital, and enable him to extend his hand still farther in the way of improvement. Hence it happened, that in proportion as the merchants extended credit to the planters, and supplied them with labourers for their lands, the profits returned to the capital yearly according to the increased number of hands employed in cultivation.

It is no easy thing to enumerate all the advantages of water carriage to a fruitful and commercial province. The lands are rendered more valuable by being situated on navigable creeks and rivers. The planters who live fifty miles from the capital, are at little more expence in sending their provisions and produce to its market, than those who live within five miles of it. The town is supplied with plenty of provisions, and its neighbourhood prevented from enjoying a monopoly of its market. By this general and unlimited competition the price of provisions is kept low, and while the money arising from them circulates equally and universally through the country, it contributes, in return, to its improvement. The planters have not only water carriage to the market far their staple commodities, but on their arrival the merchant again commits them to the general tide of commerce, and receives in return what the world affords profitable to himself, and useful to the country in which he lives. Hence it happened, that no town was better supplied than Charlestown with all the necessaries, conveniencies, and luxuries of life.

[Sidenote] Great benefits enjoyed by colonists.

Besides these advantages arising from good lands given them by the Crown, the Carolineans received protection to trade, a ready market, drawbacks and bounties, by their political and commercial connection with the mother country. The duties laid on many articles of foreign manufacture on their importation into Britain were drawn back, sometimes the whole, almost always a great part, on their exportation to the colonies. These drawbacks were always in favour of the consumers, and supplied the provincial markets with foreign goods at a rate equally cheap as if they had been immediately imported from the place where they were manufactured. Hence the colonists were exempted from those heavy duties which their fellow-subjects in Britain were obliged to pay, on most articles of foreign manufacture which they consumed. Besides, upon the arrival of such goods in the country, the planters commonly had twelve months credit from the provincial merchant, who was satisfied with payment once in the year from all his customers. So that to the consumers in Carolina, East-India goods, German manufactures, Spanish, Portugal, Madeira and Fyal wines came cheaper than to those in Great Britain. We have known coals, salt, and other articles brought by way of ballast, sold cheaper in Charlestown than in London.

But the colonists had not only those drawbacks on foreign goods imported, but they were also allowed bounties on several articles of produce exported. For the encouragement of her colonies Great Britain laid high duties on several articles imported from foreign countries, and gave the colonists premiums and bounties on the same commodities. The planting tobacco was prohibited in England, in order to encourage it in America. The bounties on naval stores, indigo, hemp, and raw silk, while they proved an encouragement to industry, all terminated in favour of the plantations. Nor ought the Carolineans to forget the perfect freedom they enjoyed with respect to their trade with the West Indies, where they found a convenient and most excellent market for their Indian corn, rice, lumber, and salt provisions, and in return had rum, unclayed sugar, coffee and molasses much cheaper than their fellow-subjects in Britain. I mention these things because many of the colonists are ignorant of the privileges and advantages they enjoy; for, upon a general view of their circumstances, and a comparison of their case with that of their fellow-subjects in Britain and Ireland, they must find they had much ground for contentment, and none for complaint.

Another circumstance we may mention to which few have paid sufficient attention. It is true, Great Britain had laid the colonists under some restraints with respect to their domestic manufactures and their trade to foreign ports, but however much such a system of policy might affect the more northern colonies, it was at this time rather serviceable than prejudicial to Carolina. It served to direct the views of the people to the culture of lands, which was both more profitable to themselves and beneficial to the mother country. Though they had plenty of beaver skins, and a few hats were manufactured from them, yet the price of labour was so high, that the merchant could send the skins to England, import hats made of them, and undersell the manufacturers of Carolina. The province also furnished some wool and cotton, but before they could be made into cloth, they cost the consumer more money than the merchant demanded for the same goods imported. The province afforded leather, but before it could be prepared and made into shoes, the price was equally high, and often higher, than that of shoes imported from Britain. In like manner, with respect to many other articles, it would be for the advantage of the province as well as mother country to export the raw materials and import the goods manufactured. For while the inhabitants of Carolina can employ their hands to more advantage in cultivating waste land, it will be their interest never to wear a woollen or linen rag of their own manufacture, to drive a nail of their own forging, nor use any sort of plate, iron, brass or stationary wares of their own making. Until the province shall grow more populous, cultivation is the most profitable employment, and the labourer injures himself and family by preferring the less to the more profitable branch of industry.

Few also are the restrictions upon trade, which, in effect, could be deemed hurtful; for, excepting the vessels which traded to the southward of Cape Finisterre, and were obliged to return to England to cancel their bond before they sailed for Carolina, every other restraint may be said to be ultimately in favour of the province. It was the interest of such a flourishing colony to be always in debt to Great Britain, for the more labourers that were sent to it, the more rapidly it advanced in riches. Suppose the planters this year stand much indebted to the merchants, and, by reason of an unfavourable season, are rendered unable to answer the demands against them; the merchants, instead of ruining them, indulged them for another year, and perhaps intrusted them with double the sum for which they stood indebted. This has frequently been found the most certain method of obtaining payment. In like manner the merchants must have indulgence from England, the primary source of credit. If the province could not obtain such indulgence from any part of the world as from the mother country, it must be for its interest to support its credit with those generous friends who were both able and disposed to give it. To lodge the yearly produce of the province in the hands of those English creditors as soon as possible, is the surest means of supporting this credit. Besides, the London merchants being the best judges of the markets of Europe, can of course sell the staple commodities to the best advantage. The centrical situation of that city was favourable for intelligence; her merchants are famous over the world for their extensive knowledge in trade; they well knew the ports where there was the greatest demand for the commodity; all which were manifestly in favour of the province in which it was raised. Were the planters to have the choice of their market, it is very doubtful whether such liberty would be for their interest. Were they to export their produce on their own bottom, they would certainly be great losers. Some who have made the attempt have honestly confessed the truth: While it divided their attention, it engaged them in affairs to which they were in general very great strangers. Even the provincial merchants themselves are not always perfect judges of the markets in Europe, nor could they have obtained such unlimited credit in any other channel than that circumscribed by the laws of their country. Here is a co-operation of a number of persons united for promoting the interest and advantage of one another, and placed in circumstances and situations well adapted for that purpose. So that, in fact, it is not for the interest of Carolina, in its present advancing state, to be free from debt, far less of its planters to engage in trade, or its inhabitants in manufactures.

[Sidenote] Progress of the province.

To form a right judgment of the progress of the province, and the mutual advantages resulting from its political and commercial connection with Britain, we need only attend to its annual imports and exports. We cannot exactly say what its imports amounted to at this time; but if they amounted to above one hundred and fifty thousand pounds sterling in the year 1740, as we have already seen, they must have arisen at least to two hundred thousand pounds sterling in 1754. The quantities of rice exported this year were 104,682 barrels; of indigo, 216,924 pounds weight, which, together with naval stores, provisions, skins, lumber, &c. amounted in value to two hundred and forty-two thousand, five hundred and twenty-nine pounds sterling. This shews the great value and importance of the province to Britain. And while she depends on the mother country for all the manufactures she uses, and applies her attention to such branches of business as are most profitable to herself and most beneficial to Britain, Carolina must in the nature of things prosper. Without this dependence, and mutual exchange of good offices, the colony might have subsisted, but could never have thrived and flourished in so rapid a manner.

CHAPTER X

A dispute about the limits of British and French territories.

Although the peace of Aix-la-Chapelle extended to the subjects of both Britain and France residing in America, yet the boundaries of the respective territories claimed by those rival states were by no means fixed in so clear and precise a manner as to preclude all grounds of future dispute. The limits of Nova Scotia in particular, and those of the extensive back settlements of Virginia and Pennsylvania, were neither clearly understood nor accurately marked. In consequence of which, as the colonists extended their culture backwards encroachments were made, or supposed to be made, which created jealousies and differences between the British and French subjects on that continent. Some merchants trading to Virginia and Pennsylvania having formed a project for a settlement on the Ohio, obtained a grant of six hundred thousand acres of land from the King, together with an exclusive privilege of trafficking with Indian nations nigh that river. To these territories the French claimed a right; and, to keep possession, as well as to engross the Indian trade, built a fort on the banks of the Ohio river, which they called Fort Duquesne. This situation was very convenient for preserving the friendship of Indian nations, an object of the utmost importance to the French, as the subjects of Britain in America were at that time vastly more numerous and powerful than those of France.

Tobacco being a plant which quickly exhausts the richest lands, the planters of Virginia were accustomed gradually to stretch backward, and occupy such fresh spots of ground as promised them the greatest returns. Some had even crossed the Allegany mountains, where they found rich vallies lying waste, upon which they settled plantations; and though the land-carriage of such a heavy and bulky commodity was expensive, yet they found that the superiority of their crops made them some compensation. To this territory beyond the mountains, as well as the other marked and measured out for the Ohio Company, the French laid claim, and sent a considerable garrison from Montreal to Fort Duquesne, to defend their pretended right. The commander in chief of Canada wrote a letter to the Governor of Virginia, complaining of encroachments made on his most Christian Majesty's territories, and demanding that such British planters and traders as had settled on those lands should withdraw, otherwise he would be obliged to seize both their properties and persons. No regard being paid to his complaints, the commandant of Fort Duquesne seized by force three British traders, and goods to a large amount, and carried them to Montreal. Upon which the Governor of Virginia determined to resent the injury, and immediately began to concert measures for the protection of the frontiers. He raised a body of militia, and sent them met the mountains to watch the motions of their troublesome neighbours, and obtained reinforcements from North and South Carolina to assist them against the French garrison. This detachment, under the command of Major Washington, encamped near Fort Duquesne, between whom and the French garrison hostilities commenced in America; and the flame of war afterwards spreading, involved Europe in the quarrel.

[Sidenote] A chain of forts raised by the French.

From this period the great object which the French kept in view was to strengthen their frontiers, and make all possible preparations for defending themselves against the storm which they foresaw gathering in America. Though they seemed averse from an open declaration of war, yet they continued pouring troops into the continent, and raising a line of forts to secure a communication between their colony at the mouth of the Mississippi and their great settlement in Canada. They amused the British administration with fruitless negotiations about the limits of Nova Scotia, while they were busily employed in the execution of this great plan. Their design, however, was no secret to the more discerning part of the Americans, who plainly perceived from such preparations that hostilities were approaching. In Acadia they erected a fort at Chinecto, to confine the British subjects of Nova Scotia within the peninsula. At Crown Point another was raised, on lands claimed by the King of Great Britain, well situated for harassing the back settlements of New York and Connecticut. Another was built at Niagara, on land belonging to the Six Nations in alliance with Britain. While the Canadians were falling down the Ohio river, and raising strong-holds, the forces at Pensacola and New Orleans were also forcing their way up the Mississippi, and establishing garrisons on the most advantageous posts, on purpose to meet their friends from Canada, and confine the British settlements to the space between the mountains and the Atlantic sea. The more easily to accomplish this great design, it was necessary to secure by all possible means the interest of the savage nations. For this purpose missionaries were sent among the different tribes, who conformed to the dress, manners and customs of the savages, and represented the British heretics in the most odious light, making the Indians believe that their safety and happiness depended on the total extirpation of such men from America. Though some tribes rejected their friendship, yet it is certain that many were won over by their insinuating arts and intrigues, and entered into alliances with them. When a general congress was held at Albany fewer Indians than usual at such meetings attended, which afforded grounds of suspicion, and obliged the governors of the British colonies to double their diligence for watching the motions of their enterprising neighbours.

[Sidenote] The distracted state of the British colonies.

At the same time the situation of some of the British colonies proved favourable to the hostile preparations and attempts of their enemies. Their clashing interests had bred jealousies and animosities among them, insomuch that it was no easy matter to bring them firmly to unite, in order to oppose a common enemy with vigour and spirit. They believed themselves unable to withstand the militia of Canada supported by some regiments of regular troops from France, and therefore in the most humble manner implored the protection of Britain. They were filled with terrible apprehensions of the French power, declaring that their vanity and ambition had nothing less in view at this period than to divide the western world with Spain, and make all its riches center in the house of Bourbon. But whether they had such a view or not, one thing is plain, that the reduction of the British empire in America would facilitate the accomplishment of such a design, as the Portuguese dominions must afterwards fall an easy prey to those two powerful potentates.

Though Great Britain was sensible of the danger which threatened her colonies, yet as the number of British settlers on the continent exceeded that of the French, being not less than twenty to one, she expected that they would unite among themselves, and raise a fund for the common defence. Hitherto she had nursed and protected them, and many of the colonies had arrived at a considerable degree of opulence and strength. They had the easiest taxes of any civilized people upon earth. They had enjoyed many civil privileges, and commercial advantages, from their connection with the mother country. As their resources were considerable, it was hoped their zeal would not be wanting for their own defence. To give a check to any encroachments of the French in that quarter, Great Britain was more remotely, America herself more immediately, concerned. Instructions were therefore sent to the governors of the different provinces, to recommend unanimity to the people, and the necessity of an association for their mutual defence. But when the raising of men and money was proposed to the assemblies they fell into disputes among themselves, which became more violent in proportion as the enemy approached their habitations. Some pleaded extraordinary privileges from their charters; others started frivolous and absurd objections, insisting on punctilios as pretences for delay. In short, so different were their constitutions and forms of government, so divided were they in their views and interests, that it was found impossible to unite them together, in order to give their force its due weight. The frontiers were naked and extensive, the inhabitants upon them were thin and scattered, and utterly unequal to the service requisite without the assistance of their neighbours. The flames of war had broke out on some of them, and the neighbouring provinces could no otherwise be safe than by stretching forth their hands in helping to extinguish them. Thus, while the French were acting in concert under one commander and chief, the British colonists were spending that time in barren deliberations and private disputes which they ought to have employed in fortifying their borders and checking the progress of their enemy. What was in fact the business of every man seemed to engage the attention of none, and all kept their eyes fixed on the mother country for protection, regarding themselves as disinterested in the general safety of the empire, and very unequal to their own defence.

[Sidenote] General Braddock's defeat in Virginia.

While thus one province refused help to another, Great Britain, notwithstanding the extensive dominions she had to guard in different quarters of the globe, generously undertook the protection of America. As the greatest dangers seemed to hang over the province of Virginia, General Braddock was sent out with a considerable body of men to assist the Virginians in driving the French from their frontiers. This haughty and rash leader, being possessed of considerable skill in the European arts of war, entertained a sovereign contempt for an American enemy, and advanced against Fort Duquesne without even the smallest doubt of success. However, the French had intelligence of his approach, and were prepared to receive him. Having collected a large body of Indians, they had taken possession of an advantageous ground, and placed the regulars on a rising hill in front, and the savages in the dark woods on each side. General Braddock, instead of keeping small parties before the main body, to scour the woods as he advanced, and explore every dangerous pass, marched his men, according to the custom in Europe, in a close compacted body, and unfortunately fell into the snare which his enemies had laid for him. The French regulars in the front began the attack from behind a breast-work, while the Indians kept up an irregular and scattered fire from the dark thickets on each side, which surprized and confounded the British soldiers, who were utter strangers to such methods of attack. Almost every shot took effect, and the brave men observing their neighbours falling by their side, were put into confusion and fled, refusing to return to the charge against invisible assailants, notwithstanding every effort used by the officers for that purpose. Braddock with many brave officers and men fell in this field, and the remainder retreated with precipitation to Philadelphia, leaving these frontiers in a worse condition than they were in before.

[Sidenote] Colonel Johnston's success at Lake George.

Colonel Johnston, who marched with about three thousand men against Crown Point, was indeed more successful than this rash commander in Virginia. Being better acquainted with the woods, and the various methods of attack, he could both avail himself of the advantages, and guard against the dangers arising from the nature of the country. With cautious steps he advanced against the enemy, until he reached Lake George, where a party of his advanced guard being attacked retreated to the main body. The French pursued them, and a bloody battle ensued between the two armies, equally skilled in bush-fighting, which terminated much to the honour of the British officer. The enemy was repulsed with considerable loss, leaving Baron de Diescau wounded in the field, who, with many others, fell into Johnston's hands, and were made prisoners of war. This finall advantage gained over the French served in some measure to revive the drooping spirits of the colonists; yet still they entertained the most discouraging apprehensions of the French power in the woods, and seemed ardently to long for the relief and assistance of the mother country.

While these hostilities were openly carrying on in the northern parts of America, it was judged prudent to consult the safety of the provinces to the south, and put them in the best posture of defence. To prevent the fatal influence of French emissaries among the Indian tribes, it was thought necessary to build some small forts in the heart of their country. The Indians on the Ohio river, from the success which attended their arms at Fort Duquesne, entertained the highest ideas of French courage and conduct, and were trying to seduce the Cherokees, who were at this time the firmest allies of Britain. A message was sent to Governor Glen from the chief warrior of the over-hill settlements, acquainting him that some Frenchmen and their allies were among their people, endeavouring to poison their minds, and that it would be necessary to hold a general congress with the nation, and renew their former treaties of friendship. He assured the Governor, that though he had been wounded in his younger years, and was now old, yet he would meet him half way for this purpose, if he should even be carried on the backs of his people. Accordingly, Governor Glen appointed a place for holding a congress, and agreed to meet the warrior; for as the clouds were gathering every where on the American horizon, the friendship of the Cherokees at such a time was an object of too much importance to Carolina to be overlooked or neglected.

It may be remarked, that the Cherokees differ in some respects from other Indian nations that have wandered often from place to place, and fixed their habitations on separate districts. From time immemorial they have had possession of the same territory which at present they occupy. They affirm, that their forefathers sprung from that ground, or descended from the clouds upon those hills. These lands of their ancestors they value above all things in the world. They venerate the places where their bones lie interred, and esteem it disgraceful in the highest degree to relinquish these sacred repositories. The man that would refuse to take the field in defence of these hereditary possessions, is regarded by them as a coward, and treated as an outcast from their nation. To the over-hill villages the French had an easy access by means of rivers that emptied themselves into the Ohio and Mississippi. Their middle settlements and towns in the valley lay more convenient for trading with the Carolineans. Hitherto they despised the French, whom they called light as a feather, fickle as the wind, and deceitful as serpents; and, being naturally of a very grave cast, they considered the levity of that people as an unpardonable insult. They looked upon themselves as a great and powerful nation, and though their number was much diminished, yet they could bring from their different towns about three thousand men to the field. At this time they had neither arms nor ammunition to defend themselves against their enemy, and the Governor of Carolina wanted liberty to build two forts on their lands, in order to secure their friendship and trade. As the French were tampering with them, and had shewn a keenness more than common to gain some footing with them, it behoved the province to exert itself, in order to prevent if possible any alliance with its enemies.

[Sidenote] Governor Glen holds a congress with the Cherokees.

Accordingly, in 1755, Governor Glen met the Cherokee warriors in their own country, with a view to purchase some lands from them; and, after the usual ceremonies previous to such solemn treaties were over, the Governor sat down under a spreading tree, and Chulochcullah being chosen speaker for the Cherokee nation, came and took his seat beside him. The other warriors, about five hundred in number, stood around them in solemn silence and deep attention. Then the Governor arose, and made a speech in name of his king, representing his great power, wealth and goodness, and his particular regard for his children the Cherokees. He reminded them of the happiness they had long enjoyed by living under his protection; and added, that he had many presents to make them, and expected they would surrender a share of their territories in return for them. He acquainted them of the great poverty and wicked designs of the French, and hoped they would permit none of them to enter their towns. He demanded lands to build two forts in their country, to protect them against their enemies, and to be a retreat to their friends and allies, who furnished them with arms, ammunition, hatchets, clothes, and every thing that they wanted.

When the Governor had finished his speech, Chulochcullah arose, and holding his bow in one hand, his shaft of arrows and other symbols used by them on such occasions in the other, in answer spoke to the following effect. "What I now speak our father the great king should hear—We are brothers to the people of Carolina—one house covers us all." Then taking a boy by the hand he presented him to the Governor, saying, "We, our wives and our children, are all children of the great King George—I have brought this child, that when he grows up he may remember our agreement on this day, and tell it to the next generation, that it may be known for ever." Then opening his bag of earth, and laying the same at the Governor's feet, he said, "We freely surrender a part of our lands to the great King—The French want our possessions, but we will defend them while one of our nation shall remain alive." Then shewing his bows and arrow, he added, "These are all the arms we can make for our defence—We hope the King will pity his children the Cherokees, and send us guns and ammunition—We fear not the French—Give us arms and we will go to war against the enemies of the great King." Then delivering the Governor a string of wampum in confirmation of what he had said, he added, "My speech is at an end—It is the voice of the Cherokee nation—I hope the Governor will send it to the King, that it may be kept for ever."

[Sidenote] And purchases a large tract of land from them.

At this congress a territory of prodigious extent was ceded and surrendered to the King. Deeds of conveyance were drawn up, and formally executed by their head men in name of the whole people. It contained not only much rich land, but there the air was more serene, and the climate more healthy, than in the maritime parts. It exhibited many pleasant and romantic scenes, formed by an intermixture of beautiful hills, fruitful vallies, rugged rocks, clear streams, and gentle water-falls. The hills were of a stiff and tenacious clay, but the vallies of a deep, fat mould, and were covered with perpetual verdure. The acquisition at that time was so far of importance to Carolina, as it removed the savages at a greater distance from the settlements, and allowed the inhabitants liberty to extend backwards, in proportion as their number increased.

[Sidenote] Forts built in defence of Carolina.

Soon after the cession of these lands, Governor Glen built a fort about three hundred miles from Charlestown, afterwards called Fort Prince George, which was situated on the banks of the river Savanna, and within gun-shot of an Indian town called Keowee. This fort was made in the form of a square, and had an earthen rampart about six feet high, on which stockades were fixed, with a ditch, a natural glacis on two sides, and bastions at the angles, on each of which four small cannon were mounted. It contained barracks for an hundred men, and was designed for a defence to the western frontiers of the province. About an hundred and seventy miles further down there was another strong-hold, called Fort Moore, in a beautiful commanding situation on the banks of the same river. In the year following another fort was erected, called Fort Loudon, among the Upper Cherokees, situated on Tenassee river upwards of five hundred miles distant from Charlestown; to which place it was very difficult at all times, but, in case of a war with the Cherokees, utterly impracticable to convey necessary supplies. These strong-holds, together with those of Frederica and Augusta in Georgia, were garrisoned by his Majesty's independent companies of foot, stationed there for the protection of the two provinces.

After having fortified these frontiers, the settlers of Carolina began to stretch backward, and occupied lands above an hundred and fifty miles from the shore. New emigrants from Ireland, Germany and the northern colonies obtained grants in these interior parts, and introduced the cultivation of wheat, hemp, flax and tobacco, for which the soil answered better there than in the low lands nearer the sea. The cattle, sheep, hogs and horses multiplied fast, and having a country of vast extent to range over, they found plenty of provisions in it through the whole year. From different parts new settlers were invited to those hilly and more healthy parts of Carolina, where they laboured with greater safety than among the swamps, and success crowned their industry. By degrees public roads were made, and they conveyed their produce in waggons to the capital, where they found an excellent market for all their productions, but especially the provisions which they raised.

[Sidenote] Its excellent fruits and plants.

Although the soil and climate of the province suited the finest fruits and vegetable productions, yet the garden had long been neglected, and the orchard had engaged the attention only of a few. The people of Bermuda, not many years ago, carried to the market in Charlestown cabbages raised on that island, and the northern colonies their apples and Irish potatoes. But now the Carolineans found, by chusing a spot of land with judgment for the garden, that it would furnish them with all necessaries of this kind. Every spring and autumn brought them a crop of European peas and beans. Musk and water melons thrive exceedingly well even on the sandy maritime islands, and arrive at a degree of perfection unknown in many parts of Europe. All kinds of sallad, such as lettuce, endive, cresses, parsley, radishes, onions, will grow there in all seasons of the year, excepting one, and as nature has denied the people this kind of nourishment during the summer months, it is probable it must on that account be unwholesome. The garden also yielded abundance of cabbages, brocoli, cauliflower, turnips, spinage, cucumbers, squashes, artichokes, pompions, asparagus, &c. in great perfection. The climate indeed refuses the people of Carolina currants and gooseberries, as every attempt to raise them has failed; but they have oranges, figs, peaches, apricots, nectarines and strawberries in plenty, which are exceedingly agreeable and refreshing in the summer season. Olives, grapes, cherries, citrons and plumbs will grow, though not cultivated in common; but apples, pears, pomegranates, chesnuts and walnuts are, or at least may be, raised in abundance. Many physical roots and herbs, such as China-root, snake-root, sassafras, are the spontaneous growth of the woods; and sage, balm and rosemary thrive well in the gardens. The planters distil brandy of an inferior quality from peaches; and gather berries from the myrtle bushes of which they make excellent candles. The woods will also supply them with a variety of cherries, mulberries, wild grapes and nuts. In short, nature hath denied the diligent and skilful planter few of the most useful vegetables, and many delicious fruits grow to a degree of perfection exceeded by no country in Europe.

Ar the same time it must be acknowledged, that some disadvantages attend the climate with respect to the vegetable kingdom. European grapes have been transplanted, and several attempts made to raise wine in Carolina; but so overshaded are the vines planted in the woods, and so foggy is the season of the year when they begin to ripen, that they seldom come to maturity. But as excellent grapes have been raised in gardens where they are exposed to the sun, we are apt to believe that proper methods have not been taken for encouraging that branch of agriculture, considering its great importance in a national view. Some tolerable wine has been made from the native vines, which do not ripen so early in the season as those transplanted from Europe; and perhaps in some future day, when the planters have acquired greater skill, and made trials of different soils and situations, the vineyard culture may succeed better than it has yet done, and turn to some national account, like other profitable articles of American husbandry.

In some seasons the cold blast from the north-west proves very destructive to the orange, the olive and peach trees. In mild winters the trees blossom early, sometimes by the beginning of February, often before the middle of it. After the juices begin to rise, should the north west wind bring a cold frosty night, it commonly kills every tender shoot. Governor Glen makes mention of a frost which happened on the 7th of February, 1747, which killed almost all the orange trees in the country. The trees being ready to blossom about the time the frost came, it burst all their vessels, insomuch that not only the bark, but even the bodies of many of them were split, and all on the side next the sun. Such blasts are incredibly sharp and piercing. The Governor says he found several birds frozen to death near his house. We cannot vouch for the truth of this assertion, but we know no climate where the cold is more severely felt by the human body.

[Sidenote] Its minerals undiscovered.

With respect to the mineral kingdom we may say, who can tell what rich mines lie hid in Carolina, when no person has sought for them? If it be true that mountainous countries are favorable to mines, it may be presumed that this province, in which there are many extensive and high mountains, is not without its hidden treasures, no more than the other parts of the continent. Pennsylvania hath already exhibited to the world some useful minerals, and Carolina in time will probably do the same. But while the surface of the earth yields abundance of vegetable productions for the use of the inhabitants, and a plentiful livelihood can be obtained by easier means than that of digging into its bowels, it can scarcely be expected that they will apply themselves to deep and uncertain researches. It remains for a more populous and improved state, when ingenious men will probably attempt to explore those subterranean riches, which as yet lie neglected. Mineral water has been found in several parts, and such springs will help both to lead men to the important discovery, and animate them with the hopes of success.

The province of Georgia, with respect to improvement, still remained little better than a wilderness, and the vast expence it had cost the mother country might perhaps have been laid out to greater advantage in other parts of the continent. In the government of that colony John Ellis, a Fellow of the Royal Society, succeeded Captain John Reynolds. The rich swamps on the sides of the rivers lay uncultivated; and the planters had not yet found their way into the interior parts of the country, where the lands not only exceeded those in the maritime parts in fertility, but where the climate was also more healthy and pleasant. Excepting vagabonds and fraudulent debtors, who fled to them from Carolina, few of the Georgians had any negroes to assist them in cultivation; so that, in 1756, the whole exports of the country were 2997 barrels of rice, 9335 lb. of indigo, 268 lib. of raw silk, which, together with skins, furs, lumber and provisions amounted only to 16,776 pounds sterling.

Although the hostilities which had commenced between Great Britain and France still continued, yet both potentates remained averse from an open declaration of war. William Lyttleton, now Lord Westcot, being appointed governor of South Carolina, in his way through the Bay of Biscay, was intercepted by a French squadron under the command of Count de Guay, and carried into France; but an order from the French court came to release the ship, and permit the Governor to return to England. The British commanders at sea indeed had orders to seize all French ships and bring them into port, yet as some hopes of an accommodation still remained, the crews were only confined, and the cargoes remained entire. But so soon as the news of the bare-faced invasions of our dominions in the Mediterranean, joined with the many encroachments in America, had reached the British court, all prospects of an accommodation vanished at once, and war was publicly declared against France on the 17th of May, 1756.

Before the end of that year William Pitt, who had long been distinguished in the House of Commons for a bold and powerful orator, was called to the helm, and to his uncommon popularity added the whole influence of administration. After his preferment such bold plans of operation were introduced to the council, as were calculated at once to rouze the British nation and to alarm her enemies. The city of London, having the greatest confidence in the spirit and abilities of the minister, poured in its treasures to his assistance, and so great were his resources, that his schemes, however vast, never failed for want of money. From this period vigour and decision attended almost every warlike enterprize; a martial spirit pervaded the navy and army, and every officer seemed emulous of distinction and glory in the service of his country. This new minister gave the enemy so much employment, that for the future they had scarce time to breathe, and extended the powerful arm of Britain from the centre to the extremities of the empire.

In America John Earl of London had been appointed commander in chief; but such was the state of affairs on that continent, that all he could do was not sufficient to prevent the encroachments of the enemy. So disunited were the provincials, and so different were their principles, views and interests, that each colony seemed concerned only for its own defence, and determined to act independent of its neighbour; while the French were firmly united under one commander in chief, the Governor of Canada. Lord Loudon plainly saw that nothing remained for him to achieve, and therefore pitched his camp at Albany, and there determined to continue with his little army on the defensive, until a reinforcement should arrive from Britain. The French still wore the laurel, and triumphed in the forest, having every possible advantage their heart could desire from the divided state of British America.

But although the campaign under Lord Loudon was opened under many disadvantages, this gallant officer was not idle during the year. Having made himself master of the state of affairs on the continent, he perceived that the French, though united and strong, were nevertheless vulnerable, and drew up a plan of operations for the ensuing campaign, which he transmitted to the minister in Britain. Immediately preparations were made for carrying it into execution. It had been proposed to raise some regiments in America, but the levies went on slowly. As many of the colonists fit for service were foreigners, and only understood their native language, it was thought proper to allow them foreign officers to command them upon their taking the oaths to government, which contributed not a little to the more speedy completion of the Royal American regiments.

[Sidenote: The British forces augmented.]

Early in the year following a considerable reinforcement from Britain arrived at New York. The Indians in alliance with us were furnished with arms, and encouraged to join the army. Among the British forces sent out there was a regiment of Highlanders, who were in many respects well qualified for the service. It is impossible to describe how much the savages were delighted with the dress, manners and music of this regiment. Their sprightly manner of dancing, their dexterity in the use of arms, and natural vivacity and intrepidity, the savages greatly admired, and expressed a strong inclination for attending the Scotch warriors to the field. To prevent them from joining the enemy it was not only necessity to employ those warriors, but it was thought they might be rendered useful for scouring the dark thickets before the regular army. Lieutenant Kennedy, to encourage them, entered into their humour, and, in order to head them, dressed and painted himself like an Indian. They gave him a squaw, and the nation to which she belonged having made him a king, no small service was expected from the new alliance.

[Sidenote] Their first success in America.

When General Abercrombie succeded Lord Loudon as commander in chief in America, the British force being considerably augmented, bolder enterprises were undertaken. It was agreed to attack the French settlements in different places. Though this commander met with a sharp repulse at Ticonderago, the French paid dear for this advantage by the loss of Cape Breton, which opened the way into Canada. Fort Frontenac next surrendered to Colonel Bradstreet, in which were found vast quantities of provision and ammunition, that had been designed for the French forces on the Ohio. The great loss sustained by the enemy at this place facilitated the reduction of Fort Duquesne, against which General Forbes was advancing with great vigilance and considerable force. This fortress the enemy, after a few skirmishes, determined to abandon; and having burnt their houses, and destroyed their works, fell down the Ohio river in boats to their strong-holds erected beyond the Cherokee mountains. No sooner was the British flag erected on Fort Duquesne, than the numerous tribes of Indians came in and made their submission; and, from a conviction of the superior valour and strength of the British army, joined the conquerors. Although the enemy lost few men at this place, yet their power in America received a heavy stroke by the division of their force which the loss of it occasioned. All communication between their settlements on the south parts and those of Canada being cut off, they could no longer act in concert, and their future exertions were rendered more feeble and ineffectual.

[Sidenote] The cause of the Cherokee war.

However, the flight of this French garrison to the south promised little good to Carolina. The scene of action was changed only from one place to another, and the baleful influence of those active and enterprising enemies soon appeared among the upper tribes of Cherokees. An unfortunate quarrel with the Virginians helped to forward their designs, by opening to them an easier access into the towns of the savages. In the different expeditions against Fort Duquesne, the Cherokees, agreeable to treaty, had sent considerable parties of warriors to the assistance of the British army. As the horses in those parts run wild in the woods, it was customary, both among Indians and white people on the frontiers, to lay hold on them and appropriate them to their own purposes. While the savages were returning home through the back parts of Virginia, many of them having lost their horses, laid hold of such as came in their way, never imagining that they belonged to any individual in the province. The Virginians however, instead of asserting their right in a legal way, resented the injury by force of arms, and killed twelve or fourteen of the unsuspicious warriors, and took several more prisoners. The Cherokees, with reason, were highly provoked at such ungrateful usage from allies, whose frontiers they had helped to change from a field of blood into peaceful habitations, and when they came home told what had happened to their nation. The flame soon spread through the upper towns, and those who had lost their friends and relations were implacable, and breathed nothing but fury and vengeance against such perfidious friends. In vain did the chieftains interpose their authority, nothing could restrain the furious spirits of the young men, who were determined to take satisfaction for the loss of their relations. The emissaries of France among them added fuel to the flame, by telling them that the English intended to kill every man of them, and make slaves of their wives and children. They instigated them to bloodshed, and for that purpose furnished them with arms and ammunition. The scattered families on the frontiers of Carolina lay much exposed to scalping parties of these savages, who commonly make no distinction of age or sex, but pour their vengeance indiscriminately on the innocent and guilty.

The garrison of Fort Loudon, consisting of about two hundred men, under the command of Captains Demere and Stuart, first discovered the ill humour in which the Cherokee warriors returned from the northern expedition. The soldiers, as usual, making excursions into the woods, to hunt for fresh provisions, were attacked by them, and some of them were killed. From this time such dangers threatened the garrison, that every one was confined within the small boundaries of the fort. All communication with the distant settlement from which they received supplies being cut off, and the soldiers being but poorly provided, had no other prospects left but those of famine or death. Parties of young Indians took the field, and, rushing down among the settlements, murdered and scalped a number of people on the frontiers.

[Sidenote] Governor Lyttleton prepares to march against them.

The commanding officer at Fort Prince George having received intelligence of those acts of hostility, dispatched a messenger to Charlestown to inform Governor Lyttleton that the Cherokees were gone to war, and that it would be necessary speedily to warn the people of their danger. In consequence of which orders were given to the commanders of the militia immediately to collect their men, and stand in a posture of defence, while the Governor was making preparations in Charlestown for marching against them, in order to give a speedy check to their progress. Parties of the independent companies were brought to Charlestown for this purpoise. The militia of the country had orders to rendezvous at Congarees, where the Governor, with such a force as he could procure from the lower parts, resolved to join them, and march to the relief of the frontier settlements.

[Sidenote] The Cherokees sue for peace.

No sooner had the Cherokees heard of these warlike preparations at Charlestown, than thirty-two of their chiefs set out for that place; in order to settle all differences, and prevent if possible a war with the Carolineans. For although they could not restrain some of their young men from acts of violence, yet the nation in general was still inclined to friendship and peace. As they arrived at Charlestown before the Governor had set out on the intended expedition, a council was called, and the chiefs being sent for, Mr. Lyttleton, among other things, told them, "That he was well acquainted with all the acts of hostility of which their people had been guilty, and likewise those they intended against the English, and enumerated some of them; then he added, That he would soon be in their country, where he would let them know his demands, and the satisfaction he required, which he would certainly take if they refused it. As they had come to Charlestown to treat with him as friends, they should go home in safety, and not a hair of their head should be touched; but as he had many warriors in arms in different parts of the province, he could not be answerable for what might happen to them unless they marched along with his army." After this speech Occonostota, who was distinguished by the name of the Great Warrior of the Cherokee nation, began to speak by way of reply; but the Governor being determined that nothing should prevent his military expedition, declared, he would hear no talk he had to make, neither in vindication of his nation, nor any proposals with regard to peace. Lieutenant-Governor Bull, who was better acquainted with the manners of Indians, and the dangers to which the province would be exposed from a war with them, urged the necessity of hearing the Great Warrior, and the happy consequences of an agreement before more blood was spilt. But Mr. Lyttleton remained inflexible, and put an end to the conference; with which behaviour the chiefs, however, were not a little displeased. For as they had travelled so far to obtain peace, and, after all, to be not only denied liberty to speak, but also to be disappointed with respect to the chief end of their journey, chagrined them much, and created many uneasy fears and suspicions.

[Sidenote] Governor Lyttleton marches against the Cherokees.

A few days after holding this conference with the chieftains the governor set out for Congarees, the place of general rendezvous for the militia, and about one hundred and forty miles distant from Charlestown, where he mustered in all about one thousand four hundred men. To this place the Cherokees marched along with the army, and were to appearance contented, but in reality burning with fury and resentment. When the army moved from the Congarees, the chieftains, very unexpectedly, were all made prisoners, and, to prevent their escape to the nation, a captain's guard was mounted over them, and in this manner they were obliged to march to Fort Prince George. Being not only deprived of their liberty, which an Indian values above all things, but also compelled to accompany an enemy going against their families and friends, they could now no longer conceal their resentment. They turned exceedingly sullen, and shewed that they were stung to the heart by such base treatment. The breach of promise an Indian holds an atrocious crime. To requite good intended with real evil, they with reason deemed an unpardonable injury. But what compleated the ill usage, the thirty-two Indians, upon the arrival of the army at Fort Prince George, were all shut up in a hut scarcely sufficient for the accommodation of six soldiers, where they spent their time in concerting plots for obtaining their liberty, and satisfaction for the injuries done them.

[Sidenote] Holds a congress a Fort Prince George.

Governor Lyttleton's little army being not only ill armed and disciplined, but also discontented and mutinous, he therefore judged it dangerous to proceed farther into the enemy's country. Having beforehand sent for Attakullakulla, who was esteemed both the wisest man of the nation and the most steady friend of the English, to meet him at Fort Prince George, this warrior hastened to his camp from an excursion against the French, in which he had taken some prisoners, one of whom he presented to the Governor. Mr Lyttleton knew, that, for obtaining a re-establishment of peace, there was not a man in the whole nation better disposed to assist him than this old warrior, though it was observed that he cautiously avoided making any offer of satisfaction. But so small was his influence among the Cherokees at this time, that they considered him as no better than an old woman on account of his attachment to their English enemies, and his aversion from going to war against them.

[Sidenote] His speech to Attakullakulla.

About the 18th of December, 1759, the Governor held a congress with this warrior, and by an interpreter spoke to him to the following effect: "You told me yesterday that you had a good talk to make, and expected the same from me. You know it is the will of the great King that his subjects and your people should live together in friendship, and you have said you desire not to break the chain thereof. It is a chain which our most gracious sovereign holds at one end, and you hold at the other. You know that, in order to keep this chain from contracting rust, and hinder it from being broken, it was necessary certain conditions should be made; and as all acts of the great king are kept till time shall be no more, so I now have in my hand those very conditions made with you and your people. It was agreed, that if an Indian should kill an Englishman, he shall be delivered up to be punished as the law requires. This was the ancient talk of our fathers and your fathers, and when King George took your nation under his protection he so ordered it for the future. This treaty has been since renewed by several of our King's governors of this province from time to time. It was the mercy of the great King that this way of restitution should be established, to prevent a war which might destroy your nation; whereas, at any time, by delivering up of the guilty person, the innocent might escape, and your people be suffered to live in friendship with ours.

"In the month of November, 1758, six deputies from your nation came to Charlestown, to make up all differences between our people and yours. They did then engage to observe the words of the treaty I have here, and which you know are the same with those formerly made by the great King. They received a large quantity of goods as a full compensation for the injuries done them by white people, and did solemnly promise to continue in strict friendship with all the King's subjects. Notwithstanding which they went to Statiquo under Moytoy and killed many white men, though no provocation had been given them. Thereupon I demanded satisfaction, according to the words of the great King, but they have given me none. As King Gorge loves mercy better than war, I was willing to wait; and while our people lay quietly in their houses, the Indians came, killed and scalped them. Last of all they put to death three men in the Upper nation, and drove our people, who lived in their towns to furnish them with goods, into the forts. As you know that your people have been guilty of all these crimes, and many more, I expected you would not only come down with a good talk, but also would have offered satisfaction for them. I am now come here with a great number of warriors, to take that satisfaction I have more than once demanded. Perhaps some of you thought, that, as our people put up with such injuries, they were apprehensive of your power; but you shall now see that this was owing to their patience, and not to their want of resolution. You know well the strength of our province, and that one third part of it is sufficient to destroy your nation. Besides, the white people in all the provinces are brothers, and linked together: we come not alone against you because we have suffered, for the Virginians and North Carolineans are prepared to march against you, unless satisfaction be given me. My brother the Governor of Georgia will also prevent any ammunition from coming to you. Some time ago you sent to Virginia, offering to trade with that province, and goods were on their way to you which I have stopt and they shall not proceed hither until I send directions for them. It is not necessary for me to say more to you, until you make satisfaction for killing the white people.

"Attakullakulla, you have been in England, and seen the power of the great King, and the number of his warriors. You also know, that, during these five years and more, we have been at war with the French, who were once numerous over all parts of America. You know I disdain to tell you a falsehood, and I will now inform you what success our army has had. Some of the last ships that arrived at Charlestown brought me a good deal of news. Our fleet has taken many ships of war belonging to the French. A messenger has arrived with an account that the great city of Quebec is reduced, as also, that the warriors of the great king have taken all the forts on the lakes and upon the Ohio, and beat down all things in their way, as a hurricane would have done in its passage. The Indians in those parts, fearing his power, have made their peace with the great King. The Delawares, Shawanese, and all of them that live near Fort Duquesne, have desired to be in friendship with us. The Choctaws also beg to be received under the King's protection by his beloved man Mr. Aitken, upon which a great number of traders are gone into their country with all sorts of goods. If you will not believe what I say, and imagine that the French are able to supply you with the necessaries which you want, you will be deceived, for they themselves are starving, and so much undone that they cannot furnish a blanket or a gun to the Choctaws, much less to you, who are removed at so great a distance from them.

"These things I have mentioned to show you that the great King will not suffer his people to be destroyed without satisfaction, and to let you know the people of this province are determined to have it. What I say is with a merciful intention. If I make war with you, you will suffer for your rashness; your men will be destroyed, and your women and children carried into captivity. What few necessaries you now have will soon be done, and you will get no more. But if you give the satisfaction I shall ask, the trade will be again opened with you, and all things go right. I have twice given you a list of the murderers; I will now tell you there are twenty-four men of your nation whom I demand to be delivered up to me, to be put to death, or otherwise disposed of as I shall think fit. Your people have killed that number of ours and more, therefore it is the least I will accept of. I shall give you till to-morrow morning to consider of it, and then I shall expect your answer. You know best the Indians concerned; several gangs at different times have been out, and I expect the twenty-four you shall deliver up will be those who have committed the murders."

[Sidenote] Attakullakulla's answer.

To this long speech Attakullakulla replied in words to the following effect: "That he remembered the treaties mentioned, as he had a share in making them: He owned the kindness of the province of South Carolina, but complained much of the bad treatment his countrymen had received in Virginia, which, he said, was the immediate cause of our present misunderstanding: That he had always been the firm friend of the English, of which he hoped his late fatiguing march against their enemies the French was a sufficient proof: That he would ever continue such, and would use all the influence he had to persuade his countrymen to give the Governor the satisfaction he demanded, though he believed it neither would nor could be complied with, as they had no coercive authority one over another: He desired the Governor to release some of the head men then confined in the fort to assist him; and added, that he was pleased to hear of the successes of his brothers the English, but could not help mentioning, that they shewed more resentment against the Cherokees than they had used to other nations that had disobliged them; that he remembered some years ago several white people belonging to Carolina were killed by the Choctaws, for whom no satisfaction had either been given or demanded."

Agreeable to the request of Attakullakulla, the Governor released Occonostota, Fiftoe the chief man of Keowee town, and the head warrior of Estaloe, who next day delivered up two Indians, whom Mr. Lyttleton ordered to be put in irons. After which all the Cherokees present, who knew their connections to be weak, being alarmed, fled out of the way, so that it was impossible to complete the number demanded. Attakullakulla, being then convinced that peace could not be obtained on such terms as the Governor required, resolved to go home and patiently wait the event; but no sooner was Mr. Lyttleton made acquainted with his departure, than he dispatched a messenger after him to bring him back to his camp; and being desirous of finishing the campaign with as much credit as possible, immediately on his return began to treat of peace. Accordingly a treaty was drawn up and signed by the Governor and six of the head men; in which it was agreed, that those twenty-two chieftains of the Cherokees should be kept as hostages confined in the fort, until the same number of Indians guilty of murder be delivered up to the commander in chief of the province; that trade should be opened and carried on as usual; that the Cherokees should kill, or take every Frenchman prisoner, who should presume to come into their nation during the continuance of the war; and that they should hold no intercourse with the enemies of Great Britain, but should apprehend every person, white or red, found among them, that may be endeavouring to set the English and Cherokees at variance, and interrupt the friendship and peace established between them.

After having concluded this treaty with the Cherokees, the Governor resolved to return to Charlestown. But whether the Indians who put their mark to it understood the articles of agreement or not, we cannot pretend to affirm; one thing is certain, that few or none of the nation afterward paid the smallest regard to it. The treacherous act of confining their chiefs, against whom no charge could be brought, and who had travelled several hundred miles in order to obtain peace for their nation, had made a strong impression on their minds, but particularly on that of Occonostota, who breathed nothing but fury and vengeance against such false friends. Instead of permitting them to return home without hurting a hair of their head, as the Governor promised in Charlestown, they were close confined in a miserable hut, having permission neither to see their friends nor even the light of day. It was said they were kept only as hostages, until the number of criminals he demanded was completed by their nation; but if they were robbed of their liberty, it was of little consequence to them under what denomination they were confined. It was said to be done by the consent of the nation, as six of its chiefs had signed the articles of peace; but in whatever light we view the act, it appears to be one of those base and unjustifiable advantages which policy and craft commonly take of the weakness and simplicity of more unfortunate neighbours; and nothing less could have been expected, than that these wild and independent warriors would resent such base and unmerited usage on the first opportunity that offered.

[Sidenote] The Governor returns to Charlestown.

Scarcely had Governor Lyttleton concluded the treaty of Fort Prince George when the small-pox, which was raging in an adjacent Indian town, broke out in his camp. As few of his little army had ever gone through that distemper, and as the surgeons were totally unprovided for such an accident, his men were struck with terror, and in great haste returned to the settlements, cautiously avoiding all intercourse one with another, and suffering much from hunger and fatigue by the way. The Governor followed them, and arrived in Charlestown about the beginning of the year 1760. Though not a drop of blood had been spilt during the expedition, he was received like a conqueror, with the greatest demonstrations of joy. Addresses the most flattering were presented to him by the different societies and professions, and bonefires and illuminations testified the high sense the inhabitants entertained of his merit and services, and the happy consequences which they believed would result from his expedition.

[Sidenote] The treaty of peace broken

However, those rejoicings on account of the peace were scarcely over, when the news arrived that fresh hostilities hod been committed, and the Governor was informed that the Cherokees had killed fourteen men within a mile of Fort Prince George. The Indians had contracted an invincible antipathy to Captain Coytmore, the officer whom Mr. Lyttleton had left commander of that fort. The treatment they had received at Charlestown, but especially the imprisonment of their chiefs, had now converted their former desire of peace into the bitterest rage for war. Occonostota, a chieftain of great influence, had become a most implacable and vindictive enemy to Carolina, and determined to repay treachery with treachery. Having gathered a strong party of Cherokees, he surrounded Fort Prince George, and compelled the garrison to keep within their works; but finding that he could make no impression on the fort, nor oblige the commander to surrender, he contrived the following stratagem for the relief of his countrymen confined in it.

[Sidenote] Occonostota's stratagem for killing the officer of the fort.

As that country was every where covered with woods, he placed a party of savages in a dark thicket by the river side, and then sent an Indian woman, whom he knew to be always welcome at the fort, to inform the commander that he had something of consequence to communicate to him, and would be glad to speak with him at the river side. Captain Coytmore imprudently consented, and without any suspicions of danger walked down towards the river, accompanied by Lieutenants Bell and Foster. Occonostota appearing on the opposite side, told him he was going to Charlestown to procure a release of the prisoners, and would he glad of a white man to accompany him as a safeguard; and, the better to cover his dark design, had a bridle in his hand, and added, he would go and hunt for a horse to him. The captain replied, that he should have a guard, and wished he might find a horse, as the journey was very long. Upon which the Indian, turning quickly about, swung the bridle thrice round his head, as a signal to the savages placed in ambush, who instantly fired on the officers, shot the captain dead on the spot, and wounded the other two. In consequence of which orders were given to put the hostages in irons, to prevent any farther danger from them. But while the soldiers were attempting to execute their orders, the Indians stabbed the first man who had hold of them with a knife, and wounded two more; upon which the garrison, exasperated to the highest degree, fell on the unfortunate hostages, and butchered them in a manner too shocking to relate.

[Sidenote] The war becomes general.

There were few men in the Cherokee nation that did not lose a friend or a relation by this massacre, and therefore with one voice all immediately declared for war. The leaders in every town seized the hatchet, telling their followers that the spirits of murdered brothers were flying around them, and calling out for vengeance on their enemies. From the different towns large parties of warriors took the field, painted in the most formidable manner, and arrayed with all their instruments of death. All sang the song of war, and burning with impatience to imbrue their hands in the blood of their enemies, rushed down among innocent and defenceless families on the frontiers of Carolina, where men, women and children, without distinction, fell a sacrifice to their merciless fury. Such as fled to the woods, and escaped the scalping-knife, perished with hunger; and those whom they made prisoners were carried into the wilderness, where they suffered inexpressible hardships. Every day brought fresh accounts to the capital of their ravages, murders and desolations. But while the back settlers impatiently looked to their Governor for relief, the small-pox raged to such a degree in town, that few of the militia could be prevailed on to leave their distressed families to serve the public. In this extremity an express was sent to General Amherst, the commander in chief in America, acquainting him with the deplorable situation of the province, and imploring his assistance in the most pressing terms. Accordingly a battalion of Highlanders, and four companies of the Royal Scots, under the command of Colonel Montgomery, now Earl of Eglinton, were ordered immediately to embark, and sail for the relief of Carolina.

In the mean time William Lyttleton being appointed Governor of Jamaica, the charge of the province devolved on William Bull, a man of great integrity and erudition. Application was made to the neighbouring provinces of North Carolina and Virginia for relief, and seven troops of rangers were raised to patrole the frontiers, and prevent the savages from penetrating farther down among the settlements. A considerable sum was voted for presents to such of the Creeks, Chickesaws and Catabaws as should join the province and go to war against the Cherokees. Provisions were sent to the families that had escaped to Augusta and Fort Moore, and the best preparations possible made for chastising their enemy, so soon as the regulars coming from New York should arrive in the province.

[Sidenote] Colonel Montgomery arrives.

Before the end of April, 1760, Colonel Montgomery landed in Carolina, and encamped at Monk's Corner. Great was the joy of the province upon the arrival of this gallant officer; but as the conquest of Canada was the grand object of this year's campaign in America, he had orders to strike a sudden blow for the relief of Carolina, and return to head quarters at Albany without loss of time. Nothing was therefore omitted that was judged necessary to forward the expedition. Several gentlemen of fortune, excited by a laudable zeal for the safety of their country, formed themselves into a company of volunteers, and joined the army. The whole force of the province was collected, and ordered to rendezvous at Congarees. Waggons, carts and horses were impressed for the service of his Majesty, and the colonists flattered themselves with the hopes that they would now be able to punish the insolence of their barbarous enemies.

[Sidenote] And marches against the Cherokees.

A few weeks after his arrival Colonel Montgomery marched to the Congarees, where he was joined by the internal strength of the province, and immediately set out for the Cherokee country. For a guide he was provided with an half-blooded Indian, who was well acquainted with the roads though the woods, and the passages through the rivers. Having little time allowed him, his march was uncommonly spirited and expeditious. After reaching a place called Twelve-mile River, he encamped on an advantageous ground, and marched with a party of his men in the night to surprize Estatoe, an Indian town about twenty miles from his camp. The first noise he heard by the way was the barking of a dog before his men, where he was informed there was an Indian town called Little Keowee, which he ordered the light infantry to surround, and, except women and children, to put every Indian in it to the sword. Having done this piece of service, he proceeded to Estatoe, which he found abandoned by all the savages, excepting a few who had not had time to make their escape. This town, which consisted of at least two hundred houses, and was well provided with corn, hogs, poultry, and ammunition, he reduced to ashes. Sugar Town, and every other settlement in the lower nation, afterwards shared the same fate. The surprize to every one of them was nearly equal; for as the army darted upon them like lightning, the savages could scarcely save themselves, far less any little property that they had. In these lower towns about sixty Indians were killed and forty made prisoners, and the rest driven to seek for shelter among the mountains. Having finished his business among these lower settlements with the small loss of three or four men, he then marched to the relief of Fort Prince George, which had been for some time invested by savages, insomuch that no soldier durst venture beyond the bounds of the fort, and where the garrison was in distress, not for the want of provisions, but of wood to prepare them.

[Sidenote] Chastises them near Etchoe.

While the army rested at Fort Prince George, Edmund Atkin, agent for Indian affairs, dispatched two Indian chiefs to the middle settlements, to inform the Cherokees that by suing for peace they might obtain it, as the former friends and allies of Britain. At the same time he sent a messenger to Fort Loudon, requesting Captains Demere and Stuart, the commanding officers at that place, to use their best endeavours for obtaining peace with the Cherokees in the upper towns. Colonel Montgomery finding that the savages were as yet disposed to listen to no terms of accommodation, determined to carry the chastisement a little farther. Dismal was the wilderness into which he entered, and many were the hardships and dangers he had to encounter, from dark thickets, rugged paths, and narrow passes; in which a small body of men, properly posted, might harass and tire out the bravest army that ever took the field. Having on all hands suspicious grounds, he found occasion for constant vigilance and circumspection. While he was piercing through the thick forest he had numberless difficulties to surmount, particularly from rivers fordable only at one place, and overlooked by high banks on each side, where an enemy might attack him with advantage, and retreat with safety. When he had advanced within five miles of Etchoe, the nearest town in the middle settlements, he found there a low valley, covered so thick with bushes that the soldiers could scarcely see three yards before them, and in the middle of which there was a muddy river, with steep clay banks. Through this dark place, where it was impossible for any number of men to act together, the army must necessarily march; and therefore Captain Morison, who commanded a company of rangers, well acquainted with the woods, had orders to advance and scour the thicket. He had scarcely entered it, when a number of savages sprung from their lurking den, and firing on them, killed the captain and wounded several of his party. Upon which the light infantry and grenadiers were ordered to advance and charge the invisible enemy, which they did with great courage and alacrity. A heavy fire then began on both sides, and during some time the soldiers could only discover the places where the savages were hid by the report of their guns. Colonel Montgomery finding that the number of Indians that guarded this place was great, and that they were determined obstinately to dispute it, ordered the Royal Scots, who were in the rear, to advance between the savages and a rising ground on the right, while the Highlanders marched towards the left to sustain the light infantry and grenadiers. The woods now resounded with horrible shouts and yells, but these, instead of intimidating the troops, seemed rather to inspire them with double firmness and resolution. At length the savages gave way, and in their retreat falling in with the Royal Scots, suffered considerably before they got out of their reach. By this time the Royals being in the front and the Highlanders in the rear, the enemy stretched away and took possession of a hill, seemingly disposed to keep at a distance, and always retreating as the army advanced. Colonel Montgomery perceiving that they kept aloof, gave orders to the line to face about, and march directly for the town of Etchoe. The enemy no sooner observed this movement, than they got behind the hill, and ran to alarm their wives and children. During the action, which lasted above an hour, Colonel Montgomery, who made several narrow escapes, had twenty men killed, and seventy-six wounded. What number the enemy lost is uncertain, but some places were discovered into which they had thrown several of their slain, from which it was conjectured that they must have lost a great number, as it is a custom among them to carry their dead off the field. Upon viewing the ground, all were astonished to see with what judgment and skill they had chosen it. Scarcely could the most experienced officer have fixed upon a spot more advantageous for way-laying and attacking an enemy, according to the method of fighting practised among the Indian nations.

[Sidenote] And returns to Fort Prince George.

This action, though it terminated much in favour of the British army, had nevertheless reduced it to such a situation as made it very imprudent, if not altogether impracticable, to penetrate farther into those woods. The repulse was far from being decisive, for the enemy had only retired from one to another advantageous situation, in order to renew their attack when the army should again advance. Humanity would not suffer the commander to leave so many wounded men exposed to the vengeance of savages, without any strong-hold in which he might lodge them, or some detachment, which he could not spare, to protect them. Should he proceed farther, he saw plainly that he must expect frequent skirmishes, which would increase the number, and the burning of so many Indian towns would be a poor compensation for the great risque and perhaps wanton sacrifice of so many valuable lives. To furnish horses for the men already wounded obliged him to throw so many bags of flour into the river, and what remained was no more than sufficient for his army during their return to Fort Prince George. Orders were therefore given for a retreat, which was made with great regularity, although the enemy continued hovering around them, and annoying them to the utmost of their power. A large train of wounded men was brought above sixty miles through a hazardous country in safety, for which no small share of honour and praise was due to the officer that conducted the retreat. Never did men endure greater hardships and fatigues with fewer complaints than this little army during the expedition. Such confidence did they repose in their leader, that they seemed to despise all difficulties and dangers which he shared along with them in the service of their King and country.

[Sidenote] The consternation of the inhabitants from Indians.

After Colonel Montgomery had returned to the settlements, and was preparing to embark for New York, agreeable to his orders from General Amherst, the Carolineans were again thrown under the most dreadful apprehensions from the dangers which hung over the province. This appears from the following address of the General Assembly, presented to Lieutenant-Governor Bull on the 11th of July, 1760. "We, his Majesty's most dutiful and loyal subjects, the Commons House of Assembly of this province, return your Honour our sincere thanks for the advices you have been pleased to communicate to us in the morning; and being deeply affected with the contents of Colonel Grant's letter, which imports, that Colonel Montgomery will soon embark with his Majesty's troops under his command to join General Amherst; humbly beg leave to represent to your Honour, that we apprehend the province to be in a much more dangerous situation at this juncture, than it was at the time when the said troops arrived here; as the Upper Creek Indians have since murdered several English traders in their towns, and made no offer to give up the murderers, or make any other satisfaction whatever; whence we have the greatest reason to believe they will soon break out into open war. And by what is mentioned in Colonel Grant's letter, we fear that our implacable enemies the French have already spirited up and prevailed with the Choctaws to assist the Cherokees against us. And notwithstanding the present rupture with the Cherokees has cost the province, in less than nine months, near 50,000 pounds sterling, yet all our endeavours to raise a number of forces capable of preventing the Cherokees from ravaging the back settlements have proved ineffectual. This being the situation of the province when we had only the Cherokees to contend with, how deplorable then must our case be, should Colonel Montgomery depart with the King's troops under his command, and we have the united attacks of the Cherokees, Creeks and Choctaws, (the three most powerful nations of Indians on the continent), to repel, can be better imagined than described. Being truely sensible of your Honour's good inclinations to render every service in your power to this province, we unanimously intreat your Honour to use the most pressing instances with Colonel Montgomery not to depart with the King's troops, as it may be attended with the most pernicious consequences." Accordingly the Lieutenant-Governor having given the Colonel the fullest view of those extensive dangers to which the province after his departure would be exposed, prevailed with him to leave four companies of the royal regiment, under the command of Major Frederick Hamilton, for covering the frontiers, while he embarked with the battalion of Highlanders, and sailed for New York.

[Sidenote] Great distress of the garrison at Fort Loudon.
[Sidenote] The terms obtained for the garrison.

In the mean time the distant garrison of Fort Loudon, consisting of two hundred men, was reduced to the dreadful alternative of perishing by hunger or submitting to the mercy of the enraged Cherokees. The Governor having information that the Virginians had undertaken to relieve it, for a while seemed satisfied, and anxiously waited to hear the news of that happy event. But the Virginians were equally ill qualified with their neighbours of Carolina to send them any assistance. So remote was the fort from every settlement, and so difficult was it to march an army through the barren wilderness, where the various thickets were lined with enemies, and to carry at the same time sufficient supplies along with them, that the Virginians had dropped all thoughts of the attempt. Provisions being entirely exhausted at Fort Loudon, the garrison was reduced to the most deplorable situation. For a whole month they had no other subsistence but the flesh of lean horses and dogs, and a small supply of Indian beans, which some friendly Cherokee women procured for them by stealth. Long had the officers endeavoured to animate and encourage the men with the hopes of relief; but now being blockaded night and day by the enemy, and having no resource left, they threatened to leave the fort, and die at once by the hands of savages, rather than perish slowly by famine. In this extremity the commander was obliged to call a council of war, to consider what was proper to be done; when the officers were all of opinion that it was impossible to hold out any longer, and therefore agreed to surrender the fort to the Cherokees on the best terms that could be obtained from them. For this purpose Captain Stuart, an officer of great sagacity and address, and much beloved by all the Indians that remained in the British interest, procured leave to go to Chote, one of the principal towns in the neighbourhood, where he obtained the following terms of capitulation, which were signed by the commanding officer and two of the Cherokee chiefs. "That the garrison of Fort Loudon march out with their arms and drums, each soldier having as much powder and ball as their officer shall think necessary for their march, and all the baggage they may chuse to carry: That the garrison be permitted to march to Virginia, or Fort Prince George, as the commanding officer shall think proper, unmolested; and that a number of Indians be appointed to escort them, and hunt for provisions during their march: That such soldiers as are lame, or by sickness disabled from marching, be received into the Indian towns, and kindly used until they recover, and then be allowed to return to Fort Prince George: That the Indians do provide for the garrison as many horses as they conveniently can for their march, agreeing with the officers and soldiers for payment: That the fort great guns, powder, ball, and spare arms, be delivered to the Indians without fraud or further delay, on the day appointed for the march of the troops."

[Sidenote] Treacherously broken by the savages.

Agreeable to those terms stipulated, the garrison delivered up the fort, and marched out with their arms, accompanied by Occonostota, Judd's friend, the prince of Chote, and several other Indians, and that day went fifteen miles on their way to Fort Prince George. At night they encamped on a plain about two miles from Taliquo, an Indian town, when all their attendants, upon one pretence or another, left them; which the officers considered as no good sign, and therefore placed a strict guard round their camp. During the night they remained unmolested, but next morning about break of day a soldier from an out-post came running in, and informed them that he saw a vast number of Indians, armed, and painted in the most dreadful manner, creeping among the bushes, and advancing in order to surround them. Scarcely had the officer time to order his men to stand to their arms, when the savages poured in upon them a heavy fire from different quarters, accompanied with the most hideous yells, which struck a panic into the soldiers, who were so much enfeebled and dispirited that they were incapable of making any effectual resistance. Captain Demere, with three other officers, and about twenty-five private men, fell at the first onset. Some fled into the woods, and were afterwards taken prisoners and confined among the towns in the valley. Captain Stuart, and those that remained, were seized, pinioned, and brought back to Fort Loudon. No sooner had Attakullakulla heard that his friend Mr. Stuart had escaped, than he hastened to the fort, and purchased him from the Indian that took him, giving him his rifle, clothes, and all he could command, by way of ransom. He then took possession of Captain Demere's house, where he kept his prisoner as one of his family, and freely shared with him the little provisions his table afforded, until a fair opportunity should offer for rescuing him from their hands; but the poor soldiers were kept in a miserable state of captivity for some time, and then redeemed by the province at a great expence.

[Sidenote] A proposal for attacking Fort Prince George.

During the time these prisoners were confined at Fort Loudon, Occonostota formed a design of attacking Fort Prince George, and for this purpose dispatched a messenger to the settlements in the valley, requesting all the warriors there to join him at Stickoey old town. By accident a discovery was made of ten bags of powder, and ball in proportion, which the officers had secretly buried in the fort, to prevent their falling into the enemy's hands. This discovery had nearly proved fatal to Captain Stuart, and would certainly have cost him his life, had not the interpreter had so much presence of mind as to assure the enemy that these warlike stores had been concealed without his knowledge or consent. The Indians having now abundance of ammunition for the siege, a council was called at Chote, to which the captain was brought, and put in mind of the obligations he lay under to them for sparing his life; and as they had resolved to carry six cannon and two cohorns with them against Fort Prince George, to be managed by men under his command, they told him he must go and write such letters to the commandant as they should dictate to him. They informed him at the same time, that if that officer should refuse to surrender, they were determined to burn the prisoners one after another before his face, and try if he could be so obstinate as to hold out while he saw his friends expiring in the flames. Captain Stuart was much alarmed at his situation, and from that moment resolved to make his escape or perish in the attempt. His design he privately communicated to Attakullakulla, and told him how uneasy he was at the thoughts of being compelled to bear arms against his countrymen. He acknowledged that he had always been a brother, and hoped he would assist him to get out of his present perilous circumstances. The old warrior, taking him by the hand, told him he was his friend, he had already given one proof of his regard, and intended to give another so soon as his brother should return and help him to concert the measure. He said he was well apprized of the ill designs of his countrymen, and should he go and persuade the garrison of Fort Prince George to do as he had done, what could he expect but that they should share the same dismal fate. Strong and uncultivated minds carry their friendship, as well as their enmity, to an astonishing pitch. Among savages family friendship is a national virtue, and civilized mortals may blush when they consider how much barbarians have often surpassed them in the practice of it. The instance I am going to relate is as singular and memorable as many that have been recorded in the annals of past ages.

[Sidenote] Captain Stuart escapes to Virginia.

Attakullakulla claimed Captain Stuart as his prisoner, and had resolved to deliver him from danger and for this purpose there was no time to be lost. Accordingly he gave out among his countrymen that he intended to go a-hunting for a few days, and carry his prisoner along with him to eat venison, of which he declared he was exceedingly fond. At the same time the Captain went through among his soldiers, telling them that they could never expect to be ransomed by the province, if they gave the smallest assistance to the Indians against Fort Prince George. Having settled all matters, they set out on their journey, accompanied by the warrior's wife, his brother, and two soldiers, who were the only persons in the garrison that knew how to convey great guns through the woods. For provisions they depended on what they might kill by the way. The distance to the frontier settlements was great, and the utmost expedition necessary to prevent any surprize from Indians pursuing them. Nine days and nights did they travel through a dreary wilderness, shaping their course by the light of the sun and moon for Virginia, and traversing many hills, valleys and paths that had never been crossed before but by savages and wild beasts. On the tenth they arrived at the banks of Holston's river, where they fortunately fell in with a party of three hundred men, sent out by Colonel Bird for the relief of such soldiers as might make their escape that way from Fort Loudon. On the fourteenth day the Captain reached Colonel Bird's camp on the frontiers of Virginia, where having loaded his faithful friend with presents and provisions, he sent him back to protect the unhappy prisoners till they should be ransomed, and to exert his influence among the Cherokees for the restoration of peace.

No sooner had Captain Stuart made his escape from the hands of the savages, than he immediately began to concert ways and means for the relief of his garrison. An express was dispatched to Lieutenant-Governor Bull, informing him of the sad disaster that had happened to the garrison of Fort Loudon, and of the designs of the enemy against Fort Prince George. In consequence of which orders were given to Major Thomson, who commanded the militia on the frontiers, to throw in provisions for ten weeks into that fort, and warn the commanding officer of his danger. At the same time a messenger was sent to Attakullakulla desiring him to inform the Cherokees that Fort George was impregnable, having vast quantities of powder buried under ground every where around it, to blow up all enemies that should attempt to come near it. Presents of considerable value were sent to redeem the prisoners at Fort Loudon, a few of whom had by this time made their escape; and afterwards not only those that were confined among the towns in the valley, but also all that had survived the hardships of hunger, disease and captivity in the upper towns were released, and delivered up to the commanding officer at Fort Prince George.

[Sidenote] The war continues.

It might now have been expected that the vindictive spirit of the savages would be satisfied, and that they would he disposed to listen to some terms of accommodation. This treacherous conduct to the soldiers at Fort Loudon, they intended as a satisfaction for the harsh treatment their relations had met with at Fort Prince George; and dearly had the province paid for the base imprisonment and horrid massacre of the chiefs at that place. Still, however, a great majority of the nation spurned at every offer of peace. The lower towns had all been destroyed by Colonel Montgomery; the warriors in the middle settlements had lost many friends and relations; and several Frenchmen had crept in among the uppertowns, and helped to foment their ill humour against Carolina. Lewis Latinac, a French officer, was among them, and proved an indefatigable instigator to mischief. He persuaded the Indians that the English had nothing less in view than to exterminate them from the face of the earth; and, furnishing them with arms and ammunition, urged them on to war. At a great meeting of the nation he pulled out his hatchet, and, striking it into a log of wood, called out, Who is the man that will take this up for the King of France? Saloue, the young warrior of Estatoe, instantly laid hold of it, and cried out, "I am for war. The spirits of our brothers who have been slain still call upon us to avenge their death. He is no better than a woman that refuses to follow me." Many others seized the tomahawk, yet dyed in British blood, and burnt with impatience for the field.

[Sidenote] The Highlanders return to Carolina.

Under the flattering appearance of a calm were those clouds again gathering; however, Lieutenant-Governor Bull, who knew well how little Indians were to be trusted on any occasion, kept the Royal Scots and militia on the frontiers in a posture of defence. But finding the province still under the most dreadful apprehensions from their savage neighbours, who continued insolent and vindictive, and ready to renew their ravages and murders, he made application a second time to General Amherst for assistance. Canada being now reduced; the commander in chief could the more easily spare a force adequate to the purpose intended. The brave

Colonel Montgomery, who conducted the former expedition, having by this time embarked for England, the command of the Highlanders devolved on Lieutenant-Colonel James Grant, who received orders to return to the relief of Carolina. Early in the year 1761 he landed at Charlestown, where he took up his winter quarters, until the proper season should approach for taking the field. Unfortunately during this time many of the soldiers, by drinking brackish water, were taken sick, which afforded the inhabitants an opportunity of showing their kindness and humanity. They considered themselves, and with reason, under the strongest obligations to treat men with tenderness, who came to protect them against their enemies, and therefore they brought the sick soldiers into their houses, and nursed them with the greatest care and attention.

In this campaign the province determined to exert itself to the utmost, that, in conjunction with the regular forces, a severe correction might be given to those troublesome savages. For this purpose a provincial regiment was raised, and the command of it given to Colonel Middleton. Presents were provided for the Indian allies, and several of the Chickesaws and Catabaws engaged to assist them against the Cherokees. But the Creeks, whose help was also strongly solicited, played an artful game between the English and the French, and gave the one or the other encouragement, according to the advantages they reaped from them. All possible preparations were made for supplying the army with provisions at different stages, and with such carts and horses as were thought necessary to the expedition. Great had been the expence which this quarrel with the Cherokees had already occasioned; now they flattered themselves that by one resolute exertion more they would tire the savages of war, and oblige them to accept of such terms of peace as they thought proper to dictate.

As all white men in the province, of the military age, were soldiers as well as citizens, and trained in some measure to the use of arms, it was no difficult matter to complete the provincial regiment. Their names being registered in the list of militia; on every emergency they were obliged to be ready for defence, not only against the incursions of Indians, but also against the insurrection of negroes; and although the same prompt obedience to orders could not be expected from them that is necessary in a regular army, yet the provincials had other advantages which compensated for that defect. They were better acquainted than strangers with the woods, and the nature of that country in which their military service was required. They were seasoned to the climate, and had learned from experience what clothes, meat and drink were most proper to enable them to do their duty. In common occasions, when the militia was called out, the men received no pay, but when employed, as in this Cherokee war, for the public defence, they were allowed the same pay with the King's forces.

[Sidenote] Colonel Grant marches against the Cherokees.

So soon as the Highlanders had recovered from their sickness, and were in a condition to take the field, Colonel Grant began his march for the Cherokee territories. After being joined by the Provincial regiment and Indian allies, he mustered in all about two thousand six hundred men. Having served some years in America, and been in several engagements with Indians, he was now no stranger to their methods of making war. He was sensible how ready they were to take all advantages, by surprize, stratagem, or otherwise, that the nature of their country afforded them. Caution and vigilance were not only necessary on his part, but, to prepare an army for such services, the dress, the arms, and discipline, should all be adapted to the nature of the country, in order to give the men every advantage, according to the Indian manner of attack. The eye should be habituated to perpetual watchfulness, the body should be clothed in green, the prevailing colour of the woods, that it may be difficult to distinguish it, and equipped in such light armour as is easiest managed in a thicket. The feet and legs should be fortified against prickly briers and bushes, and those men who have been accustomed to hunt in the woods, being quick-sighted, are best qualified for scouring the dark thickets, and for guards to the main body. Europeans, who are strangers to such things, are ill prepared for military services in America. Many brave officers have suffered by inattention to them, and being ignorant of the peculiar circumstances of the country, have fallen a sacrifice to their own rashness, or the numberless snares to which they are exposed in it.

On the 27th of May, 1761, Colonel Grant arrived at Fort Prince George, and Attakullakulla, having got information that he was advancing against his nation with a formidable army, hastened to his camp, to signify his earnest desire of peace. He told the Colonel that he always had been, and ever would continue to be, a firm friend to the English; that the outrages of his countrymen covered him with shame, and filled his heart with grief; yet nevertheless he would gladly interpose in their behalf, in order to bring about an accommodation. Often, he said, had he been called an old woman by the mad young men of his nation, who delighted in war and despised his counsels. Often had he endeavoured to get the hatchet buried, and the former good correspondence with the Carolineans established. Now he was determined to set out for the Cherokee towns, to persuade them to consult their safety, and speedily agree to terms of peace, and again and again begged the Colonel to proceed no farther until he returned.

Colonel Grant, however, gave him no encouragement to expect that his request could be granted; but, on the 7th of June, began his march from Fort Prince George, carrying with him provisions to the army for thirty days. A party of ninety Indians, and thirty woodmen painted like Indians, under the command of Captain Quintine Kennedy, had orders to march in front and scour the woods. After them the light infantry and about fifty rangers, consisting in all of about two hundred men, followed, by whose vigilance and activity the commander imagined that the main body of the army might be kept tolerably quiet and secure. For three days he made forced marches, in order to get over two narrow and dangerous defiles, which he accomplished without a shot from the enemy, but which might have cost him dear, had they been properly guarded and warmly disputed. On the day following he found suspicious ground on all hands, and therefore orders were given for the first time to load and prepare for action, and the guards to march slowly forward, doubling their vigilance and circumspection. As they frequently spied Indians around them, all were convinced that they should that day have an engagement. At length, having advanced near to the place where Colonel Montgomery was attacked the year before, the Indian allies in the van-guard, about eight in the morning, observed a large body of Cherokees posted upon a hill on the right flank of the army, and gave the alarm. Immediately the savages, rushing down, began to fire on the advanced guard, which being supported, the enemy were repulsed, and recovered their heights. Under this hill the line was obliged to march a considerable way. On the left there was a river, from the opposite banks of which a large party of Indians fired briskly on the troops as they advanced. Colonel Grant ordered a party to march up the hill and drive the enemy from the heights, while the line faced about and gave their whole charge to the Indians that annoyed them from the side of the river. The engagement became general, and the savages seemed determined obstinately to dispute the lower grounds, while those on the hill were dislodged only to return with redoubled ardour to the charge. The situation of the troops was in several respects deplorable; fatigued by a tedious march, in rainy weather, surrounded with woods, so that they could not discern the enemy, galled by the scattered fire of savages, who when pressed always kept aloof, but rallied again and again, and returned to the ground. No sooner did the army gain an advantage over them in one quarter, than they appeared in another. While the attention of the commander was occupied in driving the enemy from their lurking-place on the river's side, the rear was attacked, and so vigorous an effort made for the flour and cattle, that he was obliged to order a party back to the relief of the rear-guard. From eight o'clock in the morning until eleven the savages continued to keep up an irregular and incessant fire, sometimes from one place and sometimes from another, while the woods resounded with hideous shouts and yells, to intimidate the troops. At length the Cherokees gave way, and, being pursued for some time, popping shots continued till two o'clock, when they disappeared. What loss the enemy sustained in this action we have not been able to learn, but of Colonel Grant's army there were between fifty and sixty men killed and wounded; and it is probable the loss of the savages could not be much greater, and perhaps not so great, owing to their manner of fighting. Orders were given not to bury the slain, but to sink them in the river, to prevent their being dug up from their graves and scalped. To provide horses for those that were wounded, several bags of flour were thrown into the river. After which the army proceeded to Etchoe, a pretty large Indian town, which they reached about midnight, and next day reduced to ashes. Every other town in the middle settlements, fourteen in number, shared the same fate. Their magazines and corn fields were likewise destroyed, and those miserable savages, with their families, were driven to seek for shelter and provisions among the barren mountains.

It would be no easy matter to describe the various hardships which this little army endured in the wilderness, from heat, thirst, watching, danger and fatigue. Thirty days did Colonel Grant continue in the heart of the Cherokee territories, and, upon his return to Fort Prince George, the feet and legs of many of his army were so mangled, and their strength and spirits so much exhausted, that they were utterly unable to march farther. He resolved therefore to encamp at that place for a while, both to refresh his men and wait the resolutions of the Cherokees, in consequence of the heavy chastisement which they had received. Besides the numberless advantages their country afforded for defence, it was supposed that some French officers had been among them, and given them all the assistance in their power. It is true the savages supported their attack for some hours with considerable spirit; but being driven from their advantageous posts and thickets they were wholly disconcerted, and though the repulse was far from being decisive, yet after this engagement they returned no more to the charge, but remained the tame spectators of their towns in flames, and their country laid desolate.

Such engagements in Europe would be considered as trifling skirmishes, scarcely worthy of relation, but in America a great deal is often determined by them. It is no easy matter to describe the distress to which the savages were reduced by this severe correction. Even in time of peace they are destitute of that foresight, in a great measure, which provides for future events; but in time of war, when their villages are destroyed and their fields laid desolate, they are reduced to extreme want. Being driven to the barren mountains, the hunters furnished with ammunition might indeed make some small provision for themselves, but women, children, and old men, must perish, being deprived of the means of subsistence.

[Sidenote] Peace with the Cherokees

A few days after Colonel Grant's arrival at Fort Prince George, Attakullakulla, attended by several chieftains, came to his camp, and expressed a desire of peace. Severely had they suffered for breaking their alliance with Britain, and giving ear to the deceitful promises of France. Convinced at last of the weakness and perfidy of the French, who were neither able to assist them in time of war, nor supply their wants in time of peace, they resolved to renounce all connection with them for ever. Accordingly terms of peace were drawn up and proposed, which were no less honourable to Colonel Grant than advantageous to the province. The different articles being read and interpreted, Attakullakulla agreed to them all excepting one, by which it was demanded, That four Cherokee Indians be delivered up to Colonel Grant at Fort Prince George, to be put to death in the front of his camp; or four green scalps be brought to him in the space of twelve nights. The warrior having no authority from his nation, declared he could not agree to this article, and therefore the Colonel sent him to Charlestown, to see whether the Lieutenant-Governor would consent to mitigate the rigour of it.

Accordingly Attakullakulla and the other chieftains, being furnished with a safeguard, set out for Charlestown to hold a conference with Mr. Bull, who, on their arrival, called a council to meet at Ashley Ferry, and then spoke to the following effect. "Attakullakulla, I am glad to see you, and as I have always heard of your good behaviour, that you have been a good friend to the English, I take you by the hand, and not only you but all those with you also, as a pledge for their security whilst under my protection. Colonel Grant acquaints me that you have applied for peace; now that you are come, I have met with my beloved men to hear what you have to say, and my ears are open for that purpose." Then a fire was kindled, the pipe of peace was lighted, and all smoked together for some time in great silence and solemnity.

Then Attakullakulla arose, and addressed the Lieutenant-Governor and Council to the following effect. "It is a great while since I last saw your honour; now I am glad to see you, and all the beloved men present—I am come to you as a messenger from the whole nation—I have now seen you, smoked with you, and hope we shall live together as brothers.—When

I came to Keowee, Colonel Grant sent me to you—You live at the water side, and are in light—We are in darkness, but hope all will be yet clear with us.—I have been constantly going about doing good, and though I am tired, yet I am come to see what can be done for my people, who are in great distress." Here he produced the strings of wampum he had received from the different towns, denoting their earnest desire of peace; and then added, "As to what has happened, I believe it has been ordered by our Father above.—We are of a different colour from the white people—They are superior to us—But one God is father of all, and we hope what is past will be forgotten.—God Almighty made all people—There is not a day but some are coming into, and others are going out of, the world.—The great King told me the path should never be crooked, but open for every one to pass and repass.—As we all live in one land, I hope we shall all live as one people." After which peace was formally ratified and confirmed by both parties, and their former friendship being renewed, all hoped that it would last as long as the sun shall shine and the rivers run.

[Sidenote] A quarrel between the commanding officers.

Thus ended the Cherokee war, which was among the last humbling strokes given to the expiring power of France in North America, and Colonel Grant returned to Charlestown to wait further orders. But no sooner was peace concluded, and the province secured against external enemies, than an unhappy difference broke out between the two principal commanders of the regular and provincial forces. Colonel Grant, a native of Scotland, was naturally of an high spirit, to which he added that pride of rank which he held among those British soldiers who had carried their arms triumphant through the continent. During this expedition it is probable that he scorned to ask the advice of a provincial officer, whom he deemed an improper judge of military operations, and claimed the chief glory of having restored peace to the province. Colonel Middleton was equally warm and proud, and considering such neglect as an affront, resented it, and while some reflections were cast upon the provincial troops, being the chief in command, he thought himself bound to stand forth as a champion for the honour of the province. This ill-humour, which appeared between the officers on their return to Charlestown, was encouraged and fomented by persons delighting in broils, who, by malicious surmises and false reports, helped to widen the difference. The dispute became serious, and was carried on for some time in the public papers by mutual charges of misconduct, and at length terminated in a duel. Mr. Middleton called out Colonel Grant to the single combat, after they had both given the best proof of their courage against the common enemy. The duel, however, happily terminated without bloodshed, and not a little to the credit of the Scots officer, though his antagonist shewed no less spirit in the field of honour, falsely so called, than in defence of his country. The citizens of Charlestown seemed interested in the dispute, and each spoke of the conduct of the two officers as they were differently affected. Indeed, however much we may applaud the brave man who is first in the field in defence of his country, with justice we with-hold our praises from him that is first at the single combat with a private friend. Colonel Grant, with great reason, considered such treatment, after having brought the enemies of the colony to the most advantageous terms of peace, as a base recompence for his services. From this period a party-spirit appeared in Carolina. All the malicious aspersions and inflammatory accusations against the inhabitants of North Britain, which were at this time wantonly and wickedly published in England, were greedily swallowed by one party in the province, and industriously propagated. Prejudices were contracted, cherished, and unhappily gained ground among the people. Terms of reproach and abuse were collected from those factious publications in London, and poured indiscriminately upon all the natives of Scotland, who were by no means backward in retorting the abuse. In a growing province, where the utmost harmony and liberality of sentiment ought to have been cherished by all, as the most certain means of promoting the public strength and prosperity, such a party-spirit was attended, as might have been expected, with the most pernicious consequence.

[Sidenote] A whirlwind at Charlestown.

I have already observed, that the province is subject to whirlwinds, especially among the hills in the back country; but this year one of those, which was indeed the most violent and dreadful that had ever been known, passed Charlestown in the month of May. It appeared at first to the west of the town, like a large column of smoke, approaching fast in an irregular direction. The vapour of which it was composed resembled clouds rolling one over another in violent tumult and agitation, assuming at one time a dark, at another a bright flaming colour. Its motion was exceedingly swift and crooked. As it approached the inhabitants were alarmed with an uncommon sound, like the continual roaring of distant thunder, or the noise made by a stormy sea beating upon the shore, which brought numbers of people to witness the dreadful phenomenon. While it passed down Ashley river, such was its incredible velocity and force, that it plowed the waters to the bottom, and laid the channel bare. The town narrowly and providentially escaped, but it threatened destruction to a fleet consisting of no less than forty sail of loaded ships, lying at anchor in Rebellion road, about four miles below the town, and waiting a fair wind to sail for England. When it reached the fleet, five vessels were sunk in an instant by it, and his Majesty's ship the Dolphin, with eleven others, were dismasted. Such was the situation of the fleet, and so rapid was the motion of the whirlwind, that though the seaman observed it approaching, it was impossible to provide against it. In its oblique course it struck only a part of the fleet, and the damage, though computed at L. 20,000 sterling, was by no means so great as might have been expected. Nor were many lives lost, for the channel of the river not being very deep, while the ships sat down in the mud and were covered by the waves, the sailors saved themselves by running up the shrouds. The whirlwind passed the town a little before three o'clock, and before four the sky was so clear and serene, that we could scarcely have believed such a dreadful scene had been exhibited, had it not left many striking proofs behind it. Its route was not only marked in the woods, having levelled the loftiest trees, or swept them away before it like chaff, but its effects were visible in the fleet, by the number of vessels sunk and dismasted.

It has been also remarked, that the province is subject to violent storms of lightning and thunder throughout the year; but from the end of April until October they are very frequent and terrible. There are few nights during the summer in which lighting is not visible in some part of the horizon. Sometimes indeed those storms are of short duration, particularly when they come attended with brisk gales of wind; but when that is not the case, they will often last for four or five hours. While the clouds are gathering, it is surprising how quickly the atmosphere, which was formerly serene, will be covered with darkness. To the inhabitants, accustomed to view such appearances, the thunder-shower is rather welcome than alarming, as it cools the air and earth, and enables them to live comfortably during the remainder of the day; but to every stranger it is exceedingly grand and awful. As the flashes of lightning from the clouds commonly strike the highest objects, and the whole country is covered with woods, the fury of the storm for the most part falls upon them, and its amazing effects are visible from the vast number of blasted trees every where appearing throughout the forest. The country being as yet but thinly peopled, the inhabitants do not suffer so severely as might be expected, considering the violence of these storms; yet few years pass without some accidents from lightning. I never knew more than five houses in the town, but others have observed nine, two churches and five ships struck with lightning during one thunder-shower. Such storms often occasion considerable damage, particularly to the ships in the harbour, and sometimes they are attended with showers of hail, or rather solid pieces of ice, which fall with such force as to beat down the corn in the fields, to break glass windows, and occasion danger to children exposed to them. But since the inhabitants have found out the method of erecting iron rods on their houses, less damage has been done to them, and fewer lives have been lost by lightning in this province.

The climate of Georgia, like that of Carolina, is more mild and pleasant in the inland than maritime parts. Governor Ellis has left us the following account of the heat of the summer at Savanna. In the 7th of July, while he was writing in his piazza, which was open at each end, he says the mercury in Fahrenheit's thermometer stood at 102 in the shade. Twice had it risen to that height during the summer, several times to 100, and for many days together to 98; and in the night did not sink below 89. He thought it highly probable, that the inhabitants of Savanna breathed a hotter air than any other people upon earth. The town being situated on a sandy eminence, the reflection from the dry sand, when there is little or no agitation in the air, greatly increases the heat; for by walking an hundred yards from his house upon the sand, under his umbrella, with the thermometer suspended by a thread to the height of his nostrils, the mercury rose to 105. The same thermometer he had with him in the equatorial parts of Africa, in Jamaica, and in the Leeward Islands; yet by his journals he found that it had never in any of these places risen so high. Its general station was between 79 and 86. He acknowledges, however, that he felt those degrees of heat in a moist air more disagreeable than at Savanna, when the thermometer stood at 81 in his cellar, at 102 in the storey above it, and in the upper storey of his house at 105. On the 10th of December the mercury was up at 86, on then 11th down as low as 38, on the same instrument. Such sudden and violent changes, especially when they happen frequently, must make havock of the human constitution; yet he asserts that few people die at Savanna out of the ordinary course, though many were working in the open air, exposed to the sun during this extreme heat.—As this governor was a man of sense and erudition, and no doubt made his observations with great accuracy, we shall not presume to call in question the facts he relates; but we must say, we never saw the mercury rise so high in the shade at Charlestown, and believe it very seldom happens to do so in Georgia. We may add, that such is the situation of Savanna, surrounded with low and marshy lands, and so sudden and great are the changes in the weather there, as well as in Carolina, that the maritime parts of both provinces must be ranked among the most unhealthy climates in the world.

CHAPTER XI

The peace of Paris, though condemned by many in England as inadequate to the amazing success that attended the British arms during the bloody war, and below the expectation of the British nation, unquestionably placed America in the most advantageous situation. As the flames of war first kindled in that continent, by a contest about the limits of the British and French territories, to prevent all disputes of this kind for the future was made one of the first objects of attention in framing a treaty of peace. By the seventh article of this treaty it was agreed, "That, for the future, the confines between the dominions of his Britannic Majesty and those of his most Christian Majesty in that part of the world should be fixed irrevocably, by a line drawn along the middle of the river Mississippi, from its source to the river Iberville, and from thence by a line drawn along the middle of the river and the lakes Maurepas and Pontchartrain to the sea." By the twentieth article, "His Catholic Majesty ceded and guarantied in full right to his Britannic Majesty, Florida, with Fort Augustine and the Bay of Pensacola, as well as all that Spain possessed on the continent of North America to the east or south-east of the river Mississippi, and in general every thing depending on the said countries and lands, with the sovereignty, property, possession, and all rights acquired by treaties or otherwise, which the Catholic King and the Crown of Spain have had till now over the said countries, lands, places, and other inhabitants." By these articles the southern provinces were rendered perfectly secure, and, considering the nature of the country, no frontiers could be more distinctly defined.

But as the French colonies in the northern district had been the chief seat of war, the conquest of which had occasioned such an immense waste of blood and treasure to Britain, it was also judged proper to guard against the return of any danger on that side. Experience had shewn the nation, that while France possesses a single stronghold on that continent, the British subjects could never enjoy perfect repose, but must be in danger of being again plunged into those calamities from which they had been with so much difficulty delivered. Therefore it was determined to remove this ambitious and enterprising enemy entirely from the neighbourhood of these colonies, and secure them beyond a possibility of future molestation. Accordingly, by the fourth article of the treaty, "His most Christian Majesty renounced all pretensions which he had heretofore formed, or might form, to Nova Scotia, or Acadia, in all its parts, and guarantied the whole of it, with all its dependencies, to the King of Great Britain; as also Canada, with all its dependencies; Cape Breton, and all the other islands and coasts in the Gulf of St. Laurence, and every thing that depends on these countries, islands, lands, places and coasts, and their inhabitants; so that the most Christian King ceded and made over the whole to the said King and Crown of Great Britain, and that in the most ample manner and form, without restriction, and without any liberty to depart from said cession and guaranty under any pretence, or to disturb Great Britain in the possessions above mentioned; reserving only the island of New Orleans, and liberty of fishing in the Gulf of St. Laurence, which was granted, upon condition that the subjects of France do not execute the said fishery but at the distance of three leagues from all the coasts belonging to Great Britain, as well those of the continent as those of the islands situated in the Gulf of St. Laurence."

We do not pretend to pass any judgment on the value of these conquests in America, which were preferred to those of the West India islands at the peace. By giving up a little of the sugar trade, it was thought the nation lost only a luxury, and could be sufficiently supplied with all the sugar and rum she wanted from the islands which she possessed before the war; and therefore the precious conquests in the West Indies were sacrificed to the security of America. The vast territory to the east and south east of the great river Mississippi formed the British empire on the continent, which, for variety of climate as well as of soil was exceeded by no empire upon earth. As the trade of the mother country had uniformly increased with the population of her colonies, it was hoped that by freeing them from all molestation, they must increase in a still more rapid manner than they had hitherto done, to the great advantage of Britain; for while the colonists had liberty to extend their culture to the remotest desert, the trade of the mother country would be increased, her debt diminished, and at the same time the demand for manufactures would be so great, that all the hands she employed would scarcely be able to furnish the supply. These were thought to be the probable consequences which would flow from the security of our American colonies at the peace.

[Sidenote] Boundaries of East and West Florida.

With respect to the new acquisitions, great pains were taken to acquire an exact knowledge of them, not only to establish proper regulations, but also to render them as useful and flourishing as possible. They were divided into three separate independent governments, which were given to officers who had distinguished themselves during the war. The government of East Florida was bounded to the westward by the Gulf of Mexico and the river Apalachicola; to the north by a line drawn from that part of the above-mentioned river where the Catabouchee and Flint rivers meet, to the source of St. Mary's river, and by the course of the same river to the Atlantic Ocean; and to the east and south by the Atlantic Ocean; and the Gulf of Florida, including all islands within six leagues of the sea coast. The government of West Florida was bounded to the southward by the Gulf of Mexico, including all islands within six leagues of the sea coast, from the river Apalachicola to Lake Pontchartrain; to the westward by the said lake, the lake Maurepas, and the river Mississippi; to the north by a line drawn due east from that part of the river Mississippi which lies in thirty-one degrees of north latitude, to the river Apalachicola, or Catabouchee; and to the east by the said river. All the lands lying between the rivers Alatamaha and St. Mary's were annexed to the province of Georgia.

[Sidenote] The southern provinces left secure.

The possession of these two provinces of East and West Florida, though of themselves little better than an immense waste, was of great importance to the neighbouring provinces of Georgia and Carolina. It robbed the Spaniards of a strong-hold from which they could send out an armed force and harass these provinces, and of an easy avenue through which they had often invaded them. It removed troublesome neighbours out of their way, who had often instigated the savages against them, and made Augustine an asylum for fugitive slaves. It opened some convenient ports for trade with Britain and the West Indies, and for annoying French and Spanish ships coming through the Gulf of Florida, in case of any future rupture. It formed a strong frontier to the British dominions in that quarter, and furnished an immense track of improveable land for reduced officers, soldiers, and others, to settle and cultivate.

[Sidenote] Encouragement given to reduced officers and soldiers.

To testify the high sense his Majesty had of the conduct and bravery of his officers and soldiers during the late war, and to encourage the settlement of the colonies, tracks of land were offered them as the rewards of their services. Orders were given to the governors on the continent, to grant, without fee or reward, five thousand acres to every field officer who had served in America, three thousand to every captain, two thousand to every subaltern, two hundred to every non-commissioned officer, and fifty to every private man; free of quit-rents for ten years, but subject, at the expiration of that term, to the same moderate quit-rents as the lands in the other provinces, and to the same conditions of cultivation and improvement.

In the new colonies, for the encouragement of the people, they were to be allowed civil establishments, similar to those of the other royal governments on the continent, so soon as their circumstances would admit, and the same provision was made for the security of their lives, liberties and properties under the new as under the old governments.

[Sidenote] Georgia begins to flourish.

No province on the continent felt the happy effects of this public security sooner than the province of Georgia, which had long struggled under many difficulties, arising from the want of credit from friends, and the frequent molestations of enemies. During the late war the government had been given to James Wright, who wanted neither wisdom to discern, nor resolution to pursue, the most effectual means for its improvement. While he proved a father to the people and governed the province with justice and equity, he discovered at the same time the excellence of its low lands and river swamps, by the proper management and diligent cultivation of which he acquired in a few years a plentiful fortune. His example and success gave vigour to industry, and promoted a spirit of emulation among the planters for improvement. The rich lands were sought for with that zeal, and cleared with that ardour, which the prospect of riches naturally inspired. The British merchants observing the province safe, and advancing to a hopeful and flourishing state, were no longer backward in extending credit to it, but supplied it with negroes, and goods of British manufacture, with equal freedom as the other provinces on that continent. The planters no sooner got the strength of Africa to assist them than they laboured with success, and the lands every year yielded greater and greater increase. The trade of the province kept pace with its progress in cultivation. The rich swamps attracted the attention not only of strangers, but even of the planters of Carolina, who had been accustomed to treat their poor neighbours with the utmost contempt, several of whom sold their estates in that colony, and moved with their families and effects to Georgia. Many settlements were made by Carolineans about Sunbury, and upon the great river Alatamaha. The price of produce at Savanna arose as the quantity increased, a circumstance which contributed much to the improvement of the country. The planters situated on the opposite side of Savanna river found in the capital of Georgia a convenient and excellent market for their staple commodities. In short, from this period the rice, indigo and naval stores of Georgia arrived at the markets in Europe in equal excellence and perfection, and, in proportion to its strength, in equal quantities with those of its more powerful and opulent neighbours in Carolina. To form a judgment of the progress of the colony, we need only attend to its exports. In the year 1763, the exports of Georgia consisted of 7500 barrels of rice, 9633 libs. of indigo, 1250 bushels of Indian corn, which, together with deer and beaver skins, naval stores, provisions, timber, &c. amounted to no more than L. 27,021 sterling; but afterwards the colony thrived and increased in a manner so rapid, that, in the year 1773, it exported staple commodities to the value of L. 121,677 sterling.

[Sidenote] A plan adopted for encouraging emigrations to Carolina.

No less favourable and happy were the blessings of peace and security to their neighbours of Carolina; for never did any country flourish and prosper in a more astonishing degree than this province has done since the conclusion of the late war. The government had been given to Thomas Boone, who was not only a native of the province, but had a considerable estate in it, which naturally rendered him deeply interested in its prosperity. The French and Spaniards being removed out of the way, its progress was no more retarded by any molestation from them. The assembly appropriated a large fund for bounties to foreign Protestants, and such industrious poor people of Britain and Ireland as should resort to the province within three years, and settle on the inland parts. Two townships, each containing 48,000 acres, were laid out; one on the river Savanna, called Mecklenburgh, and the other on the waters of Santee at Long Canes, called Londonderry; to be divided among emigrants, allowing one hundred acres for every man, and fifty for every woman and child, that should come and settle in the back woods. The face of the country in those interior parts is variable and beautiful, and being composed of hills and vallies, rocks and rivers, there is not that stagnation in the air, which is so exceedingly hurtful to the human constitution in the flat marshy parts of the province. The hills occasion an agitation in the atmosphere, and by collecting the air in streams, these run along the earth in pleasant breezes, and mitigate the rigour of the hot season. The climate in those inland parts is not only more mild and wholesome, but the soil, particularly in the vallies, which are covered with lofty trees and luxuriant bushes, is exceedingly fertile, and promised in the amplest manner to reward the industrious labourer. In consequence of this encouragement offered, it was hoped that multitudes would resort to Carolina, and settle those extensive and fruitful territories in the back woods, by which means the frontiers of the province would be strengthened, its produce increased, and its trade enlarged.

[Sidenote] A number of Palatines seduced into England.

Not long after this a remarkable affair happened in Germany, by which Carolina received a great acquisition. One Stumpel, who had been an officer in the King of Prussia's service, being reduced at the peace, applied to the British ministry for a tract of land in America, and having got some encouragement returned to Germany, where, by deceitful promises, he seduced between five and six hundred ignorant people from their native country. When these poor Palatines arrived in England, the officer finding himself unable to perform his promises, fled, leaving them in a strange land, without money, without friends, exposed in the open fields, and ready to perish through want. While they were in this starving condition, and knew no person to whom they could apply for relief, a humane clergyman, who came from the same country, took compassion on them, and published their deplorable case in the news-papers. He pleaded for the mercy and protection of government to them, until an opportunity might offer of transporting them to some of the British colonies, where he hoped they would prove useful subjects, and in time give their benefactors ample proofs of their gratitude and affection. No sooner did their unhappy situation reach the ears of a great personage, than he immediately set an example to his subjects, which served both to warm their hearts and open their hands for the relief of their distressed fellow-creatures. A bounty of three hundred pounds was allowed them; tents were ordered from the Tower for the accommodation of such as had paid their passage and been permitted to come ashore; money was sent for the relief of those that were confined on board. The public-spirited citizens of London, famous for acts of beneficence and charity, associated, and chose a committee on purpose to raise money for the relief of these poor Palatines. A physician, a surgeon, and man-midwife, generously undertook to attend the sick gratis. From different quarters benefactions were sent to the committee, and in a few days those unfortunate strangers, from the depth of indigence and distress, were raised to comfortable circumstances. The committee finding the money received more than sufficient to relieve their present distress, applied to his Majesty to know his royal pleasure with respect to the future disposal of the German Protestants. His Majesty, sensible that his colony of South Carolina had not its proportion of white inhabitants, and having expressed a particular attachment to it, signified his desire of transporting them to that province. Another motive for sending them to Carolina was the bounty allowed to foreign Protestants by the provincial assembly, so that when their source of relief from England should be exhausted, another would open after their arrival in that province, which would help them to surmount the difficulties attending the first state of cultivation.

[Sidenote] Sent into Carolina.

Accordingly preparations were made for sending the Germans to South Carolina. When the news was communicated to them they rejoiced, not only because they were to go to one of the most fertile and flourishing provinces on the continent, but also because many of them had friends and countrymen before them. Two ships, of two hundred tons each, were provided for their accommodation, and provisions of all kinds laid in for the voyage. An hundred and fifty stand of arms were ordered from the Tower, and given them by his Majesty for their defence after their arrival in America; all which deserve to be recorded for the honour of the British nation, which has at different times set before the world many noble examples of benevolence. Every thing being ready for their embarkation, the Palatines broke up their camp in the fields behind White-Chapel, and proceeded to the ships attended by several of their benefactors; of whom they took their leave with songs of praise to God in their mouths, and tears of gratitude in their eyes.

[Sidenote] And settled at Londonderry.

In the month of April, 1764, they arrived at Charlestown, and presented a letter from the Lords Commissioners for Trade and Plantations to Governor Boone, acquainting him that his Majesty had been pleased to take the poor Palatines under his royal care and protection, and as many of them were versed in the culture of silks and vines, had ordered that a settlement be provided for them in Carolina, in a situation most proper for these purposes. Though their settlement met with some obstructions from a dispute subsisting at that time between the Governor and Assembly about certain privileges of the house; yet the latter could not help considering themselves as laid under the strongest obligations to make provision for so many useful settlers. Accordingly, in imitation of the noble example set before them in London, they voted five hundred pounds sterling to be distributed among the Palatines, according to the directions of the Lieutenant-Governor, and their necessities. That they might be settled in a body, one of the two townships, called Londonderry, was allotted for them, and divided in the most equitable manner into small tracts, for the accommodation of each family. Captain Calhoun, with a detachment of the rangers, had orders to meet them by the way, and conduct them to the place where their town was to be built, and all possible assistance was given towards promoting their speedy and comfortable settlement.

[Sidenote] Some emigrate from Britain, and multitudes from Ireland.

Besides foreign Protestants, several persons from England and Scotland resorted to Carolina after the peace. But of all other countries none has furnished the province with so many inhabitants as Ireland. In the northern counties of that kingdom the spirit of emigration seized the people to such a degree, that it threatened almost a total depopulation. Such multitudes of husbandmen, labourers and manufacturers flocked over the Atlantic, that the landlords began to be alarmed, and to concert ways and means for preventing the growing evil. Scarce a ship sailed for any of the plantations that was not crowded with men, women and children. But the bounty allowed new settlers in Carolina proved a great encouragement, and induced numbers of these people, notwithstanding the severity of the climate, to resort to that province. The merchants finding this bounty equivalent to the expenses of the passage, from avaricious motives persuaded the people to embark for Carolina, and often crammed such numbers of them into their ships that they were in danger of being stifled during the passage, and sometimes were landed in such a starved and sickly condition, that numbers of them died before they left Charlestown. Many causes may be assigned for this spirit of emigration that prevailed so much in Ireland: some, no doubt, emigrated from a natural restlessness of temper, and a desire of roving abroad, without any fixed object in view. Others were enticed over by flattering promises from their friends and relations, who had gone before them. But of all other causes of emigration oppression at home was the most powerful and prevalent. Most men have a natural fondness and partiality for their native country, and leave it with reluctance while they are able to earn a comfortable livelihood in it. That spot where they first drew the breath of life, that society in which they spent the gay season of youth, the religion, the manners and customs of those among whom they were educated, all conspire to affect the heart, and endear their native country to them. But poverty and oppression will break through every natural tie and endearment, and compel men to rove abroad in search of some asylum against domestic hardship. Hence it happened that many poor people forsook their native land, and preferred the burning sky and unwholesome climate of Carolina, to the temperate and mild air of their mother country. The success that attended some friends who had gone before them being also industriously published in Ireland, and with all the exaggerations of travellers, gave vigour to the spirit of adventure, and induced multitudes to follow their countrymen, and run all hazards abroad, rather than starve at home. Government winked at those emigrations, and every year brought fresh strength to Carolina, insomuch that the lands in Ireland were in danger of lying waste for want of labourers, and the manufacturers of dwindling into nothing.

[Sidenote] And from the northern colonies, resort to Carolina.

Nor were these the only sources from which Carolina, at this time, derived strength and an increase of population. For, notwithstanding the vast extent of territory which the provinces of Virginia and Pennsylvania contained, yet such was the nature of the country, that a scarcity of improveable lands began to be felt in these colonies, and poor people could not find spots in them unoccupied equal to their expectations. Most of the richest vallies in these more populous provinces lying to the east of the

Alleganny mountains were either under patent or occupied, and, by the royal proclamation at the peace, no settlements were allowed to extend beyond the sources of the rivers which empty themselves into the Atlantic. In Carolina the case was different, for there large tracks of the best lands as yet lay waste, which proved a great temptation to the northern colonists to migrate to the south. Accordingly, about this time above a thousand families, with their effects, in the space of one year resorted to Carolina, driving their cattle, hogs and horses over land before them. Lands were allotted them on the frontiers, and most of them being only entitled to small tracks, such as one, two or three hundred acres, the back settlements by this means soon became the most populous parts of the province. The frontiers were not only strengthened and secured by new settlers, but the old ones on the maritime parts began also to stretch backward and spread their branches, in consequence of which the demand for lands in the interior parts every year increased. The Governor and Council met once a-month for the purpose of granting lands and signing patents, and it is incredible what numbers of people attended those meetings in order to obtain them; so that; from the time in which America was secured by the peace, Carolina made rapid progress in population, wealth and trade, which will farther appear when we come particularly to consider its advanced state and annual exports.

[Sidenote] Regulations for securing the provinces against Indians.

In proportion as the province increased in the number of white inhabitants, its danger from the savage tribes grew less alarming. But to prevent any molestation from Indians, and establish the peace of the colonies on the most lasting foundation, his Majesty, by his royal proclamations after the peace, took care to fix the boundaries of their hunting lands, in as clear a manner as the nature of the country would admit. No settlements were allowed to extend any farther backward upon the Indian territories, than the sources of those great rivers which fall into the Atlantic Ocean, and all British subjects who had settled beyond these limits were ordered to remove. In this restriction his Majesty evidently made a distinction between the rights of sovereignty and those of property; having excluded his governors from all manner of jurisdiction over those lands which were not specified within the limits of their respective provinces. All private subjects were prohibited from purchasing lands from Indians; but if the latter should at any time be inclined to dispose of their property, it must for the future be done to the King, by the general consent of their nation, and at a public assembly held by British governors for that purpose. All traders were obliged to take out licences from their respective governors for carrying on commerce with Indian nations.

[Sidenote] John Stuart made superintendant for Indian affairs.

Such regulations were in many respects useful and necessary; for the French and Spaniards being excluded, it only remained to guard the provinces against the danger arising from Indians. And as they were liable to much abuse and oppression from private traders, it was thought necessary that the office of a superintendant should be continued for the southern as well as the northern district of America. Accordingly this office was given to Captain John Stuart, who was in every respect well qualified for the trust. Attakullakulla had signified to the Governor and Council, after the Cherokee war, that the province would receive no molestation from Indians were this officer appointed to reside among them, and to advise and direct them. The Assembly had not only thanked him for his good conduct and great perseverance at Fort Loudon, and rewarded him with fifteen hundred pounds currency, but also recommended him to the Governor as a person worthy of preferment in the service of the province. After his commission arrived from the King, the Carolineans rejoiced, and promised themselves for the future great tranquillity and happiness. Plans of lenity were likewise adopted by government with respect to those Indian tribes, and every possible precaution was taken to guard them against oppression, and prevent any rupture with them. Experience had shewn that rigorous measures, such as humbling them by force of arms, were not only very expensive and bloody, but disagreeable to a humane and generous nation, and seldom accompanied with any good effects. Such ill treatment rendered the savages cruel, suspicious and distrustful, and prepared them for renewing hostilities, by keeping alive their ferocious and warlike spirit. Their extirpation, even though it could easily be compleated, would be a cruel act, and all the while the growth and prosperity of the settlements would be much retarded by the attempt. Whereas, by treating Indians with gentleness and humanity, it was thought they would by degrees lose their savage spirit, and become more harmless and civilized. It was hoped that by establishing a fair and free trade with them, their rude temper would in time be softened, their manners altered, and their wants increased; and instead of implacable enemies, ever bent on destruction, they might he rendered good allies, both useful and beneficial to the trade of the nation.

[Sidenote] Decrease of Indians, and the causes of it.

It has been remarked, that those Indians on the continent of America, who were at the time of its discovery a numerous and formidable people, have since that period been constantly decreasing, and melting away like snow upon the mountains. For this rapid depopulation many reasons have been assigned. It is well known that population every where keeps pace with the means of subsistence. Even vegetables spring and grow in proportion to the richness of the soil in which they are planted, and to the supplies they receive from the nourishing rains and dews of heaven; animals flourish or decay according as the means of subsistence abound or fail; and as all mankind partake of the nature of both, they also multiply or decrease as they are fed, or have provision in plenty, luxury excluded. The Indians being driven from their possessions near the sea as the settlements multiplied, were robbed of many necessaries of life, particularly of oysters, crabs, and fish, with which the maritime parts furnished them in great abundance, and on which they must have considerably subsisted, as is apparent from a view of their camps, still remaining near the sea-shore. The women are not only much disregarded and despised, but also naturally less prolific among rude than polished nations. The men being often abroad, at hunting or war, agriculture, which is the chief means of subsistence among a civilized people, is entirely neglected by them, and looked upon as an occupation worthy only of women or slaves. That abstinence and fatigue which the men endure in their distant excursions, and that gluttony and voraciousness in which they indulge themselves in the times of plenty, are equally hurtful to the constitution, and productive of diseases of different kinds. Now that their territories are circumscribed by narrower bounds, the means of subsistence derived even from game is less plentiful. Indeed scanty and limited are the provisions they raise by planting, even in the best seasons; but in case of a failure of their crops, or of their fields being destroyed by enemies, they perish in numbers by famine. Their natural passion for war the first European settlers soon discovered; and therefore turned the fury of one tribe against another, with a view to save themselves. When engaged in hostilities, they always fought not so much to humble and conquer, as to exterminate and destroy. The British, the French and Spanish nations, having planted colonies in their neighbourhood, a rivalship for power over them took place, and each nation having its allies among the savages was zealous and indefatigable in instigating them against the allies of its neighbour. Hence a series of bloody and destructive wars has been carried on among these rude tribes, with all the rage and rancour of implacable enemies.

But famine and war, however destructive, were not the only causes of their rapid decay. The smallpox having broke out among them, proved exceedingly fatal, both on account of the contageous nature of the distemper, and their harsh and injudicious attempts to cure it by plunging themselves into cold rivers during the most violent stages of the disorder. The pestilence broke out among some nations, particularly among the Pemblicos in North Carolina, and almost swept away the whole tribe. The practice of entrapping them, which was encouraged by the first settlers in Carolina, and selling them for slaves to the West India planters, helped greatly to thin their nations. But, of all other causes, the introduction of spirituous liquors among them, for which they discovered an amazing fondness, has proved the most destructive. Excess and intemperance not only undermined their constitution, but also created many quarrels, and subjected them to a numerous list of fatal diseases, to which in former times they were entire strangers. Besides those Europeans engaged in commercial business with them, generally speaking, have been so far from reforming them, by examples of virtue and purity of manners, that they rather served to corrupt their morals, and render them more treacherous, distrustful, base and debauched than they were before this intercourse commenced. In short, European avarice and ambition have not only debased the original nature and stern virtue of that savage race, so that these few Indians that now remain have lost in a great measure their primitive character; but European vice and European diseases, the consequences of vice, have exterminated this people, insomuch that many nations formerly populous are totally extinct, and their names entirely forgotten.

[Sidenote] Present state of Indian nations in the southern district.

The principal tribes around Carolina that now remain are, the Cherokees, the Catabaws, the Creeks, the Chickesaws, and Choctaws, and a few others that scarcely deserve to be mentioned. In 1765 the Cherokees, who inhabit the mountains to the north of Charlestown, could scarcely bring two thousand men to the field. The Catabaws have fifteen miles square allotted them for hunting lands, about two hundred miles north of Charlestown, with British settlements all around them; but they are so much reduced by a long war with the Five Nations, that they could not muster one hundred and fifty warriors. The Creeks inhabit a fine country on the south-west, between four and five hundred miles distant from Charlestown, and the number of both the Upper and Lower nations does not exceed two thousand gun-men. The Chickesaw towns lie about six hundred miles due west from Charlestown, but the nation cannot send three hundred warriors to the field, owing to the incessant wars which they have carried on against the French, by which their number has been greatly diminished. The Choctaws are at least seven hundred miles west-south-west from Charlestown, and have between three and four thousand gun-men; and as their settlements border on West Florida, the greatest part of them till the late peace remained allies of France. But as these artful and insinuating rivals were removed out of the way, and the British government had adopted prudent plans of civilizing and managing those barbarous nations, the colonies for the future were in a great measure freed from all apprehensions of danger from them. I shall therefore conclude my observations respecting Indians with a speech of Mr. Stuart the superintendant, delivered at a general congress held in

Mobile, at which Governor Johnstone and many British officers and soldiers attended. For as he was so well acquainted with the humours, tempers and characters of these tribes, this speech, in which is exhibited a good specimen of the language and manner proper for addressing barbarous nations, may not be unworthy of the reader's attention.

[Sidenote] Mr. Stuart's first speech to the Indians at Mobile.

"Friends and brothers, the Supreme Being who made the world and all its inhabitants, has been pleased to permit many great warriors of the British and Indian nations to meet together in peace. The great King, who is the father of all white people in Great Britain and America, and defends them from danger, this day stretches out his arms to receive his red children into favour. He has been pleased to appoint me superintendent of the affairs of all Indian nations to the southward of Virginia. In his name I speak to you, and as the words you hear are his words, I hope you will listen to them with attention, and allow them to remain deeply impressed on your minds. They are calculated to promote not only your happiness, but that of your children and childrens children for ever.

"When the great kings of Britain and France were at variance, the storms of war raged through this great forest, the Indian nations were divided, brothers against brothers, and your country was stained with blood. Malice and revenge went forth, all paths were made crooked, and your land was covered with darkness. Now that it has pleased the Author of life to restore the blessings of light and peace, it is our duty to make a proper use and improvement of them. As fogs gathered in the night are dispersed by the rising sun, so words dictated by the rage of war should be forgotten in the time of peace. The great King, full of wisdom and magnanimity, knows the frailty of his red children, and forgives their disobedience and rebellion. He extends his love to them all, even to those that lifted up the hatchet against him. To render them secure, he has resolved that the English and French shall be for ever separated by the great river Mississippi, and that all nations on this side of it shall have him for their common father. He commands all strife and enmity between his white and red children to cease, and expects that the allies of Britain will take those Indians, the former allies of France, by the hand, and live together like brethren of one family. That his white and red children may be near one other, and mutually supply each other's wants, he has ordered some of his good subjects to come over the great waters, and live on the fruits of this land, which the Supreme Being made for the use of mankind in general. To open this friendly intercourse, I have invited you all to meet me at this place, and I rejoice that so many brothers are come to accept of the royal favour and protection.

"Ye Chickesaw warriors, I speak first to you, and I know your ears are open to my words. The great King regards you as children brought up in their father's house, who from their infancy have been dutiful and obedient, and by that means merited what you have always enjoyed, his particular care and affection. While darkness surrounded you on every side, he has defended you from all those snares and dangers to which you were exposed. Now the day is clear and unclouded. Your father continues to love you. The paths from your towns to all nations shall be made straight and plain, and nothing shall be permitted to hurt your feet. Your children shall rejoice and grow up in safety, and your houses shall be filled with abundance of corn and venison. I am come to tell you the good news, and to see that justice be done you in all commercial dealings.

"In the next place I speak to you, ye warriors of the great party of the Choctaw notion. You were like sons separated from their father, and removed at a great distance from his protection; but by persisting in obedience you were entitled to his love. The great King always acknowledged you, but now he receives you into his family, and offers you all the favours and privileges of sons. While you continue dutiful and obedient, the eye of your father shall be upon you, and his hand shall be open to relieve your wants. Under his care you shall enjoy all the blessings of peace and safety. You shall receive no injuries from friends, nor be exposed to any dangers from enemies. Your arms shall be kept bright, your hunting lands no man shall be permitted to take from you, and there shall be abundance of corn about your village.

"But as for you, ye Choctaw warriors of the Six Villages, you were like children early lost. While you were wandering out of the way, without knowing your brothers you blindly struck them. You found a father, indeed, who adopted you, and you have long served him with zeal, and shewn many proofs of your courage. You have received from your French father such poor rewards for your services as he could bestow; but all the while you remained under his care you were hungry, naked and miserable. He gave you many fair words and promises, and having long deceived you, at last is obliged to leave you in your present forlorn and wretched condition. Now your true father has found you, and this day stretches forth his arms to receive you under his protection. He has forgotten all your past offences. He knows your weakness, and forgives your errors. He knows your wants, and is disposed to relieve them. I have but one tongue, and always speak the truth; and as I bring you good news, I hope my words shall not be blown away by the wind. The great King is wise, generous and merciful, and I flatter myself with the hopes that you will never forget your obligations to his goodness.

"It is my duty to watch over Indians, and protect them against all manner of danger and oppression. For this purpose my ears shall be always open to your complaints, and it shall be my study to redress your grievances. I must warn you to beware of all quarrels and outrages, by which you will certainly forfeit the royal favour, and plunge yourselves again into misery. I hope you will always observe my advice, and conduct yourselves accordingly, that I may be able to transmit good accounts of your behaviour to England. It is only by the permission of the great King that your wants can be supplied, and that traders can come into your villages with guns, powder, balls, knives, hatchets, flints, hoes, clothes and other necessaries. These things you cannot make for yourselves, and no other nation will be allowed to furnish you with them. Therefore the great King has a right to expect your gratitude and obedience, for all he requires is with a view to your own tranquillity and happiness.

"As you are all received into the family of the great King, it is expected that Indians will not only live in friendship and peace with white men, but also with one another. In imitation of his Majesty's good example, you must forget all injuries and offences, and throw aside all national jealousies and antipathies. The King expects that the great chieftains, to whom he has given medals and gorgets, will consider them not merely as ornaments, but as emblems of the high offices they bear, and the great trust reposed in them. All presents made you are in consideration of the good services expected from you. Therefore, ye wise and great leaders, I expect you will use your authority like fathers, and restrain your young men from all acts of violence and injustice, and teach them that the only way to merit honour and preferment is to be just, honest and peaceable, and that disgrace and punishment will be the consequences of disorderly practices, such as robbing plantations, and beating or abusing white people.

"Ye warriors who have no commissions, I speak to you also in name of the King, and I hope you will reverence his authority and love your brethren. Listen at all times to your wise rulers, and be careful to follow their advice and example. By their wisdom and justice they have arrived at an high pitch of preferment, and stand distinguished by great and small medals. If, like them, you wish to be great, like them, you must first be good. You must respect them as children do their father, yielding submission to their authority, and obedience to their commands. Without the favour of your chiefs, you will neither get your wants supplied nor reach the station of honour. An armourer will be sent into your nation to clean and repair your rifles, but he will have instructions to mend arms to none but such as shall be recommended by their chiefs, it being proper that such leaders should have it in their power to distinguish those that are peaceable and obedient from the obstinate and perverse.

"I am to inform you all, that I will send a beloved man into your towns, who will be vested with authority to hear and determine all differences between you and the traders, to deliver all messages from me to you, and all talks from you to me. And as he will come to promote your welfare and tranquillity, I hope you will receive him kindly, protect him against all insults, and assist him in the execution of his office.

"When the French governor took his leave of you, he advised you to look upon yourselves as the children of the King of Great Britain. The advice was good, I hope you will remember it for ever. The great King has warriors numerous as the trees of the forest, and stands in no need of your assistance; but he desires your friendship and alliance to render you happy. He loves peace and justice, but he will punish all murders and rebellion. Be careful, therefore, to keep your feet far from the crooked and bloody path. Shun all communication with Indian tribes who lift the hatchet against their white brethren. Their talks, their calamets, their belts of wampum, and their tobacco are all poisonous. If you receive them into your towns, be assured you will be infected with their madness, and be in danger of rushing into destruction. Be cautious; above all things, of permitting great quantities of rum to be brought into your villages. It poisons your body, enervates your mind, and, from respectable warriors, turns you into furious madmen, who treat friends and enemies alike. Mark those persons, whether they be white or red, that bring rum among you, for bad men, who violate the laws, and have nothing else in view but to cheat, and render you despicable and wretched.

"Lastly, I inform you that it is the King's order to all his governors and subjects, to treat Indians with justice and humanity, and to forbear all encroachments on the territories allotted for them. Accordingly, all individuals are prohibited from purchasing any of your lands; but as you know that your white brethren cannot feed you when you visit them unless you give them grounds to plant, it is expected that you will cede lands to the King for that purpose. But whenever you shall be pleased to surrender any of your territories to his majesty, it must be done for the future at a public meeting of your nation, when the governors of the provinces, or the superintendent shall be present, and obtain the consent of all your people. The boundaries of your hunting grounds will be accurately fixed, and no settlement permitted to be made upon them. As you may be assured that all treaties with you will be faithfully kept, so it is expected that you also will be careful strictly to observe them. I have now done, and I hope you will remember the words I have spoken. Time will soon discover to you the generosity, justice and goodness of the British nation. By the bounty of the King, and a well-ordered trade with his subjects, your houses shall be filled with plenty, and your hearts with joy. You will see your men and women well clothed and fed, and your children growing up to honour you, and add strength to your nation; your peace and prosperity shall be established, and continue from generation to generation."

Having now endeavoured to give some account of the rise and progress of this colony for the first century after its settlement, or rather from the time the Proprietors received their second charter in 1665 to the year 1765, we shall add a general view of its present state and condition. I have purposely delayed speaking of several things, particularly of the temper, manners and character of the people, until this period, when they come more immediately under my own notice; and such observations as I have made shall now be submitted to the public view for the use of strangers, leaving all men acquainted with provincial affairs to judge for themselves, according to the different lights in which matters may have occurred to them.

[Sidenote] A description of Charlestown.

With respect to the towns in Carolina, none of them, excepting one, merit the smallest notice. Beaufort, Purisburgh, Jacksonburgh, Dorchester, Camden, and George-town, are all inconsiderable villages, having in each no more than twenty, thirty, or, at most, forty dwelling houses. But Charlestown, the capital of the province, may be ranked with the first cities of British America, and yearly advances in size, riches and population. It is situated upon a neck of land at the continence of Ashley and Cooper rivers, which are large and navigable, and wash at least two third parts of the town. These rivers mingle their streams immediately below the town, and, running six or seven miles farther, empty themselves at Sullivan's island into the Atlantic Ocean. By means of such broad rivers the sea is laid open from east to southeast, and the town fanned by gentle breezes from the ocean, which are very refreshing to the inhabitants during the summer months. The tide flows a great way above the town, and occasions an agitation in the air which is also productive of salutary effects. So low and level is the ground upon which Charlestown is built, that the inhabitants are obliged to raise banks of earth, as barriers, to defend themselves against the higher floods of the sea. The streets from east to west extend from river to river, and, running in a straight line, not only open a beautiful prospect, but also afford excellent opportunities, by means of subterranean drains, for removing all nuisances; and keeping the town clean and healthy. These streets are intersected by others, nearly at right angles, and throw the town into a number of squares, with dwelling houses on the front, and office-houses and little gardens behind them. Some of the streets are broad, which in such a climate is a necessary and wise regulation, for where narrow lanes and alleys have been tolerated, they prove by their confined situation a fruitful nursery for diseases of different kinds. The town, which was at first entirely built of wood, as might be expected, has often suffered from fire; but such calamities, though they fell heavy on individuals, have given the inhabitants frequent opportunities of making considerable improvements in it. Now most houses are built of brick, three storeys high, some of them elegant, and all neat habitations; within they are genteelly furnished, and without exposed as much as possible to the refreshing breezes from the sea. Many of them are indeed encumbered with balconies and piazzas, but these are found convenient and even necessary during the hot season, into which the inhabitants retreat for enjoying the benefit of fresh air, which is commonly occasioned, and always increased, by the flux and reflux of the sea. Almost every family have their pump-wells, but the water in them being at no great distance from the salt river, and filtered only through sand, is brackish, and commonly occasions severe griping and purging to every person not accustomed to it. The town consisted at this time of, at least, twelve hundred dwelling houses, and was in at advancing state. The public buildings are, an Exchange, a State-House, an Armoury, two churches for Episcopalians, one for Presbyterians, two for French and Dutch Protestants; to which may be added, meeting-houses for Anabaptists, Independents, Quakers and Jews. Upon the sides of the rivers wharfs are built, to which all ships that come over the bar may lie close; and having stores and ware-houses erected upon them, are exceedingly convenient for importing and exporting all kinds of merchandise.

The harbour is also tolerably well fortified, the King having at different times presented the province with great guns for that purpose. Towards Cooper river the town is defended by a number of batteries, insomuch that no ships of an enemy can approach it without considerable hazard. Besides these, the passage up to it is secured by Fort Johnson, built on James's Island, about two miles below the town. This fort stands in a commanding situation, within point-blank shot of the channel, through which every ship, in their way to and from Charlestown, must pass. The commander of Fort Johnson is commissioned by the King, and has authority to stop every ship coming in until the master or mate shall make oath that there is no malignant distemper on board. It has barracks for fifty men; but, in case of emergency, it obtains assistance from the militia of the island. During the late Cherokee war a plan was also formed for fortifying the town towards the land, with a horn-work built of tappy, flanked with batteries and redoubts at proper distances, and extending from river to river; but, after having spent a great sum of money on this work, peace being restored, the design was dropt.

In 1765 the number of white inhabitants in Charlestown amounted to between five and fix thousand, and the number of negroes to between seven and eight thousand. With respect to the number of white inhabitants in the province we cannot be certain, but we may form some conjecture from the militia roll; for as all male persons from sixteen to sixty are obliged by law to bear arms and muster in the regiments, and as the whole militia formed a body of between seven and eight thousand, reckoning the fifth person fit for military duty, the whole inhabitants in the province might amount to near forty thousand. But the number of negroes was not less than eighty or ninety thousand. As no exact register of the births and funerals has been kept at Charlestown for several years, we cannot ascertain the proportion between them. Formerly, when bills of mortality were annually printed, the common computation was, that, while no contagious disorder prevailed in town, one out of thirty-five died yearly, or one out of each family in the space of seven years. However, the list of deaths is often increased by the sailors and transient persons that die in the town, and by malignant distempers imported into it. It is generally believed, that the number of births among the settled inhabitants exceeds that of funerals; but we shall affirm nothing with respect to this matter without better authority than common observation and conjecture.

[Sidenote] A general view of the manners &c. of the people.

With respect to temper and character, the inhabitants of Carolina differ little from those of Great Britain and Ireland; I mean, such as derived their origin from those islands, for the descendents of other nations still retain something of the complexion, manners and customs of those countries from whence they came. In stature, the natives of Carolina are about the middle size; for in Europe we meet with men both taller and shorter. They are, generally speaking, more forward and quick in growth than the natives of cold climates. Indeed we may say, there are no boys or girls in the province, for from childhood they are introduced into company, and assume the air and behaviour of men and women. Many of them have an happy and natural quickness of apprehension, especially in the common affairs of life, and manage business with ease and discretion; but want that steadiness, application and perseverance necessary to the highest improvements in the arts and sciences. Several natives who have had their education in Britain, have distinguished themselves by their knowledge in the laws and constitution of their country; but those who have been bred in the province, having their ideas confined to a narrower sphere, have as yet made little figure as men of genius or learning. Agriculture being more lucrative than any other employment, all who possess lands and negroes apply their chief attention to the improvement of their fortune, regardless of the higher walks of science. They commonly marry early in life, and of course are involved in domestic cares and concerns before their minds have had time to ripen in knowledge and judgment. In the progress of society they have not advanced beyond that period in which men are distinguished more by their external than internal accomplishments. Hence it happens, that beauty, figure, agility and strength form the principal distinctions among them, especially in the country. Among English people they are chiefly known by the number of their slaves, the value of their annual produce, or the extent of their landed estate. For the most part they are lively and gay, adapting their dress to the nature of the climate in which they live, and discover no small taste and neatness in their outward appearance. Their intercourse and communication with Britain being easy and frequent, all novelties in fashion, dress and ornament are quickly introduced; and even the spirit of luxury and extravagance, too common in England, was beginning to creep into Carolina. Almost every family kept their chaises for a single horse, and some of the principal planters of late years have imported fine horses and splendid carriages from Britain. They discover no bad taste for the polite arts, such as music, drawing, fencing and dancing; and it is acknowledged by all, but especially by strangers, that the ladies in the province considerably outshine the men. They are not only sensible, discreet and virtuous, but also adorned with most of those polite and elegant accomplishments becoming their sex. The Carolineans in general are affable and easy in their manners, and exceedingly kind and hospitable to all strangers. There are few old men or women to be found in the province, which is a sure sign of the unhealthiness of the climate. We cannot say that there are many in the country that arrive at their sixtieth year, and several at thirty bear the wrinkles, bald head and grey hairs of old age. As every person by diligence and application may earn a comfortable livelihood, there are few poor people in the province, except the idle or unfortunate. Nor is the number of rich people great; most of them being in what we call easy and independent circumstances. It has been remarked, that there are more persons possessed of between five and ten thousand pounds sterling in the province, than are to be found any where among the same number of people. In respect of rank, all men regarded their neighbour as their equal, and a noble spirit of benevolence pervaded the society. In point of industry the town was like a bee-hive, and there were none that reaped not advantages more or less from the flourishing state of trade and commerce. Pride and ambition had not as yet crept into this community; but the province was fast advancing to that state of power and opulence, when some distinctions among men necessarily take place.

With respect to the manner of living in Charlestown, it is nearly the same as in England; and many circumstances concur to render it neither very difficult nor expensive to furnish plentiful tables. They have tea from England, and coffee, chocolate and sugar from the West Indies, in plenty. Butter is good, especially at that season when the fields are cleared of rice, and the cows are admitted into them; and it is so plentiful that they export a good deal of it to the Leeward Islands. The province produces some flour for bread; but it being of an inferior quality, the inhabitants chiefly make use of that imported from New York and Philadelphia. In the market there is plenty of beef, pork, veal, poultry and venison, and a great variety of wild-fowls and salt-water fish. The mutton from the low lands is not so good as that from the hills in the interior parts, but as the back country is now well settled, it is hoped that the market in time will be likewise well supplied with mutton from it. They have also a variety of the finest fruits and vegetables in their season. Their principal drink is punch, or grog, which is composed of rum well diluted with water. With respect to wine, Madeira is not only best suited to the climate, in which it improves by heat and age, but also most commonly used by the people in general, though French, Spanish and Portuguese wines are likewise presented at the tables of the most opulent citizens. Besides these, they have porter and beer from England, and cyder and perry from the northern colonies. Where rum is cheap, excess in the use of it will not be uncommon, especially among the lower class of people; but the gentlemen in general are sober, industrious and temperate. In short, the people are not only blessed with plenty, but with a disposition to share it among friends and neighbours; and many will bear me witness, when I say, that travellers could scarcely go into any city where they could meet with a society of people more agreeable, intelligent and hospitable than that at Charlestown.

[Sidenote] The arts and sciences only of late encouraged.

Though the arts and sciences had been long neglected, and have as yet made no great progress in the province, yet of late years they have met with great encouragement. The people in general stand not only much indebted to an ingenious bookseller, who introduced many of the most distinguished authors among them, but several of the most respectable citizens also united and formed a society for the promotion of literature, having obtained a charter of incorporation for that purpose. All the new publications in London, and many of the most valuable books, both ancient and modern, have been imported for the use of this society the members of which were ambitious of proving themselves the worthy descendants of British ancestors, by transporting not only their inferior arts of industry and agriculture, but also their higher improvements in philosophy and jurisprudence. Their design was not confined to the present generation, but extended to posterity, having the institution of a college in view, so soon as the funds of the society should admit of it. News-papers were also printed, for supplying the province with the freshest and most useful intelligence of all that passed in the political and commercial world. For amusement the inhabitants of Charlestown had not only books and public papers, but also assemblies, balls, concerts and plays, which were attended by companies almost equally brilliant as those of any town in Europe of the same size.

[Sidenote] The militia and internal strength of the province.

Charlestown had its armoury, magazine, and militia, and every citizen, like those of ancient Sparta, joined the military to the civil character. The officers of the militia are appointed by the Governor, who commonly nominates such men from among the inhabitants to command the rest as are most distinguished for their courage and capacity. All men of the military age being registered in the militia roll, each person knows the company to which he belongs, the captain who commands it, and is obligated to keep his arms in order, and to appear properly equipped in case of any alarm or other emergency. We cannot say that the militia in general made a good appearance, or seemed expert at the use of arms; but the companies of grenadiers, light infantry, and artillery, were extravagantly gay, and tolerably well disciplined. As most of the men were equally independent as their officers, that prompt obedience to orders, necessary in a regular army, could not be expected from them; but being conscious that union of strength was necessary to the common safety, on all emergencies they appeared under arms with alacrity and expedition. By the militia law the merchants and tradesmen of the city were subjected to some temporary inconveniencies and interruptions of business; but as agriculture was chiefly carried on by slaves, and nature brought the fruits of the earth to maturity, the planters in the country had abundance of time to spare for military exercises. Their rural life, and the constant use of arms, promoted a kind of martial spirit among them, and the great dangers to which they were always exposed, habituated them to face an enemy with resolution. Fortunately a natural antipathy subsisted between Indians and negroes, and prevented the two from uniting and conspiring the destruction of the colony. Therefore, while Indians remained quiet and peaceable, it was not the interest of the province to have them removed at a great distance; for had they been driven over the Mississippi, or extirpated, their place would probably have been supplied by fugitive slaves, who, by taking shelter in the mountains, would have proved an enemy equally, if not more, cruel and formidable to Carolina than the Indians themselves; or had the savage nations given encouragement to slaves to fly to them for liberty and protection, fatal must the consequences have been to the settlement.

[Sidenote] Of its societies formed for mutual support and relief.

Thus exposed to barbarians, the members of this little community knew that union of strength was not only requisite to the common safety, but both interest and duty naturally led them to establish societies with a particular view of raising funds for relieving each others wants. Though every person was obliged by law to contribute, in proportion to his estate, for the relief of the poor of the province, yet, besides this, there were several societies formed and incorporated for the particular purpose of assisting such families belonging to them as might happen to be unfortunate in trade, or in any other way reduced to an indigent state. Among these there is one called The South-Carolina Society, which merits particular notice. At first it consisted not of the most opulent citizens, though many of these afterwards joined it, but of persons in moderate stations, who held it an essential duty to relieve one another in such a manner as their circumstances would admit; accordingly they united, elected officers, and, by trifling weekly contributions, donations and legacies, together with good management, in process of time accumulated a considerable stock. A common seal was provided, with the device of a hand planting a vine, and the motto *Posteritati*. The Heavens smile on humane and generous designs. Many observing the great usefulness of this society, petitioned for admission into it; and as its numbers increased its stock enlarged. In 1738, their capital amounted to no more than L.213: 16 s.; but, in 1776, it had arisen to a sum not less than L. 68,787: 10: 3, current money. All the while their works of charity have likewise been conspicuous and extensive. Many unfortunate and sinking families have been supported by them in a decent and respectable manner. Many helpless orphans have been educated, and prepared for being useful members of society. Several other societies in Charlestown have been founded upon the same plan, and on many occasions the inhabitants in general, (it may be mentioned to their honour), have discovered a benevolent and charitable spirit, not only to poor people in the province, but also to unfortunate strangers.

[Sidenote] Of its merchants and trade.

The merchants in Carolina are a respectable body of men, industrious and indefatigable in business, free, open and generous in their manner of conducting it. The whole warehouses in Charlestown were like one common store, to which every trader had access for supplying his customers with those kinds of goods and manufactures which they wanted. The merchants of England, especially since the late peace, observing the colonies perfectly secure, and depending on the strength of the British navy for the protection of trade, vied with each other for customers in America, and stretched their credit to its utmost extent for supplying the provinces. Hence every one of them were well furnished with all kinds of merchandise. But as the staples of Carolina were valuable, and in much demand, credit was extended to that province almost without limitation, and vast multitudes of negroes, and goods of all kinds, were yearly sent to it. In proportion as the merchants of Charlestown received credit from England, they were enabled to extend it to the planters in the country, who purchased slaves with great eagerness, and enlarged their culture. Though the number of planters had of late years much increased, yet they bore no proportion to the vast extent of territory, and lands were still easily procured, either by patent or by purchase. According to the number of hands employed in labour, agriculture prospered and trade was enlarged. An uncommon circumstance also attended this rapid progress, which was favourable to the planting interest, and proved an additional incentive to industry. The price of staple commodities arose as the quantity brought to market increased. In 1761 rice sold at forty shillings per barrel, and indigo at two shillings per lib.; but in 1771 in so flourishing a state was the commerce of this country, that rice brought at market three pounds ten shillings per barrel, and indigo three shillings per lib. At the same time the quantity increased so much, that the exports of Carolina amounted, upon an average of three years after the peace, to L. 395,666: 13: 4; but, in 1771, the exports in that year alone arose to a sum not less than L. 756,000 sterling. How great then must the imports have been, when the province, notwithstanding this amazing increase, still remained in debt to the mother country.

[Sidenote] Of its planters and agriculture.

To this advanced state had Carolina arrived in point of improvement. Agriculture, beyond doubt, is of such importance to every country, that, next to public security and the distribution of justice and equity, it is the interest of every government to encourage it. Nothing could more manifestly promote industry and agriculture, than that fair and equitable division of lands among the people which took place in this province. Immense tracts of ground in possession of one man, without hands to cultivate and improve them, are only unprofitable deserts: but when lands are judiciously parcelled out among the people, industry is thereby encouraged, population increased, and trade promoted. The lands first yield abundance for the inhabitants, and then more than they can consume. When this is the case, the overplus can be spared for procuring foreign articles of exchange, and the province is thereby furnished with the conveniencies and luxuries of another climate and country. Then the planter's views are turned to the advantages of trade, and the merchant's, in return, to the success of husbandry. From which time a mutual dependence subsists between them, and it is the interest of the one to encourage the other. For when the merchants receive nothing from the province, it is impossible they can afford to import anything into it. Without cultivation commerce must always languish, being deprived of its chief supplies, the fruits of the earth. Without credit from the merchant there would have been little encouragement to emigrate to Carolina. A single arm could make little impression on the forest. A poor family, depending for support on the labour of one man, would have long remained in a starving condition, and scarcely ten of an hundred emigrants, obliged to work in such a climate, would have survived the tenth year after their arrival. To what causes then shall we ascribe the prosperity of the province? The answer is plain. Under the royal care the people, being favoured with every advantage resulting from public security, an indulgent government, abundance of land, large credit, liberty to labour and to reap the whole fruits of it, protection to trade, and an excellent market for every staple, laboured with success. These were powerful motives to emigrate, strong incentives to industry, and the principal causes of its rapid advances towards maturity. No colony that ever was planted can boast of greater advantages. Few have, in the space of an hundred years, improved and flourished in an equal degree.

Notwithstanding the favourable situation for agriculture in which the Carolineans stood, they remained slovenly husbandmen, and every stranger was astonished at the negligent manner in which all estates in the province were managed. Those planters who had arrived at easy or affluent circumstances employed overseers; and having little to do but to ride round their fields now and then, to see that their affairs were not neglected, or their slaves abused, indulge themselves in rural amusements, such as racing, mustering, hunting, fishing, or social entertainments. For the gun and dog the country affords some game, such as small partridges, woodcocks, rabbits, &c. but few of the planters are fond of that kind of diversion. To chace the fox or the deer is their favourite amusement, and they are forward and bold riders, and make their way through the woods and thickets with astonishing speed. The horses of the country, though hardy and serviceable animals, make little figure; and therefore, to improve the breed, many have been of late years imported from England. The planters being fond of fine horses, have been at great pains to raise them, so that they now have plenty of an excellent kind, both for the carriage and the turf.

In every plantation great care is taken in making dams to preserve water, for overflowing the rice-fields in summer, without which they will yield no crops. In a few years after this pond is made, the planters find it stocked with a variety of fishes; but in what manner they breed, or whence they come, they cannot tell, and therefore leave that matter to philosophical inquirers to determine. Some think that the spawn of fishes is exhaled from the large lakes of fresh water in the continent, and being brought in thunder-clouds, falls with the drops of rain into these reservoirs of water. Others imagine that it must have remained every where among the sand since that time the sea left these maritime parts of the continent. Others are of opinion, that young fish are brought by water-fowls, which are very numerous, from one pond to another, and there dropt, by which means the new-made pools receive their supply. But be the cause what it will, the effect is visible and notorious all over the country. When the ponds are stocked with fishes, it becomes an agreeable amusement to catch them, by hawling a sene[*] through the pool. Parties of pleasure are formed for this purpose, so that the young planters, like gentlemen of fortune, being often abroad at these rural sports and social entertainments, their domestic affairs by such means are much neglected, and their plantations carelessly managed.

[note: The word 'sene' appears thus in the original. Might be an uncommon misprint of 'sieve'.]

But even among the most diligent and attentive planters we see not that nice arrangement and order in their fields observable in most places of Europe, probably owing to the plenty and cheapness of land. In every country where landed estates are easily procured, they engross not that care and attention requisite for making them yield the greatest returns. The freeholds in Carolina are not only easily obtained by patent or purchase, but also all alienable at pleasure; so that few of the present generation of planters regulate their system of husbandry upon any established principles or plans, much less with any views to posterity. In no country have the finest improvements been found in the first ages of cultivation. This remains for a future day, and when lands shall be more scarce and valuable, and the country better peopled; then, it is probable, Carolina will cover, like other countries, the effects of the nice art and careful management of the husbandman.

At present the common method of cultivation is as follows. After the planter has obtained his tract of land, and built a house upon it, he then begins to clear his field of that load of wood with which the land is covered. Nature points out to him where to begin his labours; for the soil, however various, is every where easily distinguished, by the different kinds of trees which grow upon it. Having cleared his field, he next surrounds it with a wooden fence, to exclude all hogs, sheep and cattle from it. This field he plants with rice or indigo, year after year, until the lands are exhausted or yield not a crop sufficient to answer his expectations. Then it is forsaken, and a fresh spot of land is cleared and planted, which is also treated in like manner, and in succession forsaken and neglected. Although there are vast numbers of cattle bred in the province, yet no manure is provided for improving the soil. No trials of a different grain are made. No grass seeds are sown in the old fields for enriching the pastures, so that either shrubs and bushes again spring up in them, or they are overgrown with a kind of coarse grass, grateful or nourishing to no animal. Like farmers often moving from place to place, the principal study with the planters is the art of making the largest profit for the present time, and if this end is obtained, it gives them little concern how much the land may be exhausted. The emulation that takes place among the present generation, is not who shall put his estate in the most beautiful order, who shall manage it with most skill and judgment for posterity; but who shall bring the largest crop to the market. Let their children provide for themselves. They will endeavour to leave them plenty of labourers, and they know they can easily obtain abundance of lands; vain and absurd, therefore, would it be to bestow much pains and time in preparing this or that landed estate for them, and laying it out in fine order, which they are certain will be deserted so soon as the lands are exhausted.

Such is the present method of carrying on agriculture in Carolina, and it may do for some time, but every one must clearly see that it will be productive of bad effects. The richness of the soil, and the vast quantity of lands, have deceived many, even those men who had been bred farmers in England, and made them turn out as careless husbandmen as the natives themselves. Wherever you go in this province, you may discover the ignorance of the people with respect to agriculture, and the small degree of perfection to which they have yet attained in this useful art. This will not be the case much longer, for lands will become scarce, and time and experience, by unfolding the nature of the soil, and discovering to the planters their errors, will teach them, as circumstances change, to alter also their present rules, and careless manner of cultivation. In every country improvements are gradual and progressive. In such a province as Carolina, where the lands are good, new staples will be introduced, new sources of wealth will open; and, if we may judge from what is past, we may conclude, that, if no misunderstandings or quarrels shall interrupt its future progress, it certainly promises to be one of the most flourishing settlements in the world. We have seen that its exports are already very great, even while the lands are negligently cultivated and ill managed; but how much greater will they be when the art of agriculture shall hare arrived at the same degree of perfection in that province as in England.

[Sidenote] An interruption of the harmony between Britain and her colonies, and the causes of it.

Such, at this period, was the happy situation of the people and province of South Carolina; safe under the royal care and protection, and advancing to an opulent state by the unlimited credit and great indulgence granted by Britain. However, if we proceed a little farther, we shall see the face of things gradually changing. We shall behold the mother country, as the wealth of her colonies increased, attempting some alteration in their political and commercial system: and the different provinces, infected with pride and ambition, aspiring after independence. Let us take a slight view of the causes of that unhappy quarrel which at this time began between them, and afterwards proceeded to such a degree of violence as to threaten a total dissolution of all political union and commercial intercourse.

It might have been expected that those colonies would not soon forget their obligations to the mother country, by which they had been so long cherished and defended. As all the colonies were in themselves so many independent societies, and as in every state protection and allegiance are reciprocal and inseparable duties, one would have thought that subjects would yield obedience to the laws, and submission to the authority of that government under which they claimed protection. Such was the constitution of the provinces, that each, by its own legislature, could only regulate the internal police within the bounds of its territory. Thus far, and no farther, did its authority extend. Not one of them could either make or execute regulations binding upon another. They had no common council, empowered by the constitution, to act for and to bind all, though perhaps good policy now required the establishment of such a council, for the purpose of raising a revenue from them. Every member of the vast empire might perceive, that some common tax, regularly and impartially imposed, in proportion to the strength of each division, was necessary to the future defence and protection of the whole. In particular, the people of Great Britain, when they looked forward to the possible contingency of a new war, and considered the burdens under which they groaned, had a melancholy and dreadful prospect before them; and the parliament considered it as their indispensible duty to relieve them as much as possible, and provide for the safety of the state by a proportionable charge on all its subjects. For as the exemption of one part from this equal charge was unreasonable and unjust, so it might tend to alienate the hearts of these subjects residing in one corner of the empire from those in another, and destroy that union and harmony in which the strength of the whole consisted.

Such were probably the views and designs of the parliament of Great Britain at this juncture, with respect to America. At the same time, if we consider the genius, temper and circumstances of the Americans, we will find them jealous of their liberties, proud of their strength, and sensible of their importance to Britain. They had hitherto obeyed the laws of the British parliament; but their great distance, their vast extent of territory, their numerous ports and conveniencies for trade, their increasing numbers, their various productions, and consequently their growing power, had now prepared and enabled them for resisting such laws as they deemed inconsistent with their interest, or dangerous to their liberty. Some of these colonists even inherited a natural aversion to monarchy from their forefathers, and on all occasions discovered a strong tendency towards a republican form Of government, both in church and state. So that, before the parliament began to exert its authority for raising a revenue from them, they were prepared to shew their importance, and well disposed for resisting that supreme power, and loosening by degrees their connection with the parent state.

America was not only sensible of her growing strength and importance, but also of the weakness of the mother country, reduced by a tedious and expensive war, and groaning under an immense load of national debt. The colonies boasted of the assistance they had given during the war, and Great Britain, sensible of their services, was generous enough to reimburse them part of the expences which they had incurred. After this they began to over-rate their importance, to rise in their demands, and to think so highly of their trade and alliance, as to deem it impossible for Britain to support her credit without them. In vain did the mother country rely upon their gratitude for past favours, so as to expect relief with respect to her present burdens. We allow, that the first generation of emigrants retained some affection for Britain during their lives, and gloried in calling her their home and their mother country; but this natural impression wears away from the second, and is entirely obliterated in the third. Among the planters in all the colonies this was manifestly the case; the sons of Englishmen in America by degrees lost their affection for England, and it was remarkable, that the most violent enemies to Scotland were the descendants of Scotchmen.

But among merchants, the attachment to any particular country is still sooner lost. Men whose great object is money, and whose business is to gather it as fast as possible, in fact retain a predilection for any country no longer than it affords them the greatest advantages. They are citizens of the world at large, and provided they gain money, it is a matter of indifference to them to what country they trade, and from what quarter of the globe it comes. England is the best country for them, so long as it allows them to reap the greatest profits in the way of traffic; and when that is not the case, a trade with France, Spain, or Holland will answer better. If the laws of Great Britain interfere with their favourite views and interests, merchants will endeavour to elude them, and smuggle in spite of legal authority.

Of late years, although the trade of the colonies with the mother country had increased beyond the hopes of the most sanguine politicians, yet the American merchants could not be confined to it, but carried on a contraband trade with the colonies of France and Spain, in defiance of all the British laws of trade and navigation. This illicit trade the people had found very advantageous, having their returns in specie for their provisions and goods, and the vast number of creeks and rivers in America proved favourable to such smugglers. During the late war this trade had been made a treasonable practice, as it served to supply those islands which Britain wanted to reduce; but, after the conclusion of the war, it returned to its former channel, and increased beyond example in any past period.

[Sidenote] The new regulations made in the trade of the colonies give great offence.

To prevent this illicit commerce, it was found necessary, soon after the peace, to establish some new regulations in the trade of the colonies. For this purpose some armed sloops and cutters were stationed on the coasts of America, whose commanders had authority to act as revenue officers, and to seize all ships employed in that contraband trade, whether belonging to foreigners or fellow-subjects. And to render these commercial regulations the more effectual, courts of admiralty were erected, and invested with a jurisdiction more extensive than usual. In consequence of the restrictions laid on this trade, which the smugglers found so advantageous, it suffered much, and, notwithstanding the number of creeks and rivers, was almost annihilated. This occasioned some very spirited representations to be sent across the Atlantic by merchants, who declared that the Americans bought annually to the amount of three millions of British commodities: That their trade with the French and Spanish colonies took off such goods as remained an encumbrance on their hands, and made returns in specie, to the mutual advantage of both parties concerned in it. They complained, that the British ships of war were converted into Guarda Costas, and their commanders into custom-house officers; an employment utterly unworthy of the exalted character of the British navy: That naval officers were very unfit for this business in which they were employed, being naturally imperious in their tempers, and little acquainted with the various cases in which ships were liable to penalties, or in which they were exempted from detention: That that branch of trade was thereby ruined, by which alone they were furnished with gold and silver for making remittances to England; and that though the loss fell first upon them, it would ultimately fall on the commerce and revenue of Great Britain.

[Sidenote] A vote passed for charging stamp-duties on the Americans.

Soon after this an act of parliament was passed, which, while it in some respects rendered this commercial intercourse with the foreign settlements legal, at the same time loaded a great part of the trade with duties, and ordered the money arising from them to be paid in specie to the British exchequer. Instead of giving the colonists any relief, this occasioned greater murmurs and complaints among them, as it manifestly tended to drain the provinces of their gold and silver. At the same time another act was passed, for preventing such paper bills of credit as might afterwards be issued for the conveniency of their internal commerce, from being made a legal tender in the payment of debts. This served to multiply their grievances, and aggravate their distress. But that the provinces might he supplied with money for their internal trade, all gold and silver arising from these duties were to be reserved, and applied to the particular purpose of paying troops stationed in the colonies for their defence. Several new regulations for encouraging their trade with Great Britain were also established. In consequence of a petition for opening more ports for the rice trade, leave was granted to the provinces of South Carolina and Georgia to carry their rice for a limited time into foreign parts, on its paying British duties at the place of exportation. A bounty was given on hemp and undressed flax imported into Britain from the American colonies; and a bill was passed for encouraging the whale-fishery on the coasts of America: which advantages, it was thought, would amply compensate for any loss the colonies might sustain by the duties laid on their foreign trade. But the colonists, especially those in New England, who had advanced to such a degree of strength as rendered troops unnecessary for their defence, were too much soured in their tempers, to allow that Great Britain had any other than self-interested views in her whole conduct towards them. They murmured and complained, and resolved on a plan of retrenchment with respect to the purchasing of British manufactures; but still they presumed not openly to call in question the authority of the British legislature over them. But the time was at hand when their affection to the mother country, which was already considerably weaned, should undergo a greater trial, and when their real dispositions with respect to the obedience due to the British parliament would no longer be concealed. A vote passed in the House of Commons, and very unanimously, "That, towards the farther defraying of the necessary expences of protecting the colonies, it may he proper to charge certain stamp-duties upon them."

[Sidenote] Upon which the people of New-England discover their disaffection to government.

When the news of this determination reached America, all the colonies were in some degree uneasy at the thoughts of paying taxes; but the colonists of New England, as if ripe for some commotion, were alarmed with the most terrible apprehensions and suspicions, openly affirming, that the King, Lords and Commons had formed a design for enslaving them, and had now begun deliberately to put it in execution. Immediately they entered into associations for distressing the mother country, from a principle of resentment, as some thought, agreeing to purchase as few clothes and goods from her as possible, and to encourage manufactures of all kinds within themselves. They pretended that they were driven to such measures by necessity; but in reality they had nothing less in view than their favourite plan of independence, for the accomplishment of which it required time to secure the union and help of the other colonies, without which they plainly perceived all attempts of their own would be vain and fruitless. Accordingly they established a correspondence with some leading men in each colony, representing the conduct of Great Britain in the most odious light, and declaring that nothing could prevent them and their posterity from being made slaves but the firmest union and most vigorous opposition of every colony, to all laws made in Great Britain on purpose to raise a revenue in the plantations. A few discontented persons, who are commonly to be found in every legislature, joined the disaffected colonists of New England; and though at this time the party was inconsiderable, yet being more firmly cemented together by the prospect of a stamp-act, which equally affected the interest of all, it by degrees gained strength, and at length became formidable.

[Sidenote] An opportunity given the colonies to offer a compensation for the stamp-duty.

Such measures, however, did not intimidate the British ministers, who imagined that an association entered into from a principle of resentment would be of short duration, and that the colonies in general would be averse from any serious quarrel with the mother country, upon which they depended for safety and protection. And although they were well apprised of this sullen and obstinate disposition of the colonists before the bill was introduced, yet they took no measures for preventing that opposition, which they had reason to believe would be made to the execution of their law. On the contrary, time was imprudently given to sound the temper of the colonies with respect to it, and to give them an opportunity of offering a compensation for it in their own way, in case they were dissatisfied with that method of raising a revenue for their defence. The minister even signified to the agents of the colonies his readiness to receive proposals from them for any other tax that might be equivalent to the stamp-duty. This he did although he thought that the parliament not only had a right to tax them, but also that it was expedient and proper to exercise that right. For as the colonies had no common council empowered by their constitution to bind all, their taxing themselves equally and impartially would be a matter of great difficulty, even although they should be disposed to agree to it. But the colonies, instead of making any proposal for raising a revenue by a stamp-duty or any other way, sent home petitions to be presented to King, Lords, and Commons, questioning, in the most direct and positive terms, the jurisdiction of Parliament over their properties.

[Sidenote] The stamp-act passes in parliament.

In this situation of affairs, the Parliament, sensible of the heavy burden which already lay on the people of Great Britain, and of the addition to it which another war must occasion, thought it their indispensable duty to exert that authority, which before this time had never been called in question, for relieving this oppressed part of the nation, and providing for the common safety, by a charge impartially laid upon all subjects, in proportion to their abilities. The tender indulgence exercised by a parent over her children in their infant state, was now considered as both unreasonable and unnecessary in that state of maturity to which the colonies had advanced. All were obliged to confess, that the people of America were favoured with the same privileges and advantages with their fellow-subjects of Britain, and justice required that they should contribute to the necessary expences of that government under which they lived, and by which they were protected. A revenue was necessary to the future security of America; and on whom should it be raised, but those colonists who were to enjoy the benefit of such protection. Therefore the bill for laying a stamp-duty upon the colonies was brought into parliament; which, after much debate, and many strong arguments urged on both sides, passed through both houses, and received the royal assent by commission, on the 22d of March, 1765. At the same time, to compensate for the operations of the stamp-act, another was made to encourage the importation of all kinds of timber from the colonies into Britain: and as the estimated produce of the stamp-act amounted only to L. 60,000 *per annum*, and timber was so plentiful over all the plantations, it was thought that the great advantage which the colonies must reap from the latter act, would be an ample recompense for the loss they might sustain from the former.

[Sidenote] Violent measures taken to prevent its execution.

In the mean time the inhabitants of New England were industrious in spreading an alarm of danger over all the continent, and making all possible preparations for resistance. They had turned a jealous eye towards the mother country, where they had many friends employed to watch her conduct, who failed not to give them the earliest intelligence of what was doing in parliament. While they received the news that the stamp-act had passed, they at the same time had intelligence of that violent opposition it had met with from a strong faction in the House of Commons. And if their friends in Britain had the boldness to call in question both the right of the British legislature to impose taxes on the colonies, and the expediency of exercising that right, they thought that they had much better reason to do so; and that none deserved the blessing of liberty who had not courage to assert their right to it. Accordingly, no means were neglected that could inflame and exasperate the populace. Bold and seditious speeches were made to stir up the people to resistance; by representing the act in the most odious light, and affirming that it would be attended with consequences subversive of all their invaluable rights and privileges. They declared that silence was a crime at such a critical time, and that a tame submission to the stamp-act would leave their liberties and properties entirely at the disposal of a British parliament. Having obtained a copy of the act, they publicly burnt it. The ships in the harbours hung out their colours half-mast high, in token of the deepest mourning; the bells in the churches were muffled, and set a-ringing, to communicate the melancholy news from one parish to another. These flames, kindled in New England, soon spread through all the capital towns along the coast; so that there was scarcely a sea-port town in America in which combinations were not framed for opposing the introduction of stamp-paper.

When the vessels arrived which carried those stamp-papers to America, the captains were obliged to take shelter under the stern of some ships of war, or to surrender their cargoes into the hands of the enraged populace. The gentlemen appointed to superintend the distribution of stamps, were met by the mob at their landing, and compelled to resign their office. All men suspected of having any desire of complying with the act, or of favouring the introduction of stamps into America, were insulted and abused. The governors of the provinces had no military force to support civil authority. The magistrates connived at these irregular and riotous proceedings of the people. The assemblies adopted the arguments of the minority in parliament, and took encouragement from them to resist the authority of the supreme legislature. Though each colony in respect of another was a separate and independent society, without any political connection, or any supreme head to call the representatives of the people together, to act in concert for the common good; yet in this case almost all, of their own authority, sent deputies to meet in congress at New York, who drew up and signed one general declaration of their rights, and of the grievances under which they laboured, and transmitted a petition to the King, Lords and Commons, imploring relief.

[Sidenote] The assembly of Carolina study ways and means of eluding the act.

Among the rest a party in South Carolina, which province at this time, from inclination, duty and interest, was very firmly attached to the mother country, entered warmly into the general opposition. Lieutenant-governor Bull, a native of the province, manifested a desire of complying with the act, and supporting the legal and constitutional dependency of the colony on the crown and parliament of Great Britain; but wanted power sufficient for maintaining the dignity and authority of his government, and carrying that act into execution. Several old and wise men joined him, and declared that they had formerly taken an active part in bringing the province under his majesty's care, but would now be very cautious of resisting the authority of parliament, and robbing it of that protection which it had so long and so happily enjoyed. The members of assembly, finding the Lieutenant-governor determined to transact no public business but in compliance with the act of parliament, began to deliberate how they might best elude it. For this purpose they addressed him, begging to be informed whether the stamp act, said to be passed in parliament, had been transmitted to him by the Secretary of State, the Lords of Trade; or any other authentic channel, since he considered himself as under obligations to enforce it. He replied, that he had received it from Thomas Boone, the Governor of the province. The assembly declared, that they could consider Mr. Boone, while out of the bounds of his government, in no other light than that of a private gentleman, and that his receiving it in such a channel was not authority sufficient to oblige him to execute so grievous an act. But Mr. Bull and his council were of opinion, that the channel in which he had received it was equally authentic with that in which he had formerly received many laws, to which they had quietly submitted. Upon which the assembly came to the following resolutions, which were signed by Peter Manigault their speaker, and ordered to be printed, that they might be transmitted to posterity, in order to shew the sense of that house with respect to the obedience due by America to the British parliament.

[Sidenote] Their resolutions respecting the obedience due to the British parliament.

"Resolved, That his Majesty's subjects in Carolina owe the same allegiance to the crown of Great Britain that is due from its subjects born there. That his Majesty's liege subjects of this province are entitled to all the inherent rights and liberties of his natural born subjects within the kingdom of Great Britain. That the inhabitants of this province appear also to be confirmed in all the rights aforementioned, not only by their character, but by an act of parliament, 13th George II. That it is inseparably essential to the freedom of a people, and the undoubted right of Englishmen, that no taxes be imposed on them but with their own consent. That the people of this province are not, and from their local circumstances cannot be represented in the House of Commons in Great Britain; and farther, that, in the opinion of this house, the several powers of legislation in America were constituted in some measure upon the apprehension of this impracticability. That the only representatives of the people of this province are persons chosen therein by themselves; and that no taxes ever have been, or can be, constitutionally imposed on them but by the legislature of this province. That all supplies to the Crown being free gifts of the people, it is unreasonable and inconsistent with the principles and spirit of the British constitution for the people of Great Britain to grant to his Majesty the property of the people of this province. That trial by jury is the inherent and invaluable right of every British subject in this province. That the act of parliament, entitled, An act for granting and applying certain stamp-duties and other duties on the British colonies and plantations in America, &c. by imposing taxes on the inhabitants of this province; and the said act and several other acts, by extending the jurisdiction of the courts of admiralty beyond its ancient limits, have a manifest tendency to subvert the rights and liberties of this province. That the duties imposed by several late acts of parliament on the people of this province will be extremely burdensome and grievous; and, from the scarcity of gold and silver, the payment of them absolutely impracticable. That as the profits of the trade of the people of this province ultimately center in Great Britain, to pay for the manufactures which they are obliged to take from thence, they eventually contribute very largely to all the supplies granted to the Crown; and besides, as every individual in this province is as advantageous at least to Great Britain as if he were in Great Britain, as they pay their full proportion of taxes for the support of his Majesty's government here, (which taxes are equal, or more, in proportion to our estates, than those paid by our fellow subjects in Great Britain upon theirs), it is unreasonable for them to be called upon to pay any further part of the charges of government there. That the assemblies of this province have from time to time, whenever requisitions have been made to them by his Majesty, for carrying on military operations, either for the defence of themselves or America in general, most cheerfully and liberally contributed their full proportion of men and money for these services. That though the representatives of the people of this province had equal assurances and reasons with those of the other provinces, to expect a proportional reimbursement of those immense charges they had been at for his Majesty's service in the late war, out of the several parliamentary grants for the use of America; yet they have obtained only their proportion of the first of those grants, and the small sum of L. 285 sterling received since. That, notwithstanding, whenever his Majesty's service shall for the future require the aids of the inhabitants of this province, and they shall be called upon for this purpose in a constitutional way, it shall be their indispensable duty most cheerfully and liberally to grant to his Majesty their proportion, according to their ability, of men and money, for the defence, security, and other public services of the British American colonies. That the restrictions on the trade of the people of this province, together with the late duties and taxes imposed on them by act of parliament, must necessarily greatly lessen the consumption of British manufactures amongst them. That the increase, prosperity and happiness of the people of this province, depend on the full and free enjoyment of their rights and liberties, and on an affectionate intercourse with Great Britain. That the readiness of the colonies to comply with his Majesty's requisitions, as well as their inability to bear any additional taxes beyond what is laid on them by their respective legislatures, is apparent from several grants of parliament, to reimburse them part of the heavy expences they were at in the late war in America. That it is the right of the British subjects of this province to petition the King, or either house of parliament. Ordered, That these votes be printed and made public, that a just sense of the liberty, and the firm sentiments of loyalty of the representatives of the people of this province, may be known to their constituents, and transmitted to posterity."

[Sidenote] The people become more violent in opposition to government.

Notwithstanding these resolutions, few of the inhabitants of Carolina, even the most sanguine, entertained the smallest hopes of a repeal; but expected, after all their struggles, that they would be obliged to submit. Indeed a very small force in the province at that time would have been sufficient to quell the tumults and insurrections of the people, and enforce obedience to legal authority. But to the imprudence of ministers, the faction in parliament, and the weakness of the civil power in America, the resistance of the colonies may be ascribed. Had the stamp-duty been laid on them without any previous notice of the resolution of parliament, it is not improbable that they would have received it as they had done other acts of the British legislature. Or had the parliament been unanimous in passing the act, and taken proper measures for carrying it into execution, there is little doubt but the colonies would have submitted to it. For however generally the people might be indisposed for admitting of that or any other tax, yet a great majority of them at this time were averse from calling in question the supreme authority of the British parliament. But a small flame, which at first is easily extinguished, when permitted to spread, has often been productive of great conflagrations. The riotous and turbulent party, encouraged by the minority in England, set the feeble power of government in America at defiance. The better sort of people mingled with the rioters, and made use of the arguments of their friends in England to inflame and exasperate them. At length, they not only agreed to adhere to their former illegal combinations for distressing and starving the English manufactures, but also to with-hold from British merchants their just debts. This they imagined would raise such commotions in Britain as could not fail to overturn the ministry, or intimidate the parliament.

[Sidenote] The merchants and manufacturers in England join in petitioning for relief.

In consequence of these disturbances and combinations in America, great evils began to be felt in England, and still greater to be feared. The temporary interruption of commercial intercourse between the mother country and the colonies was very prejudicial to both. That large body of people engaged in preparing, purchasing and sending out goods to the continent were deprived of employment, and consequently of the means of subsistence; than which nothing could be conceived more likely to excite commotions in England. The revenue suffered by the want of the export and import duties. Petitions flowed into parliament from all quarters, not only from the colonies in America, but also from the trading and manufacturing towns in Great Britain, praying for such relief as to that house might seem expedient, at a juncture so alarming. The ministers having neglected to take the proper measures to enforce their law, while the matter was easy and practicable, were now obliged to yield to the rising current, and resign their places. By the interposition of the duke of Cumberland, such a change in the administration took place as promised an alteration of measures with respect to America. Mr. Pitt, who highly disapproved of the scheme for raising a revenue from the colonies, having long been detained by indisposition from parliament, had now so much recovered as to be able to attend the house.—The history of what follows is disgraceful to Great Britain, being entirely composed of lenient concessions in favour of a rising usurpation, and of such shameful weakness and timidity in the ministry, as afterwards rendered the authority of the British parliament in America feeble and contemptible.

[Sidenote] The stamp-act repealed.

No sooner had this change in administration taken place, than all papers and petitions relative to the stamp-act, both from Great Britain and America, were ordered to be laid before the House of Commons. The house resolved itself into a committee, to consider of those papers, about the beginning of the year 1766. Leave was given to bring in a bill for repealing an act of last session of parliament, entitled, An act for granting and applying certain stamp-duties and other duties, in the British colonies and plantations in America, towards defraying the expenses of protecting and securing the same. When this bill came into parliament a warm debate ensued, and Mr. Pitt with several more members strongly urged the necessity of a repeal. He made a distinction between external and internal taxes, and denied not only the right of parliament to impose the latter on the colonies, but also the justice, equity, policy and expediency of exercising that right. Accordingly, while it was declared that the King, by and with the consent of the Lords spiritual and temporal, and Commons of Great Britain in parliament assembled, had, have, and of right ought to have, full power and authority to make laws and statutes of sufficient force and validity to bind the colonies and people of America, subjects of the crown of Great Britain, in all cases whatsoever; the stamp-act was repealed, because it appeared that the continuance of it would be attended with many inconveniences, and might be productive of consequences detrimental to the commercial interest of these kingdoms.

[Sidenote] Which proves fatal to the jurisdiction of the British parliament in America.

This concession in favour of the rising usurpation, instead of proving favourable to the commercial interests of the nation, had rather the contrary effect, and served to set the colonies in some measure free from the legislative authority of Britain. It gave such importance to the licentious party in America, and such superiority over the good and loyal subjects as had a manifest tendency to throw the colonies into a state of anarchy and confusion. It served to promote a doctrine among them subversive of all good government, which plainly implied, that the obedience of subjects was no longer due to the laws of the supreme legislature, than they in their private judgments might think them agreeable to their interest, or the particular notions which they may have framed of a free constitution. While it gave countenance and encouragement to the riotous and turbulent subjects in America, who at that time were neither an opulent nor respectable party in the colonies, it exposed the real friends of government to popular prejudice, and rendered their affections more cool, and their future endeavours in support of government more feeble and ineffectual. For after repealing the stamp-act, without any previous submission on the part of the colonies, how could it be expected that any gentleman would risque his domestic peace, his fortune, or his life, in favour of a distant government ready to desert him, and leave him subjected to all the insults and outrages of future insurgents? How could it be imagined that these colonies, that had set the power of Great Britain at defiance, and obtained what they aimed at by tumults and insurrections, would afterwards remain quiet? As they had opposed the stamp-act, assigning for reason that they were not represented in parliament, was it not evident that the same reason would extend to all other laws which the parliament might enact to bind them in times to come, or had enacted to bind them in times past? The repeal of the stamp-act upon such a principle, and in such circumstances of tumult, unquestionably served to encourage the colonies in disobedience, and to prepare their minds for asserting their independence.

[Sidenote] And gives occasion of triumph to the colonies.

When the news of the repeal of this act reached America, it afforded the colonists, as might have been expected, matter of great triumph. The most extravagant demonstrations of joy, by bonfires, illuminations and ringing of bells, were exhibited in every capital. The Carolineans sent to England for a marble statue of Mr. Pitt, and erected it in the middle of Charlestown, in grateful remembrance of the noble stand he had made in defence of their rights and liberties. Addresses were sent home to the King, acknowledging the wisdom and justice of his government in the repeal of the grievous act, and expressing their happiness that their former harmony and commercial intercourse, so beneficial to both countries, were restored. But soon after it appeared that the power of Great Britain in America had received a fatal blow, such as she would never be able to recover without the severest struggles and boldest exertions. For whatever fair professions of friendship some colonies might make, the strongest of them retained their natural aversion to monarchy, and were well disposed for undermining the civil establishments, and paving the way for their entire subversion. The British government, formerly so much revered, was now deemed oppressive and tyrannical. The little island, they said, had become jealous of their dawning power and splendour, and it behoved every one to watch her conduct with a sharp eye, and carefully guard their civil and religious liberties. Accordingly, for the future, we will find, that the more Great Britain seemed to avoid, the more the colonies seemed to seek for, grounds of quarrel; and the more the former studied to unite, by the ties of common interest, the more the latter strove to dissolve every political and commercial connection. Their minds and affections being alienated from the mother country, they next discovered an uneasiness under the restraints of legal authority. They quarrelled almost with every governor, found fault with all instructions from England which clashed with their leading passions and interests, and made use of every art for weakening the hands of civil government. Their friends in Britain had gloried that they had resisted; and now subjection of every kind was called slavery, and the spirit of disorder and disobedience which had broke out continued and prevailed. At length, even the navigation-act was deemed a yoke, which they wished to shake off, and throw their commerce open to the whole world. Several writers appeared in America in defence of what they were pleased to call their natural rights, who had a lucky talent of seasoning their compositions to the palate of the bulk of the people. Hence the seeds of disaffection which had sprung up in New England spread through the other colonies, insomuch that multitudes became infected with republican principles, and aspired after independence.—But here we shall stop for the present time, and leave the account of their farther struggles towards the accomplishment of this favourite plan to some future opportunity.